P9-CMW-240

Photoshop® Elements 5 FOR DUMMIES

Cheat Sheet

Getting Familiar with the Elements Workspace

Shortcuts bar

Order Online

Tools palette

Sharing

Menu bar

Make Creations

Go to Quick Fix

Go to Organizer

Search help topic

Foreground and Background colors

Image window

Photo Bin

Palette Bin

- ✔ Open an image in the Elements Editor by choosing File➪Open.

- ✔ Get information about your image by looking at the status bar. Click the right-pointing arrow to get more details regarding your document.

- ✔ Need to see detail in your image? Zoom into your image by pressing Ctrl/⌘+spacebar and clicking. Zoom back out by pressing Alt/Option+spacebar and clicking.

- ✔ Easily switch between open documents by clicking images in the Photo Bin.

- ✔ Access palettes as needed by choosing them from the Window menu or the Palette Bin.

- ✔ Execute common tasks, such as Open, Save, Print, and Share photos, by clicking buttons on the Shortcuts bar. You can also jump into making creations or dive into the Elements Organizer by clicking the buttons shown in the workspace figure.

For Dummies: Bestselling Book Series for Beginners

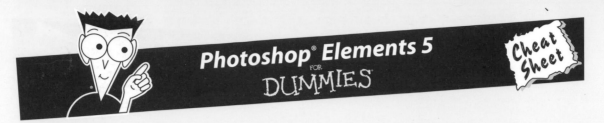

Photoshop® Elements 5 FOR DUMMIES

Cheat Sheet

Toolbox Shortcuts

V —		Z	Q —	J	G —		U
H —		I	Y —	J	R —		U
M —		L	S —	E	R —		U
M —		L	S —	E	R —		U
W —		L		E	X		O
T —		F	B —	K	D		O
T —		A	B —	U			O
T —		C	B —	U			
T —		P	N —	U			

Selection Tricks

	Windows	Mac (Elements 4)
Add to selection	Shift+drag	Shift+drag
Deselect from a selection	Alt+drag	Option+drag
Deselect all but intersected area	Shift+Alt+drag	Shift+Option+drag
Deselect	Ctrl+D	⌘+D
Reselect last selection	Ctrl+Shift+D	⌘+Shift+D
Select everything	Ctrl+A	⌘+A
Hide selection outline	Ctrl+H	⌘+H
Cut selection	Ctrl+X	⌘+X
Copy selection	Ctrl+C	⌘+C
Paste last cut or copied image	Ctrl+V	⌘+V
Paste into a selection	Ctrl+Shift+V	⌘+Shift+V
Adjust levels	Ctrl+L	⌘+L
Adjust hue or saturation	Ctrl+U	⌘+U
Adjust image size	Ctrl+Alt+I	⌘+Option+I

For Dummies: Bestselling Book Series for Beginners

Photoshop® Elements 5

FOR

DUMMIES®

by Barbara Obermeier and Ted Padova

BICENTENNIAL
1807
WILEY
2007
BICENTENNIAL

Wiley Publishing, Inc.

Photoshop® Elements 5 For Dummies®

Published by
Wiley Publishing, Inc.
111 River Street
Hoboken, NJ 07030-5774
www.wiley.com

DEC 15 2007

WILEY

About the Authors

Barbara Obermeier: Barbara Obermeier is principal of Obermeier Design, a graphics design studio in Ventura, California. She's the author of *Photoshop CS2 All-in-One Desk Reference For Dummies* and has contributed as author or coauthor on numerous books on Photoshop, Illustrator, and PowerPoint. Barb is also a faculty member in the Visual Communication Department at Brooks Institute of Photography.

Ted Padova: In addition to writing several books on Adobe Photoshop and Adobe Illustrator, Ted is the world's leading author of books on Adobe Acrobat. He is also a coauthor of *Adobe Creative Suite Bible* and *Adobe Creative Suite 2 Bible* (Wiley), *Color Correction For Digital Photographers Only* (Wiley), and *Color Management for Digital Photographers For Dummies* (Wiley). Ted spends most of his time writing and speaking at conferences and expos nationally and internationally.

Dedication

Barbara Obermeier: I would like to dedicate this book to Gary, Kylie, and Lucky, who constantly remind me of what's really important in life.

Ted Padova: For Arnie

Authors' Acknowledgments

The authors would like to thank our excellent project editor, Kim Darosett, who kept us and this book on track; Bob Woerner, our great Sr. Acquisitions Editor; Andy Cummings, Dummies Royalty; Dennis Cohen, technical editing wizard, who made what we wrote sound better; and all the dedicated production staff at Wiley. Additionally, we would like to thank Don Mason of Don Mason Photography (Bakersfield, California) for helping us out with some tone corrections and for his expert advice on digital color correction.

Barbara Obermeier: A special thanks to Ted Padova, my coauthor, and friend, who always reminds me there is still a 1-in-53-million chance that we can win the lottery.

Ted Padova: My first choice always in coauthoring a book is to do the job with Barbara Obermeier. There's no one I'd rather work with, and I thank Barbara for initially putting together this project and asking me to join her.

Publisher's Acknowledgments

We're proud of this book; please send us your comments through our online registration form located at www.dummies.com/register/.

Some of the people who helped bring this book to market include the following:

Acquisitions, Editorial, and Media Development

Project Editor: Kim Darosett

Senior Acquisitions Editor: Bob Woerner

Copy Editor: Rebecca Whitney

Technical Editors: Dennis Cohen, Alfred DeBat

Editorial Manager: Leah Cameron

Media Development Manager: Laura VanWinkle

Editorial Assistant: Amanda Foxworth

Sr. Editorial Assistant: Cherie Case

Cartoons: Rich Tennant (www.the5thwave.com)

Composition Services

Project Coordinator: Adrienne Martinez

Layout and Graphics: Jonelle Burns, Denny Hager, Barry Offringa, Melanee Prendergast, Heather Ryan, Alicia B. South, Erin Zeltner

Proofreader: Betty Kish

Indexer: Slivoskey Indexing Services

Anniversary Logo Design: Richard Pacifico

Publishing and Editorial for Technology Dummies

    Richard Swadley, Vice President and Executive Group Publisher

    Andy Cummings, Vice President and Publisher

    Mary Bednarek, Executive Acquisitions Director

    Mary C. Corder, Editorial Director

Publishing for Consumer Dummies

    Diane Graves Steele, Vice President and Publisher

    Joyce Pepple, Acquisitions Director

Composition Services

    Gerry Fahey, Vice President of Production Services

    Debbie Stailey, Director of Composition Services

Contents at a Glance

Table of Contents

Introduction

*W*hat was once a consumer-grade, low-level program for beginning image editors and a junior cousin to the powerful Adobe Photoshop program has evolved and matured to stand on its own merits now in version 5.0 for Windows. As of this writing, Elements is available on the Mac in version 4.

You won't find much comparison between Adobe Photoshop Elements and Adobe Photoshop in this book, nor will you see any suggestions that you should consider using Photoshop for one thing or another. We don't make suggestions, simply because Photoshop Elements is a powerful tool that satisfies many needs of amateurs and professionals alike.

Who should buy Elements (and, ultimately, this book)? The range of people who can benefit from using Elements is wide and includes a vast audience. From beginning image editors to intermediate users to more advanced amateurs and professionals, Elements has something for everyone. We'll even stick our necks out a little and suggest that many Photoshop users can benefit greatly by adding Elements to their software tool cabinets. Why? Because Elements offers some wonderful creation tools that Photoshop hasn't yet dreamed of supporting. For example, in Photoshop Elements 5 on Windows, you can create post cards, greeting cards, calendars, and photo albums with just a few mouse clicks. You can place orders with online service centers that professionally print your photo creations. All these opportunities are available in Elements, and we cover these and many more creation ideas in Chapters 15 and 16.

The downside to the Photoshop Elements program is that version 5 is supported only in Windows. Adobe was a little late in releasing a Macintosh version, which now is released only in version 4. Whether we see version 5 for the Mac is yet to be seen. You may find version 5 released by Adobe after this book has been published. However, all the references to the Organizer in this book apply only to Windows. Adobe left the file management options to iPhoto in the Mac version, and you can expect a Photoshop Elements 5 version for the Mac to continue with iPhoto file handling. In the meantime, we did our best to write this book with a cross-platform audience in mind.

To set your frame of mind to thinking in Photoshop Elements terms, don't think of the program as a scaled-down version of Adobe Photoshop. Those days are gone. If you're a digital photographer and you shoot your pictures in JPEG or Camera Raw format, Elements has the tools for you to open, edit, and massage your pictures into professional images. If you worry about color profile embedding, forget it. Elements can handle the task for you, as we explain in Chapter 4, where we talk about Camera Raw, and in Chapter 14, where we talk about color profiling and printing. For the professional, Photoshop Elements has just about everything you need to create final images for color printing and commercial printing.

If you're a beginner or an intermediate user, you'll find some of the Photoshop Elements quick-fix operations a breeze to use to help you enhance your images, as we explain in Chapters 9 and 10. And, when it comes time for you to print some homemade greeting cards, calendars, and photo albums — whether you're a beginner, an intermediate user, or a professional user — Elements provides you with easy-to-follow steps to package your creations, as we cover in Chapters 15 and 16.

About This Book

This book is an effort to provide, in about 400 pages, as much of a comprehensive view of a wildly feature-rich program as we can. There's a lot to Elements, and we try to offer you as much as possible within our limited amount of space. We begged for more pages, but alas, our publisher wants to get this book in your hands in full color and with an attractive price tag. Therefore, even though we may skip over a few little things, all you need to know about using Photoshop Elements for designing images for print, sharing, Web hosting, versatile packaging, e-mailing, and more is covered in the pages ahead.

As we said, Photoshop Elements has something for just about everyone. Hence, we know that our audience is large and that not everyone will use every tool, command, or method described in this book. Therefore, we added a lot of cross-references in the text, in case you want to jump around. You can go to just about any chapter and start reading; and, if some concept needs more explanation, we point you in the right direction for getting some background when it's necessary.

Conventions Used in This Book

Throughout this book, we point you to menus where commands are accessed frequently. A couple of things to remember are the references for where to go when we detail steps in a procedure. For accessing a menu command, you may see a sentence like this one:

Choose File⟹Get Photos⟹From Files and Folders.

When you see commands like this one mentioned, we're asking you to click the File menu to open the drop-down menu, click the menu command labeled Get Photos, and then choose the command From Files and Folders from the submenu that appears.

Another convention we use refers to context menus. A context menu jumps up at your cursor position and shows you a menu similar to the menu you select at the top of the Elements workspace. To open a context menu, click the right mouse button. On the Mac, press the Control key and click the mouse to open a context menu.

A third item relates to using keystrokes on your keyboard. When we mention that some keys need to be pressed on your keyboard, the text is described like this:

> Press Alt+Shift+Ctrl+S (Option+Shift+⌘+S on the Mac).

In this case, you hold down the Alt key on Windows (or the Option key on the Mac), the Shift key, and the Control key in Windows (or the ⌘ key on the Mac) and then press the S key. Then release all the keys at the same time.

How This Book Is Organized

This book is divided into logical parts where related features are nested together in chapters within six different parts of the book:

Part 1: Getting Started

If you just bought a digital camera and you're new to image editing in a program like Photoshop Elements, you're probably tempted to jump into fixing and editing your pictures. The essentials usually aren't the most exciting part of any program or book. That's true with this book, too: The more mundane issues related to understanding some basics are assembled in the first three chapters. Although some bits of information aren't as exciting as in many other chapters, you must understand them before you start editing images. Be sure to review the first three chapters before you dive into the other chapters.

In Part I, we talk about the tools, menus, commands, preferences, workspaces, and features that help you move around easily in the program. The more you pick up in the preliminary chapters, the more easily you can adapt to the Elements way of working.

Part II: Getting Organized

In Part II, we talk about getting photos in Elements, organizing your files, searching for files, and grouping your photos, and we give you much more information related to the Photoshop Elements Organizer. The Organizer is your central workplace, and knowing a great deal about using the Organizer window helps you move around much faster in the program.

Part III: Selecting and Correcting Photos

Part III relates to creating and manipulating selections. There's a lot to making selections in photos, but after you figure it out (by reading Chapter 7), you can cut out a figure in a picture and drop it into another picture, drop different backgrounds into pictures, or isolate an area that needs some brightness and contrast adjustment. In Chapter 8, we talk about layers and how to create and manage them in Elements. In many other chapters, we refer you to Chapter 8 because you need to work with layers for many other tasks you do in Elements.

In Chapter 9, we talk about fixing image flaws and problems. That picture you took with your digital camera may be underexposed or overexposed, or it may need some work to remove dust and scratches. Maybe it needs a little sharpening, or some other imperfection requires editing. All the know-hows and how-tos are in this chapter.

In Chapter 10, we cover how to correct color problems, brightness, and contrast. We show you ways to quickly fix photos as well as some methods for custom image corrections.

Part IV: Exploring Your Inner Artist

This part is designed to bring out the artist in you. Considering the easy application of Elements filter effects, you can turn a photo image into a drawing or apply a huge number of different effects to change the look of your image.

In Chapter 12, we talk about drawing and painting so that you can let your artistic expression run wild. We follow up in Chapter 13 by talking about adding text to photos so that you can create your own layouts, posters, cards, and more.

Part V: Printing, Creating, and Sharing

One critical chapter in this book is Chapter 14, where we talk about printing your pictures. If your prints don't look the way they do on your monitor, you need to read and reread this chapter.

If screen viewing is of interest to you, we cover in Chapter 15 a number of different options for viewing your pictures on-screen. For slide shows, Web-hosted images, animated images, photo viewing on your TV, and even creating movie files, this chapter shows you the many ways you can view your Elements images on-screen.

We wrap up this part with Chapter 16, in which we describe how to make creations and share files. You have a number of different options for making creations to share or print.

Part VI: The Part of Tens

We wrap up this book with the Part of Tens chapters. We offer ten tips for composing better images and give you ten more project ideas to try with Elements.

Icons Used in This Book

In the margins throughout this book, you'll see icons indicating that something important is stated in the respective text.

This icon informs you that the item discussed is a new feature in Photoshop Elements 5.

A tip tells you about an alternative method for a procedure, by giving you a shortcut, a workaround, or some other type of helpful information related to working on tasks in the section being discussed.

Pay particular attention when you see the Warning icon. This information informs you when you may experience a problem performing your work in Elements.

This icon is a heads-up for something you may want to commit to memory. Usually, it tells you about a shortcut for a repetitive task, where remembering a procedure can save you time.

Elements is a computer program, after all. No matter how hard we try to simplify our explanation of features, we can't entirely avoid the technical information. If we think that a topic is complex, we use this icon to alert you that we're moving into a complex subject. You won't see many of these icons in the book because we try our best to bring the details to nontechnical terms.

Where to Go from Here

As we say earlier in the Introduction, the first part of this book serves as a foundation for all the other chapters. Try to spend a little time reading through the three chapters in Part I. After that, feel free to jump around and pay special attention to the cross-referenced chapters, in case you get stuck on a concept.

When you need a little extra help, refer to Chapter 1, where we talk about using the online help documents available in Elements.

If you have some questions, comments, suggestions, or complaints, go to

```
http://support.wiley.com
```

We wish you much success and enjoyment in using Adobe Photoshop Elements 5, and it is our sincere wish that the pages ahead provide you with an informative and helpful view of the program.

Part I
Getting Started

In this part . . .

Here you have it: a computer book specifically designed to help you get the most out of a computer software program — and not just any software program, but a powerful one with many complicated features. You probably want to jump in and perform some spiffy editing operations to get that prize photo looking the best you can. Inasmuch as we try to accommodate you in setting forth a how-to book in a nonlinear fashion, where you can freely move around and read about the techniques you want to use without having to read each chapter in linear order, you have to understand a few basics for editing your photos.

In this first part of the book, we talk about some essentials to help you fully understand all the parts ahead. We first talk about your Photoshop Elements working environment and describe the many tools and features you can use for all your Elements sessions. We also cover the very important task of getting color set for optimum viewing on your computer monitor and describe some essentials you need to know about color as it relates to photo images. Part I contains some important information that you should plan to carefully review and understand before going too far into all the Elements features. Don't pass up this part. Turn the page and start getting acquainted with the Adobe Photoshop Elements basics.

Getting to Know the Work Area

*I*n the Elements work areas, you find quite a collection of tools, palettes, buttons, and options. Just a quick glance at the Elements workspace when you enter Full Edit mode shows you some of the power that Elements offers with just a click of your mouse. With all the possibilities, the Elements workspace can be intimidating. To ease your introduction to the many options for editing your pictures, we break them down for you in this chapter.

Elements has several work areas, and we start off by introducing you to the one you'll likely use most often, Full Edit mode. In this mode, you can be creative with all the tools and features Photoshop Elements is known for, such as filters, drawing tools, layers, and more. We then introduce other work areas and tools you may not be as familiar with — Quick Fix mode for making common corrections to photos, Creation Setup mode for collecting your photos into creations such as calendars, and the Photo Bin for navigating among all your open images.

Before you start working in Elements, you'll find it helpful to know how to undo edits so that you can start over easily and find additional sources of help within Elements. We also explain one of the handiest ways to select tools and enter common commands: keyboard shortcuts.

Elements 5 also has the Organizer, a powerful tool for acquiring your images and keeping them organized. The Organizer includes features that help you view and search for images, too. We introduce the Organizer in Part II.

Getting Around in Full Edit Mode

Full Edit mode offers bundles of tools for editing your images, from correction tools for fixing color and clarity to filters, layers, and more for creating entirely original images either from existing photos or from scratch. But all these tools also make Full Edit mode complex.

Figure 1-1 shows Elements in Full Edit mode, highlighting all the tools and features we discuss in this section.

Jumping to Full Edit mode

You can move into Full Edit mode in a couple of ways:

- **From the initial Welcome screen,** click Edit and Enhance Photos and open a photo. Your Elements window appears in Full Edit mode, as shown in Figure 1-1.

- **From the Organizer,** click Edit on the Shortcuts bar and choose Go to Full Edit from the drop-down menu.

Examining the Image window

Not surprisingly, the Image window's tools and features are most useful when an image is open in the window. To get an image into the image window (refer to Figure 1-1), follow these steps:

1. **Click the Open tool on the Shortcuts bar.**

   The standard Open dialog box appears. It works like any ordinary Open dialog box you find in other applications.

2. **Move around your hard drive by using methods you know to open folders and select a picture.**

   If you haven't yet downloaded digital camera images or acquired scanned photos and want an image to experiment with, you can use an image found in your My Pictures folder that was installed with Windows or select a photo on the Mac.

3. **After selecting a picture, click Open.**

   The photo opens in a new image window in Elements.

Automatically
tile windows

Maximize mode

Close

Maximize

Automatically
cascade windows | Minimize

Title bar | Menu bar

Full Edit | Quick Fix | Shortcuts bar | Search Help topic

Tools palette | Photo bin | Image window | Palette bin

Figure 1-1: The Photoshop Elements workspace is shown when you open a file in Full Edit mode.

You can open as many image windows in Elements as your computer memory can handle. As each new file is opened, a thumbnail image is added to the Photo Bin at the bottom of the screen (see Figure 1-1), and the image windows are stacked, with the current active image in the topmost window. To bring another open file to the foreground and make it active, click the respective thumbnail in the Photo Bin.

Here's a quick look at important items in the image window, shown in Figure 1-2:

Image area　Title bar

- **Scroll bars** become active when you zoom in on an image. You can click the scroll arrows, move the Scroll bar, or grab the Hand tool in the Tools palette and drag within the window to move the image around.

- The **Magnification box** shows you at a glance how much you zoom in or out.

- The **Information box** shows you a readout for a particular tidbit of information. You can choose what information you want to see in this area by choosing one of the options from the pop-up menu, which we discuss in more detail later in this section.

Information box　　　　　　Size box

Magnification box

Figure 1-2: The image window displays an open file within the Elements workspace.

When you're working on an image in Elements, you always want to know the physical image size, the image resolution, and the color mode. (These terms are explained in more detail in Chapters 3 and 4.) Regardless of which menu option you choose from the status bar, you can get a quick glimpse at these essential stats by clicking the Information box, which displays a pop-up menu like the one shown in Figure 1-3.

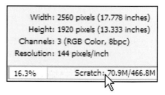

Figure 1-3: Click the readout on the status bar, and a pop-up menu shows you important information about your file.

- The **Size box** enables you to resize the window. Move the cursor to the box, and a diagonal line with two opposing arrows appears. When the cursor changes, drag in or out to size the window smaller or larger.

  You can also resize the window by dragging any of the other corners in or out.

- Click the **Minimize button** (the _ button in the upper-right corner of the image window), and the window hides from view. It's still open; you just click the image in the Photo Bin to maximize the window. On the Mac, it's the yellow minus (–) button in the top-left corner.

- If you click the **Maximize button** (the button with the box-shaped icon), the Title bar shown at the top of the window disappears and provides you with a little more room for viewing images in the window. On the Mac, it's the green plus sign (+) in the top-left corner.

✔ You can click the **Close button** (it's shaped like an X) to close the active image window and keep Elements open. Alternatively, you can use the keyboard shortcut Ctrl+W/⌘+W or the menu command File⇨Close to close the active window. On the Mac, it's the red button in the top-left corner.

Now that you're familiar with the overall image window, we want to introduce you to the Information box's pop-up menu, which enables you to choose the type of information you want to view in the Information box. Click the right-pointing arrow to open the menu, as shown in Figure 1-4.

Here's the lowdown on the options you find on the pop-up menu:

Click here to open pop-up menu

Figure 1-4: From the pop-up menu on the status bar, you select commands that provide information about your file.

✔ **Document Sizes:** Shows you the saved file size.

✔ **Document Profile:** Shows you the color profile used with the file.

✔ **Document Dimensions:** Shows you the physical size in your default unit of measure, such as inches.

✔ **Scratch Sizes:** As shown in Figure 1-4, displays the amount of memory on your hard drive that's consumed by all documents open in Elements. For example, 20M/200M indicates that the open documents consume 20 megabytes and that a total of 200 megabytes are available for Elements to edit your images. As you add more content to a file, such as new layers, the first figure grows while the second figure remains static.

✔ **Efficiency:** Indicates how many operations you're performing in RAM as opposed to using your scratch disk. When the number is 100%, you're working in RAM. When the number drops below 100%, you're using the scratch disk. If you continually work below 100%, it's a good indication that you need to buy more RAM to increase your efficiency.

✔ **Timing:** Indicates the time it took to complete the last operation.

✔ **Current Tool:** Shows the name of the tool selected from the Tools palette.

Don't worry about trying to understand all these terms. The important thing to know is that you can visit the pop-up menu and change the items at will during your editing sessions.

Moving through the menu bar

Like just about every program you launch in Windows or on the Mac, Elements supports drop-down menus. The menus are logically constructed and identified to provide commands for working with your pictures (commands that you don't find supported in tools and on palettes). A quick glimpse at the menu names gives you a hint of what might be contained in a given menu list.

The ten different menus are described in this list:

- **File menu:** Just as you might suspect, the File menu contains commands for working with your picture as a file. You find commands in the menu list for saving, opening, processing, importing, exporting, and printing. We cover saving files in Chapter 3 and printing or exporting for other output in Part V.

- **Edit menu:** As you might guess, the old-fashioned Copy, Cut, and Paste commands are located here. Additionally, you have some important file settings commands on the menu, including preferences, which we cover in more detail in Chapter 2.

- **Image menu:** You find yourself using the Image menu when you want to effect changes to the entire image, such as changing a color mode or cropping, rotating, and resizing the image. For details about sizing and color modes, check out Chapter 3. For more about cropping and rotating images, flip to Chapter 9.

- **Enhance menu:** Just the name of this menu should tell you what commands to expect here. This is where you go to change the appearance of an image, such as changing its brightness and contrast, adjusting its color and lighting, and doing some other smart fix-up work to improve its appearance. On the Enhance⇨Adjust Color submenu, you find a new adjustment introduced in Elements 5: Color Curves. Look to Chapter 10 for some detail on using this new command. In Chapters 9 and 10, you find out how to use correction tools so that your images look their best.

- **Layer menu:** As we describe in great detail in Chapter 8 (a whole chapter just about layers), most kinds of editing you do in Elements are best handled by using layers. Elements neatly tucks away all the relevant commands associated with working in layers right here.

- **Select menu:** Of just about equal importance to layers are selections. Whereas the Image menu contains commands that are applied to the entire image, you can edit isolated areas of an image by using the commands on the Select menu. To isolate an area, you need to create a selection, as we explain in Chapter 7. This menu contains commands to help you with all the essential tasks related to working with selections.

- ✔ **Filter menu:** The Filter menu is where you leave the world of photography and explore the world of a fine artist. With tons of different filter commands, you can create some extraordinary effects. Find out all about filters in Chapter 11.

- ✔ **View menu:** Zooming in and out of images, turning on a grid, exposing horizontal and vertical rulers, adding annotations, and checking out the print size of your pictures are handled on the View menu. Chapter 5 unearths secrets of the Zoom tool, rulers, and more.

- ✔ **Window menu:** Elements supports a number of different palettes, as we explain later in this chapter. Elements has so many palettes that keeping them all open at one time is impractical. Thanks to the Window menu, you can easily view and hide palettes, reopen the Welcome window, tile and cascade open windows, and bring inactive windows to the foreground.

- ✔ **Help menu:** We hope that you get all the help you need right here in this book; but just in case we miss something (or your neighbor has borrowed it, fine book that it is), you have some interactive help, right at your mouse-tip, on the Help menu. The menu also offers links to the Adobe Web site for more information and a little assistance, courtesy of the tutorials accessible from this menu. (Find a little more detail about accessing help later in this chapter.)

Uncovering the context menus

Context menus are common to many programs, and Photoshop Elements is no exception. They're those little menus that appear when you right-click, offering commands and tools related to whatever area or tool you right-clicked.

The context menus are your solution when you may be in doubt about where to find a command on a menu. You just right-click an item, and a pop-up menu opens. As you become familiar with Photoshop Elements and struggle to find a menu command, always try to first open a context menu and look for the command you want in the menu list.

Because context menus provide commands respective to the tool you're using, the menu commands change according to what tool or feature you're using at the moment you open a context menu. For example, in Figure 1-5, you can see the context menu that appears after we create a selection marquee and right-click that marquee in the Image window. Notice that the commands are all related to selections.

Deselect
Select Inverse
Feather...
Layer via Copy
Layer via Cut
New Layer...
Free Transform
Fill Selection...
Stroke (Outline) Selection...
Last Filter

Figure 1-5: A context menu for selections.

Using the Tools palette

Elements provides a good number of palettes for different purposes. The one that you'll find you use most is the Tools palette. In palette hierarchy terms, you typically first click a tool in the Tools palette and then use another palette for additional tool options or use the Options bar for fine-tuning your tool instruments. More often than not, clicking a tool in the Tools palette is your first step in most editing sessions.

Tools can be easily accessed in Elements by pressing shortcut keys on your keyboard. For a quick glance at the Tools palette and the keystrokes needed to access the tools, look over Figure 1-6.

If you accidentally press the Tab key on your keyboard, the Tools palette hides from view. Press Tab again and the Tools palette reappears.

Notice in the Tools palette that several tools appear with a tiny arrow pointing right and downward in the lower-right corner of each tool. Whenever you see this arrowhead, remember that more tools are nested within that tool group. Click a tool with an arrowhead and hold down the mouse button. A pop-up toolbar opens, as shown in Figure 1-7, and offers you more tool selections within that group.

To select tools within a tool group by using keystrokes, press the Shift key and strike the respective key (shown in Figure 1-6) to access the tool. Keep the Shift key down and repeatedly press the shortcut key to scroll through all tools in a given group.

The shortcuts work for you at all times except when you're typing text. Be certain to click the Tools palette to select a tool if your last edit was made with one of the Type tools.

The tools are varied, and you may find that you don't use all the tools in the Tools palette in your workflow. Rather than describe the tool

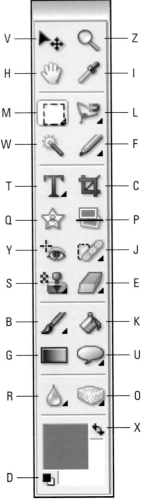

Figure 1-6: You access tools by clicking the tool in the Tools palette or typing the respective character on your keyboard.

Figure 1-7: Click and hold the mouse button on a tool that has a tiny arrowhead, and a pop-up toolbar opens.

functions here, we address the tools in the remaining chapters in this book as they pertain to the respective Elements tasks.

Playing with palettes

Elements provides you with a bunch of palettes that contain settings and options used to refine the tools you select in the Tools palette and tasks you perform to edit images. Assume for a moment that you want to let your creative juices loose and create a Picasso-esque painting — something that you can easily do in Photoshop Elements.

You first click the Brush tool and then click a color in the Color Swatches palette. On a new canvas, you begin to paint. When you want to change color, you click again in the Color Swatches palette on a different color. This kind of interactivity between the Tools palette and another palette is something you frequently use in Elements.

Palettes are accessed from either the Palette Bin or the Window menu. Many options in palettes are intuitive. To become familiar with various palette options, just poke around a little, and most of the options will become familiar to you.

Selecting tool options from the Options bar

When you click a tool in the Tools palette, the Options bar offers you choices specific to a selected tool. Figure 1-8 shows the options available when the Clone Stamp tool is selected.

Figure 1-8: The Options bar provides attribute choices for a tool selected in the Tools palette.

Juggling all your interface options

With all the settings you can use for any given tool, trying to figure out exactly where to select an option for the edit you want to make can become downright frustrating. To help simplify the process of using tools and selecting options for the tools, here's what you might do in your normal workflow:

1. **Select a tool in the Tools palette.**

   Obviously, you need to know what task you want to perform, so selecting the proper tool to complete the task is important to know upfront.

2. **Take a quick look at the Options bar.**

Before moving to other option choices, be certain that you look over the choices on the Options bar. If you want to use a tool like the Brush tool or the Clone Stamp tool, perhaps you want to make a decision about what size brush tip you want to use. This choice is specific to the selected tool and therefore appears as an Options bar choice.

3. **Open a palette for more options.**

   If you want to use the Brush tool, for example, to apply some color to an image, after selecting the Brush tip on the Options bar, open the Color Swatches palette and select a color.

4. **Open the More menu.**

   Maybe the color you want to use doesn't appear in the Color Swatches palette. Your next stop is the More menu. By using the menu choices, you can load different swatch libraries that provide more color options.

Try following the same sequence when you want to edit images in Elements by first selecting a tool and then checking out the Options bar, opening palettes related to providing choices for the task at hand, and, finally, clicking the More button for additional choices in the palettes.

Looking at the Shortcuts bar

You find the Shortcuts bar just above the Options bar and below the Menu bar. The Shortcuts bar, shown in Figure 1-9, serves two purposes:

- ✔ **Quick access to common tasks:** Tools on the Shortcuts bar are available for quick access to some of the most common tasks you perform in Elements.

- ✔ **Quick access to other Elements functions:** Buttons appear for quick access to other Elements functions that involve organizing documents, browsing photos, or viewing calendars.

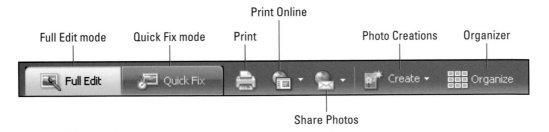

Figure 1-9: In Full Edit mode, the Shortcuts bar provides tools and viewing options.

Depending on your editing mode, such as Full Edit, Quick Fix, or one of the other viewing modes, the Shortcuts bar changes to provide different tools and buttons. Figure 1-9 shows how the Shortcuts bar appears when you view it in Full Edit mode.

The Shortcuts bar contains tools and buttons grouped as follows:

- ✔ The first group includes tools to toggle the Full Edit and Quick Fix modes.

- ✔ Click the Print tool to print a file.

- ✔ The new Print Online icon on the Shortcuts bar is used to open a drop-down menu where you make choices for making online orders for printing photos.

- ✔ Click the Share tool to open a drop-down menu where you can make choices for sharing photos by e-mail, with mobile phones, and with several online services.

- ✔ Click the Create tool to open a menu where you can choose from a number of options for making creations such as greeting cards, photo albums, CD/DVD labels and jackets, slide shows, photo stamps, calendars, and more.

- ✔ For a quick jump to all the wonderful organizing features provided in Elements, such as managing photos in collections, sorting photos, cataloging photos, tagging photos, and more, click this tool, and you jump to the Photoshop Elements 5 Organizer.

Changing Workspaces

When you're in Full Edit mode, discussed in preceding sections, you can apply any kind of edits to a picture, improve the picture's appearance, and apply all that Elements offers you. This mode is the richest editor in Elements in terms of accessing all features. Because Elements has so many different kinds of editing opportunities, the program offers you other workspace views, tailored to the kinds of tasks people typically want to perform.

Using Quick Fix mode

Quick Fix mode is designed to provide you with just those tools that are needed to prepare a picture for its intended destination, whether it's printing, on-screen viewing, or one of the other organizing items. Use this mode to make your pictures look good. You don't find tools for adding text, painting with brushes, or applying gradients in Quick Fix mode. Rather, what you find is a completely different set of palettes for balancing contrast and brightness, lighting, and sharpening, for example. This mode is like having a digital darkroom on your desktop, where you take care of perfecting an image like you would in analog photography darkrooms.

To enter Quick Fix mode while you're in Full Edit mode, click the Quick Fix button adjacent to the Shortcuts bar; the view changes, as shown in Figure 1-10.

If you want to start up Elements in Quick Fix mode, click the Quick Fix button on the Welcome screen when you first launch the program.

Figure 1-10: Click Quick Fix in Full Edit mode, and the workspace changes.

There are several differences between Full Edit mode and Quick Fix mode:

- **Completely different sets of palettes are docked in the Palette Bin.** All the palettes in Quick Fix mode are related to adjusting brightness controls and are designed to improve the overall appearance of your pictures. In addition, all the Windows menu commands for accessing palettes are grayed out. While you work in Quick Fix mode, Elements insists on limiting your use of palettes to just the ones docked in the Palette Bin. Moreover, you cannot undock palettes from the Palette Bin by dragging them out, as you can in other modes.

- **The Tools palette disappears.** Quick Fix mode offers you only these tools in the Tools palette:

  - Zoom
  - Hand
  - Magic Selection Brush
  - Crop
  - Red Eye Removal

  None of the other Elements tools is accessible while you work in this mode.

- **Multiple viewing options are available.** Notice in Figure 1-10 that you see two views of the same image. One view displays the raw, unedited image. The After view shows you the results of changes you make with palette options and menu commands.

If you want to return to Full Edit mode, click the Full Edit button.

Using Creation Wizards

To organize your pictures for display in a variety of different ways, you begin by accessing a wizard window respective to a particular creation you want. From the drop-down menu shown in Figure 1-11, you make a choice for a particular creation, and a wizard window opens where you follow some easy steps to produce creations such as photo books, album pages, CD/DVD jackets, and more.

Figure 1-11: Click Create in either Full Edit or Quick Fix mode to open the Creation Setup window.

We cover each option available in the various wizard windows in greater detail in Chapter 16.

Using the Photo Bin

The Photo Bin displays thumbnail views of all your open images. Regardless of whether you work in Full Edit or Quick Fix mode, you can immediately see a small image of all the pictures you have open at one time, as shown in Figure 1-12. You can also see thumbnail views of all the different views you create for a single picture. Find out all the details in this section.

Figure 1-12: All open pictures and new views are displayed as thumbnails in the Photo Bin.

If you want to rearrange the thumbnails in the Photo Bin, just click and drag horizontally to reorganize the order of the thumbnails.

Creating different views of an image

What? Different views of the same picture, you say? Yes, indeed. You might create a new view when you want to zoom in on an area for some precise editing and then want to switch back to a wider view. Here's how you do it:

1. **Click a thumbnail image in the Photo Bin.**

   The respective photo appears in the image window as the active document.

2. **Choose View⇨New Window for *<filename>*.**

   Note that *<filename>* is the name of the file in the image window.

3. **Zoom to the new view.**

   A new view appears for the active document, and you see another thumbnail image added to the Photo Bin.

To zoom quickly, click the Zoom tool and click a few times on the picture in the image window to zoom into the photo.

4. **Toggle views of the same image.**

   Click one thumbnail and you see the opening view; click the other thumbnail and you see the zoomed view.

Hiding the Photo Bin

The Photo Bin takes up a lot of room at the bottom of the image window, and you're not likely to want it open all the time while editing some pictures. Fortunately, Elements provides you with two methods for hiding the Photo Bin when you want to create a little more editing real estate.

To temporarily hide the Photo Bin, do one of the following:

- ↙ Place the cursor over the separator bar between the Image window and the Photo Bin. When the cursor changes to two horizontal lines with vertical opposing arrowheads, drag down to collapse the Photo Bin. When the bin is collapsed, drag up the separator bar to open the bin.

- ↙ To auto-hide the Photo Bin, open a context menu (right-click inside the Photo Bin) and select Auto-hide from the menu choices. (Alternatively, you can just click the separator bar where you see the tiny arrowhead to show or hide the bin.) When you use Auto-hide, the Photo Bin automatically hides when the cursor appears in the image window. The Photo Bin automatically opens when you move the cursor below the separator bar.

Retracing Your Steps

Ever since Apple's Macintosh brought a windows interface to the masses, the Undo command has been one of the most frequently used menu commands in every program developed. You make a change to your document, and if you don't like it, you simply choose Edit⇨Undo or press the keyboard shortcut Ctrl+Z/⌘+Z.

In Elements, your options to undo your work have expanded, as we explain in this section.

Using the Undo History palette

Elements takes the Undo command to new levels by offering you a palette in which all (well, almost all) your changes in an editing session are recorded and available for undoing at any step in an editing sequence.

Each edit you make is recorded in the Undo History palette. To open the palette, choose Window⇨Undo History. Make changes to your document, and each step is recorded in the palette, as you see in Figure 1-13.

If Elements slows down and you're moving along at a snail's pace, open the More drop-down menu in the Undo History palette and choose Clear Undo History. Elements flushes all the recorded history and frees up some precious memory that often enables you to work faster.

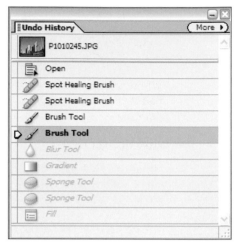

Figure 1-13: The Undo History palette records steps in an editing session.

We said *almost all* steps are recorded because the number of steps the History palette can record is controlled by a preference setting that tops out at 1,000 steps. If you choose Edit⇨Preferences (Windows) or Photoshop Elements Preferences (Mac) and look at the General preferences, as we explain in more depth in Chapter 2, the number of *history states* (times you can go back in history and undo) defaults to 50. You can change the number to the maximum 1,000, if you like. But realize that the more history states you record, the more memory that Elements requires.

To undo the last edit, you can use the keyboard shortcut Ctrl+Z/⌘+Z. When you want to undo multiple edits, open the Undo History palette and click any item listed in the palette. Elements takes you to that last edit while scrubbing all edits that follow the selected item. If you want to bring back the edits, just click again on any step appearing grayed out in the palette to redo up to that level.

All your steps are listed in the Undo History palette as long as you remain in Elements and don't close the file. When the file is closed, all history information is lost.

Reverting to the last save

As you work away in Elements, you should always plan on saving your work regularly. Each time you save in an editing session, the Undo History palette preserves the list of edits you made before the save and up to the maximum number of history states defined in the General preferences.

If you save, and then perform more edits, and then want to return to the last saved version of your document, Elements provides you with a quick, efficient way to do so. Choose Edit⇨Revert, and Elements eliminates your new edits and takes you back to the last time you saved your file.

When you choose Revert, the word *Revert* appears in the Undo History palette. You can eliminate the Revert command from the Undo History palette by right-clicking Revert in the Undo History palette and choosing Delete from a context menu. This command returns you to the edits made after the last save.

Getting a Helping Hand

You can reach for this book whenever you want some details about accomplishing a task while working in Elements. However, for those little annoying moments, and just in case some coffee stains blot out a few pages in this book, you may want to look for an alternative feature description from another source.

Rather than accumulate a library of Elements books, all you need to do is look at Elements itself to find some valuable help information quickly and easily. If you're stuck on understanding some feature, ample help documents that are a mouse click away can help you overcome some frustrating moments.

Using Help

Your first stop for exploring the helpful information Elements provides is on the Help menu. There, you find several menu commands that offer information:

- **Photoshop Elements Help:** Choose Help⇨Photoshop Elements Help or press the F1 key to open the Elements Help file. You can type a search topic and press Enter to open a list of items that provide helpful information about the searched words.

  For quick access to the Help document, type the text you want to search into the text box on the right side of the menu bar in Full Edit or Quick Fix mode.

- **Glossary of Terms:** As you read this book, if we use a term that you don't completely understand, open the Photoshop Elements glossary. There, you find definitions of terms commonly used in photography and image editing as well as terms related specifically to Elements.

- ✔ **Tutorials:** If you want to explore some advanced learning, check out the online tutorials provided by Adobe Systems.
- ✔ **Photoshop Elements Online:** This menu command launches your default Web browser and takes you to the Adobe Web site, where you can find information about Elements, problems reported by users, and some work-around methods for getting a job done.

Using PDFs from the installation CD

A number of bonus files are stored in PDF form on your installation CD. PDF files require the free Adobe Reader program or one of the commercial Acrobat viewers. Adobe Reader can be installed from the CD during the installation process.

Depending on when you purchased your Elements installer CD, the version of Adobe Reader on the CD may be outdated. If you want to stay with the latest upgrade of Adobe Reader, open your Web browser and type this address on the Location bar:

```
www.adobe.com/products/acrobat/readermain.html
```

Adobe Systems provides easy, step-by-step instructions for downloading the most current, free Adobe Reader program and installing it on your computer.

Using ToolTips

As you move your cursor around tools and palettes, pause a moment before clicking the mouse. A slight delay in your actions produces a ToolTip, as shown in Figure 1-14. Elements provides this sort of dynamic help as you move the cursor around the workspace and pause before moving to another location.

Figure 1-14: Place the cursor over a tool and pause a moment to open a ToolTip.

Using the How To palette

The default Palette Bin in Full Edit mode contains the How To palette at the top of the bin. The How To palette lists some of the more common tasks you're likely to perform in Elements. Click the right-pointing arrowhead to expand a list, and then click an item to open help information in the palette. You can scroll pages by clicking the arrows, return to the opening How To page by clicking the house icon, and print a topic by clicking the printer icon if you want to create hard copy of some help information.

Taking Charge with Shortcuts

As Emeril says, "It's time to kick it up a notch." Kicking it up a notch in Elements terms means leaving the pick-and-poke editing method of the novice and graduating to techniques used by the swift keyboard master.

Using keyboard shortcuts greatly reduces your time in Elements and makes you much more proficient. The upside is that most of what you can do by moving the mouse and clicking a tool or menu command can be performed right from your keyboard by using combinations of keystrokes. The downside is that, because Elements has so many keyboard shortcuts, remembering all of them is nearly impossible.

The best way to remember keyboard shortcuts is to practice using them. After that, you may want to browse the resources where shortcuts are defined. Here are some considerations to help you remember shortcuts and find more information about them:

- **For common tasks, always take special note of ToolTips and commands on a menu.** ToolTips provide descriptions of what tools do and often display the keyboard shortcuts used to access the tools. Menu commands that support keyboard shortcuts list the shortcut keys to the right of command names.

- **Look over all the tips and alternative methods for performing an action that we describe throughout this book.** As you're introduced to more features in Elements, we try to offer you the keyboard shortcut options as well as tools and commands. Rather than give you a list here, we provide keyboard shortcuts when we explain features.

- **Search the Help document.** Open the Elements Help document (choose Help⇨Photoshop Elements Help or press F1) and search for **keyboard shortcuts.** The Help document provides a comprehensive list of all the keyboard shortcuts you can use in Elements.

- **Stick with the essentials.** Try to commit to memory only those shortcuts that produce actions for your most common editing tasks.

The Cheat Sheet at the front of this book lists some common keyboard shortcuts so that you can reference them quickly and easily.

Memorizing keyboard shortcuts isn't critical to your work in Photoshop Elements. You can do everything the program was designed for without ever using a shortcut. However, when you become familiar with keyboard shortcuts, you'll zoom through editing sessions with much more speed and efficiency. As a matter of fact, many advanced and professional users often forget where a menu command is contained because they rely so much on shortcut keys.

2

Getting Ready to Edit

In This Chapter

▶ Specifying editing preferences

▶ Specifying organizing preferences

▶ Working with presets

▶ Understanding color in Photoshop Elements

▶ Setting up your color management system

*A*lthough not as exciting as firing up Elements and working on your precious pictures, customizing Elements for your personal work habits and properly setting up color management is critical to everything else you do in the program. This chapter explains how to take charge of Elements and customize your work environment by adjusting preference settings and setting up a color management system. If you're new to Elements or image editing in general, you might not know just how you want to set up certain features right away. However, you can always refer to this chapter and review and update settings and options later as you become familiar with other features in Elements.

Controlling the Editing Environment

Opening Elements for the first time is like moving into a new office. Before you begin work, you need to organize the office. At minimum, you need to set up the desk and computer before you can do anything. In Elements terms, the office organization consists of specifying Preference settings. *Preferences* are settings that provide a means to customize your work in Elements and to fine-tune the program according to your personal work habits.

What we offer here is a brief description of the preference options available to you. When you need some detail regarding one preference option or another, look at the help documents we discuss in Chapter 1. Use the help documents as a reference and you won't need to memorize the vast number of settings Elements provides.

Launching and navigating Preferences

Preferences are all contained in a dialog box that's organized into ten panes. By default, when you open the Preferences dialog box, the opening pane is the General pane. To open the Preferences dialog box, choose Edit⇨Preferences (Windows) or Elements⇨Preferences (Mac). Alternatively, press Ctrl+K/⌘+K. Using either method opens the dialog box to the General pane in the Preferences dialog box, as shown in Figure 2-1.

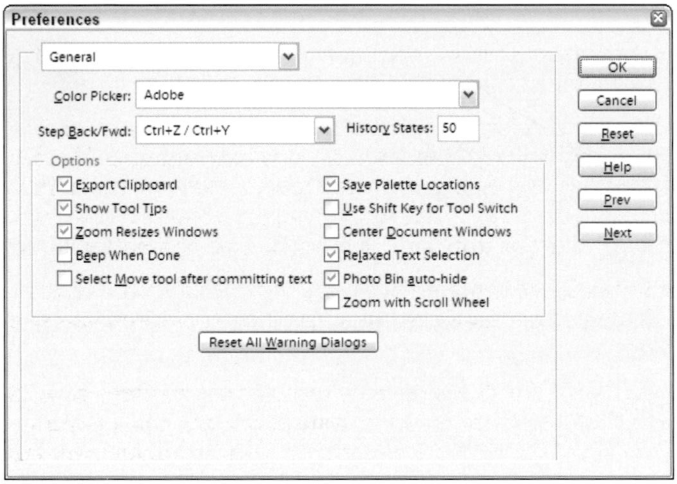

Figure 2-1: The General pane in the Preferences dialog box.

In Figure 2-1, you see items that are common to all preference panes. Here's a quick introduction to what these items are and how they work:

- **Drop-down pane menu:** Click the topmost downward-pointing arrow and you see all individual panes listed. You can select from the menu to jump to another pane.

- **OK:** Click OK to accept any changes made in any pane.

- **Cancel:** Click Cancel to return to the same settings as when you opened a pane. If you hold down the Alt/Option key, the Cancel button changes to Reset and performs the same action as clicking the Reset button.

- **Reset:** If you change the settings options and click Reset, the action takes you back to the same settings as when you opened the Preferences dialog box.

- **Learn about Preferences:** Click the blue text and the Adobe Help Center opens, where you find help information that's specific to this dialog box.

✓ **Prev:** Switch to the previous pane.

✓ **Next:** Switch to the next pane. You can also press Ctrl/⌘+(1 through 0 keys) to jump to another pane.

Checking out all the Preferences panes

The settings in the Preferences dialog box are organized into different panes that reflect key categories of preferences. The following list briefly describes the types of settings you can adjust in each of the Preferences panes:

✓ As the name implies, **General** preferences apply to overall general settings you adjust for your editing environment.

✓ **Saving Files** preferences relate to options available for saving files. You can choose to add extensions to filenames, save files with layers or flatten layers when you're saving a file (as we explain in Chapter 8), save files with image previews that appear when you're viewing files as icons on your desktop, and save with some compatibility options.

✓ **Display & Cursors** preferences offer options for how certain tool cursors are displayed and how you view the Crop tool when you're cropping images.

✓ Working with the **Transparency** preferences requires an understanding of how Elements represents transparency. Imagine painting a portrait on a piece of clear acetate. The area you paint is opaque, and the area surrounding the portrait is transparent. To display transparency in Elements, you need some method to represent transparent areas. (Chapter 7 has more details.) Open the Transparency preferences and make choices for how transparency is viewed in your 2-D Elements environment.

✓ **Units & Rulers** preferences let you specify settings for ruler units, column guides, and document preset resolutions.

✓ The **Grid** preferences offer options for gridline color, divisions, and subdivisions. A *grid* shows you nonprinting horizontal and vertical lines. You use a grid to align objects, type, and other elements. You can snap items to the gridlines to make aligning objects much easier.

✓ The **Plug-ins & Scratch Disks** preferences contain options for selecting an additional Plug-ins folder for storing third-party utilities to work with Elements and scratch disks.

Assume that you have 100MB of free RAM (your internal computer memory) and you want to work on a picture that consumes 200MB of hard disk space. Elements needs to load all 200MB of the file into RAM. Therefore, an auxiliary source of RAM is needed in order for you to work on the image; Elements uses your hard drive. When a hard drive is used as an extension of RAM, we call this source a *scratch disk*.

If you have more than one hard drive connected to your computer, you can instruct Elements to use all hard drives, and you can select the order of the hard drives Elements uses for your extension of RAM. All disks and media sources appear on the drop-down menus you see for First, Second, Third, and Fourth.

Don't use USB 1.1 external hard drives or other drives with connections slower than FireWire. Using slower drives slows the performance of Elements.

✔ Memory — and the need to conserve and manage it well — is important to Elements. Another preference item for managing memory is the **Memory & Image Cache** settings.

Cache is a memory location on your hard drive that Elements uses to remember things like image levels, screen redraws, and histogram displays. (We explain more about using histograms in Chapters 4 and 10.) When one of these items is loaded in memory, it's stored in a cache location. The next time you use the same operation, Elements pulls the item from the cache. The result is much faster access to frequently used items.

You can set the cache level from 0 to 8 by typing a number in the text box. Setting the number to a lower value can help you free up memory so that you can work on large images. If you have a lot of RAM and hard drive memory to work with, caching isn't a concern; you can set the cache to 8 for faster operations.

✔ **Type** preferences provide options for setting text attributes. You have options for using different quote marks, showing Asian characters, showing font names in English, and previewing font sizes.

✔ When you open the **Organize & Share** (Windows) preferences pane, you lose the Preferences dialog box, and another Preferences dialog box opens, in which choices are made for the organizing environment itself. Because this set of preferences is handled in a completely different dialog box, we describe it in the next section.

Controlling the Organizing Environment (Windows only)

A whole different set of Preferences appears when you select Organize & Share in the Preferences dialog box. Initially, you may be confused because the dialog box that opens when you select Organize and Share is also named Preferences. However, a quick glance at the dialog box shows you a different set of Preferences choices. In the following sections, you find a brief introduction to the Organizer and discover all the different organization preferences that Elements has to offer.

Understanding the Photoshop Elements Organizer

We cover all you need to know about the wonderful Adobe Photoshop Elements Organizer tool in Chapter 6. Rather than describe in this chapter all that the Organizer offers you, we just want you to be aware that when you're setting the Organize & Share preferences, you're setting preference options for the Organizer. To take a quick peek at the Organizer, click the Photo Browser button while in Standard Edit or Quick Fix mode.

Navigating Organize & Share preferences

You can open the Organize & Share Preferences dialog box directly from the Edit menu while in either Standard Edit or Quick Fix mode. Choose Edit⇨Preferences⇨Organize & Share. Doing so bypasses the Editing Preferences dialog box and takes you directly to the dialog box shown in Figure 2-2.

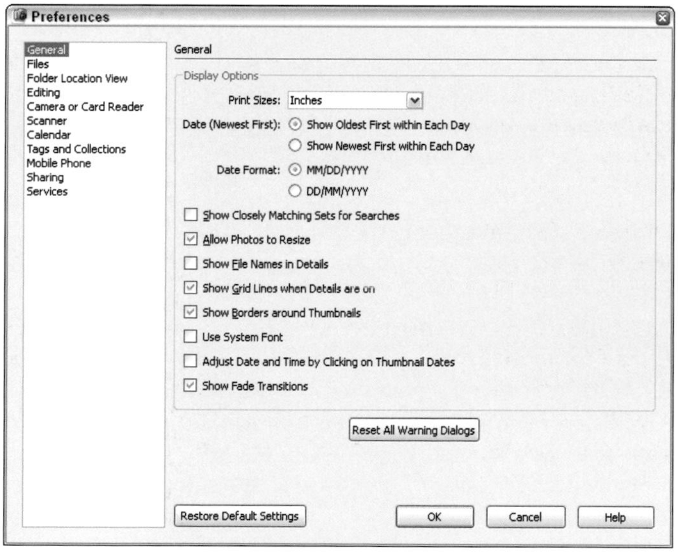

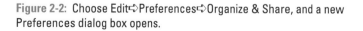

Figure 2-2: Choose Edit⇨Preferences⇨Organize & Share, and a new Preferences dialog box opens.

The Organize & Share Preferences dialog box uses the same metaphor to toggle through a number of panes that the main Preferences dialog box uses. However, selecting the individual panes is handled by clicking the names in the list on the left side of the dialog box rather than selecting panes from a drop-down menu. Options common to all preferences panes include:

✔ **Restore Default Settings:** Click Restore Default Settings to change all panes to their original defaults.

✔ **OK:** Click OK to accept new changes.

✔ **Cancel:** Click Cancel in any pane, and any changes made aren't registered.

✔ **Help:** Click Help to open the Help window and find information about Organize & Share preferences.

Setting preferences in all the panes

With the Organize & Share Preferences dialog box open, here's a quick overview of what you find there:

✔ The items in the **General** preferences pane affect a miscellaneous group of settings that are applied to files when you're using the Create tool. Chapter 16 explains this tool in detail.

✔ **Files** preferences offer options for managing file data, connecting to missing files, prompting for backing up your data, saving catalogs, choosing file and folder locations for saved files, and adjusting proxy file (a low-resolution display of a higher-resolution image) sizes.

✔ **Folder Location View** preferences provide options for showing files and folders in groups and selected folders.

✔ With the **Editing** preferences, you can enable another application that provides some editing features not found in Elements to edit an image based on its file type. One good example for adding another editor is when you're editing video clips. If you have Adobe Premiere Elements, you can add Premiere as another editor. If you don't have Premiere installed, you can use another editor, like Microsoft Media Maker or the Apple iMovie.

✔ The **Camera or Card Reader** preferences handle acquiring images from digital cameras and media storage cards. Your computer may have built-in card readers in which you can insert a media card, such as CompactFlash or Smart Media, or a USB card reader that supports a media card. In other cases, you may have a cable that connects from your camera to a USB port on your computer. These preference options are used with media cards and camera connections.

✔ If you scan images with a scanner connected to your computer (as opposed to downloading them from your camera), the **Scanner** preferences hold all the options you may want to set.

✔ **Calendar** preferences relate to calendar creations. You have several options from which to choose for your calendar design. In Chapter 16, we cover creating calendars and explain a little more about these preference options.

✓ **Tags and Collections** preferences help you find and sort your images, as we explain in much more detail in Chapters 5 and 6. Tag preferences offer options for sorting tags and icon views for tags.

✓ If you have a mobile phone capable of taking pictures, check out the **Mobile Phone** preferences. You can copy pictures from your phone to your computer, as we explain in Chapter 4. These preferences offer options for a folder location where mobile phone files are stored and an option for correcting red-eye automatically as files are opened. See Chapter 10 for more information on red-eye correction.

✓ **Sharing** preferences relate to sharing files online and in e-mail. Options are available for setting e-mail and sharing settings.

✓ **Services** preferences offer choices for handling program updates and online service orders. You can choose to check for program updates automatically or manually choose options for printing and sharing images, and update creations, accounts, and more.

Customizing Presets

Part of the fun of image editing is choosing brush tips, swatch colors, gradient colors, and patterns to create the look you want. To get you started, Elements provides you with a number of different preset libraries that can be loaded and used at your will. For example, you can load a Brushes library to acquire different brush tips you use with the Brush tool. But you're likely to want to customize the preset libraries at least a little bit, too.

You can change libraries individually in respective palettes where the items are used. For example, you can change color swatch libraries on the Color Swatches palette or brush tips from Options bar choices. Another way you can change libraries is to use the Preset Manager, shown in Figure 2-3.

We cover using the presets in Chapter 12, which is where you can find out how to use the many different presets Elements provides. The important thing to note here is

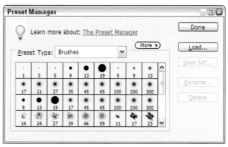

Figure 2-3: The Preset Manager dialog box provides a central area where libraries can be changed.

that you can change the presets according to your editing needs.

To open the Preset Manager dialog box, choose Edit➪Preset Manager. The options you have available include:

- ↙ **Preset Type:** Open the drop-down menu to choose from Brushes, Swatches, Gradients, and Patterns.

- ↙ **More:** The More drop-down menu lists different viewing options. You can view the library items as text lists or as thumbnail views.

- ↙ **Done:** Any changes you make in the Preset Manager are recorded and saved when you click Done.

- ↙ **Load:** Click this button to open another library. Elements provides you with several libraries from which to choose for each preset type.

- ↙ **Save Set:** Any changes you make in the Preset Manager can be saved as a new library. Use this option if you make a change so that you don't disturb the original presets.

- ↙ **Rename:** Each item in a library has a unique name. If you want to rename an item, click the thumbnail in the Preview window, click Rename, and type a new name in the dialog box that appears.

- ↙ **Delete:** Click an item in the Preview window and click Delete to remove the item from the library.

- ↙ **Help:** Click the blue *The Preset Manager* text to open the Help document and find out more about managing presets.

Getting Familiar with Color

We could spend a whole lot of time and many pages in this book delving into the complex world of color theory and definitions. You wouldn't likely read it, and we're not so inclined to reduce this book from a real page-turner to something that's likely to sedate you. Rather, in the following sections, we offer some fundamental principles to make your work in Elements easier when you're editing color images.

Introducing color channels

Your first level of understanding color is to understand what RGB is and how it comes about. *RGB* stands for *Red, Green,* and *Blue.* These are the primary colors in the computer world. Forget about what you know about primary colors in an analog world; computers see primary colors as RGB.

RGB color is divided into *color channels.* Although you can't see the individual channels in Elements, you still need to understand just a little about color channels.

When you see a color pixel (a tiny, square dot), the color is represented as different levels of gray in each channel. This may sound confusing at first, but stay with us for just a minute. When you have a color channel, like the red channel, and you let all light pass through the channel, you end up with a bright red. If you screen that light a little with a gray filter, you let less light pass through, thereby diluting the red color. This is how channels work. Individually, they all use different levels of gray that permit up to 256 levels of light to pass through them. When you change the intensity of light in the different channels, you ultimately change the color.

Each channel can have up to 256 levels of gray that mask out light. The total number of possibilities for creating color in an RGB model is achieved by multiplying the values for each channel (256 x 256 x 256). The result is more than 16.7 million; that's the total number of colors a computer monitor can display in RGB color.

This is all well and good as far as theory goes, but what does that mean in practicality? Actually, you see some of this information in tools and dialog boxes you work with in Elements. As an experiment, open a file in Elements and choose Enhance⇨Adjust Lighting⇨Levels; the dialog box shown in Figure 2-4 opens.

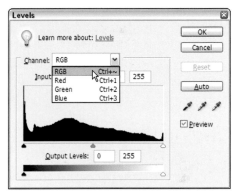

Notice that the Channel drop-down menu shows you Red, Green, and Blue as individual channels as well as a composite RGB selection. Furthermore, the Output Levels area

Figure 2-4: Choose Enhance⇨Adjust Lighting⇨ Levels to open the Levels dialog box.

shows you values ranging from 0 on the left to 255 on the right. Considering that 0 is a number, you have a total of 256 different levels of gray.

What's important is that you know that your work in color is related to RGB images that comprise three different channels. There are 256 levels of gray that can let through or hold back light and change brightness values and color. See Chapters 9 and 10 for more on using tools like levels to adjust color in this way.

Understanding bit depth

Another important item to understand about channels is bit depth. A *bit* holds one of two values; one value is for black, the other for white.

When you have 256 levels of gray, you're working with an 8-bit-per-channel image — 8 bits with two possible values each = 2^8 = 256 possible levels of gray. Multiply 8 bits per channel times your 3 channels and you get 24 bits, which is the common bit depth of images you print on your desktop printer.

Now, take a look at the Image⇨Mode menu. You should see a menu selection that says 8 Bits/Channel, as shown in Figure 2-5. When you open an image in Elements, if this menu command is grayed out, you're working with a 24-bit image, or an image of 8 bits per channel.

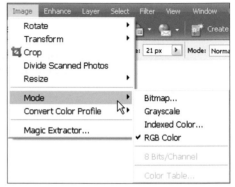

What does it mean when you can select the 8 Bit/Channel menu command? You can be certain that your image isn't an 8-bit-per-channel image. You may be able to select this command because some digital cameras and most low-end, consumer-grade scanners can cap-

Figure 2-5: When you can choose 8 Bits/Channel, you know that your image bit depth is higher than 8 bits per channel.

ture images at higher bit depths. You can scan a photo on a scanner at 16 bits per channel. When you do, you end up with many more levels of gray. When you take a picture with a quality digital camera, you can capture 32-bit-per-channel images, and you end up with a file containing 32,768 levels of gray. That's a lot!

Now, here's the catch. All files need to be reduced to 8 bits per channel before you print them because that's all the information any printer uses. In addition, many tools, commands, and palette options work with only 8-bit-per-channel images. So you ask, "What's the benefit of acquiring images at higher bit depths than I can print them?"

If you attempt to adjust brightness and contrast or other image enhancements in an 8-bit-per-channel image, you often destroy some data. You can cause some noticeable image degradation if you move adjustment sliders too far while working with 8-bit-per-channel images. When you edit your 16-bit and 32-bit images, you don't destroy data — you simply inform Elements which 256 of the total available levels of gray you want to use. The result is an image with more continuous gray tones than you can achieve in 8 bit-per-channel images. (For more on image bit-depth, see Chapter 3.)

Getting Color Right

In Elements, when it comes to color, the challenge isn't understanding color theory or definitions, but rather matching the RGB color you see on your computer monitor as closely as possible to your output. *Output* can be a printout from a color printer or a screen view on a Web page.

We say match "as closely as possible" because you can never expect to achieve a perfect match. You have far too many printer and monitor variables to deal with. The best you can hope for is a very close match.

To match color between your monitor and your output, you need to first calibrate your monitor and then choose a color workspace profile. In the following sections, you find all the details.

Calibrating your monitor

Your monitor needs to be calibrated to adjust the gamma and brightness, correct any color tints or colorcasts, and generally get your monitor to display, as precisely as possible, accurate colors on your output. You have a few choices for which tool you can use to adjust monitor brightness, ranging from a low-cost hardware device that costs less than $100 to expensive calibration equipment of $3,000 or more — or you can skip the hardware and use tools provided by Adobe or your OS developer, depending on which platform you use, to set up your monitor.

Gamma is the brightness of midlevel tones in an image. In technical terms, it's a parameter that describes the shape of the transfer function for one or more stages in an imaging pipeline.

We skip the high-end costly devices and software utilities that don't do you any good and suggest that you make, at the very least, one valuable purchase for creating a monitor profile: a hardware profiling system. On the low end, some affordable devices go a long way in helping you adjust your monitor brightness and color balance:

- ✔ **ColorVision Spyder2express:** This is one of the newer calibration devices on the market. For as low as $69 US, you can purchase an easy-to-use, three-step device to balance the color on your monitor and adjust it for optimum brightness (PC/Mac). This device is receiving five-star ratings at online resellers, including www.amazon.com.

- ✔ **Pantone Huey Monitor Color Correction:** This is another new, low-cost calibration system used for calibrating both CRTs and LCDs. It supports both Mac and Windows. This unit retails for $88 US and sells for $74.95 at Amazon.com as of this writing.

✔ **GretagMacBeth Eye-One Display 2:** For a little more money, you can order a calibration device from GretagMacBeth — a company that has long been a leader in sophisticated hardware equipment for creating calibrations and color profiles. Our choice for a low-end device with superb capabilities is the GretagMacBeth Eye-One Display 2 (www.gretagmacbeth.com), which costs a little more: $249 as of this writing.

✔ **Eye-One Display 2:** This device, like the Spyder2express and Huey, is an easy-to-use profiling tool that works with CRT displays, LCDs, and laptop computers. You attach the suction cup to your monitor (see Figure 2-6) and click a few buttons in the software application accompanying the hardware, and Eye-One Display 2 eventually prompts you to save a monitor profile. The profile you create is automatically used by your operating system when you start up your computer. When the profile kicks in, your monitor is balanced using the settings that were determined when the calibration was performed by the device.

Photo: Courtesy Don Mason Photography

Figure 2-6: The Eye-One Display 2 calibration device.

On LCD monitors, you need to adjust some of the hardware controls to bring your monitor into a match for overall brightness between your monitor and your photo prints. Be certain to run many test prints and match your prints against your monitor view to bring the two together as closely as possible.

You have a lot to focus on to calibrate monitors and get color right on your monitor and your output. We talk more about color output in Chapter 14. For a good resource for color correction and printing, we recommend that you look at *Color Management For Digital Photographers For Dummies,* by Ted Padova and Don Mason (Wiley Publishing).

Choosing a color workspace

After you get your monitor color adjusted by using a hardware profiling system, your next step is to choose your color workspace. In Elements, you have a choice between choosing one of two workspace colors: either sRGB or Adobe RGB (1998). You access your color workspace settings by choosing Edit⇨Color Settings. The Color Settings dialog box opens, as shown in Figure 2-7.

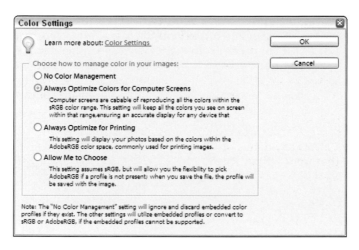

Figure 2-7: The Color Settings dialog box.

The options you have in the Color Settings dialog box include:

- ✔ **No Color Management:** This choice turns off all color management. Don't choose this option for any work you do in Elements.

- ✔ **Always Optimize Colors for Computer Screens:** Checking this radio button sets your workspace to sRGB. sRGB color is used quite often for viewing images on your monitor. But this workspace often results in the best choice for color printing too. Many color printers can output all the colors you can see in the sRGB workspace. In addition, many photo services, such as the Kodak EasyShare services we talk about in Chapter 16, prefer this workspace color.

- ✔ **Always Optimize for Printing:** Checking this option sets your color workspace to Adobe RGB (1998). The color in this workspace has more available colors than can be seen on your monitor. If you choose this workspace, you need to be certain that your printer is capable of using all the colors in this color space.

- ✔ **Allow Me to Choose:** When you choose this option, Elements prompts you for a profile assignment when you open images containing no profile. This setting is handy if you work back and forth between screen and print images.

Understanding how profiles work

You probably created a monitor color profile when you calibrated your monitor. You probably also selected a color profile when you opened the Color Settings dialog box and selected your workspace color. When you start your computer, your monitor color profile kicks in and adjusts your overall monitor brightness and correction for any colorcasts. When you open a photo in Elements, color is automatically converted from your monitor color space to your workspace color.

At print time, you use another color profile to output your photos to your desktop color printer. Color is then converted from your workspace color to your printer's color space. In Chapter 14, we show you how to use color profiles for printing. For now, just realize that each one of these color profiles, and using them properly, determines whether you can get good color output.

3

Working with Resolutions, Color Modes, and File Formats

In This Chapter

▶ Understanding resolution

▶ Resampling images

▶ Changing resolutions

▶ Understanding color modes

▶ Working with file formats

*W*hen you open a picture in Photoshop Elements, you're looking at a huge mass of pixels. These *pixels* are tiny, colored squares, and the number of pixels in a picture determines the picture's *resolution*. This relationship between pixels and resolution, which is important for you to understand in all your Elements work, relates to creating selections (as we explain in Chapter 7), printing files (Chapter 14), and sharing files (Chapter 16).

Color modes are also represented as collections of pixels. Color modes are also important when you're using tools and printing and sharing files.

This chapter explains some essential points about resolution, color modes, and the file formats you use to save your Elements images. We talk about changing resolution by resizing images, converting color modes, and saving the results in different file formats.

The Ubiquitous Pixels

Files you open in Elements are composed of thousands or maybe millions of tiny, square pixels. Each pixel has one, and only one, color value. The arrangement of the pixels of different shades and colors creates an illusion to your eyes when you're viewing an image on-screen. For example, you may have black and white pixels arranged in an order that creates the impression that you're looking at something gray — not at tiny black and white squares.

Just about everything you do in Elements has to do with changing pixels. You surround them with selection tools to select what appear to be objects in your image, you make pixels darker or lighter to change contrast and brightness, you change shades and tints of pixels for color correction, and you perform a host of other editing possibilities.

We also have another term to throw at you when talking about pixels and Elements files: Your pictures are called *raster images.* When you have pixels, you have raster data. If you open a file in Elements that wasn't made up of pixels, Elements *rasterizes* the data. In other words, Elements converts other data to pixels if the document wasn't originally composed of pixels.

In addition to raster data, there's also vector data, which we talk more about in Chapter 13. For this chapter, you just need to focus on raster data.

To use most of the tools and commands in Elements, you must be working on a raster image file. If your data isn't rasterized, many tools and commands are unavailable.

Understanding resolution

The number of pixels in a file determines its image resolution. If you have 72 pixels across a 1-inch horizontal line, your image is 72 pixels per inch (ppi). If you have 300 pixels in 1 inch, your image resolution is 300 ppi.

Image resolution is critical to properly outputting files in these instances:

- **When you print images:** If the resolution is too low, the image prints poorly. If the image resolution is too high, you waste time processing all the data that needs to be sent to your printer.

- **When you show images on-screen:** Just as images have resolution inherent in their files, your computer monitor displays everything you see on it in a fixed resolution. Computer monitors display images at 72 ppi. That's all you get. What's important to know is that the best viewing of photos on your computer monitor is always when you're viewing images at a 72 ppi image size in a 100 percent view.

As an example, take a look at Figure 3-1. You see an image reduced to 50 percent and then at different zoom sizes. As the sizes change, the resolution display on your monitor changes. When the size is 100 percent, you see the image exactly as it will print. The 100 percent size represents the image displayed on your monitor at 72 ppi, regardless of the resolution of the file.

This relationship between the image resolution and viewing at different zoom levels is an important concept to grasp. If you grab an image off the Web and zoom in on it, you may see a view like the 800 percent view shown in Figure 3-1. If you acquire a digital camera image, you may need to zoom out to a 16 percent view to fit the entire image in the Image window.

The reason that these displays vary so much is all image resolution. That Web page image you grabbed off the Web might be a 2-inch-square image at 72 ppi, and that digital camera image might be a 10-x-15-inch image at 240 ppi. To fill the entire window with the Web image, you need to zoom in on the file. As you zoom in, the resolution is lowered. The more you zoom, the lower the resolution on your monitor.

50%   100%   200%

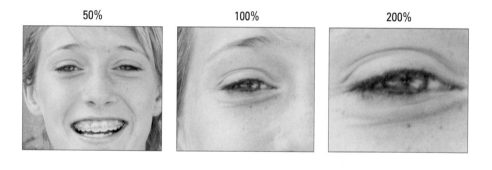

400%   800%

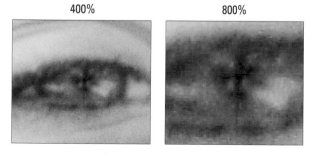

Figure 3-1: The same image is viewed at different zoom levels.

As you zoom in or out of an image, you change the resolution as it appears on your monitor. No resolution changes are made to the file. The image resolution remains the same until you use one of the Elements tools to reduce or add to image resolution.

Understanding image dimensions

Image dimensions involve the physical size of your file. If the size is 4 x 5 inches, for example, the file can be any number of different resolution values. After the file is opened in Elements, you can change the dimensions of an image, the resolution, or both.

When you change only the dimensions of an image (not the number of pixels it contains), an inverse relationship exists between the physical size of your image and the resolution. As image size is increased, resolution decreases. Conversely, as you raise resolution, you lower image size.

The Art of Resampling

In some cases, images are too large and you need to reduce their resolution and physical size. In other cases, you might need a higher resolution to output your images at larger sizes. This method of sizing — changing the size as well as the number of pixels — is referred to as *resampling* an image.

Specifically, reducing resolution is called *downsampling,* and raising resolution is known as *upsampling.*

Use caution when you resample images; when you resample, you toss away pixels or manufacture new pixels. We discuss the details later in this section.

Changing image size and resolution

You can change an image's size and resolution in a couple of different ways. One method is cropping images. You can use the Crop tool with or without resampling images. For more information on using the Crop tool, see Chapter 9. Another method is to use the Image Size dialog box, which you use in many of your editing sessions in Elements.

To resize an image with the Image Size dialog box, follow these steps:

1. **Choose Image⇨Resize⇨
   Image Size.**

   Alternatively, you can use the
   keyboard shortcut Ctrl+Alt+I
   (or ⌘+Option+I on the Mac).
   The Image Size dialog box
   opens, as shown in Figure 3-2.

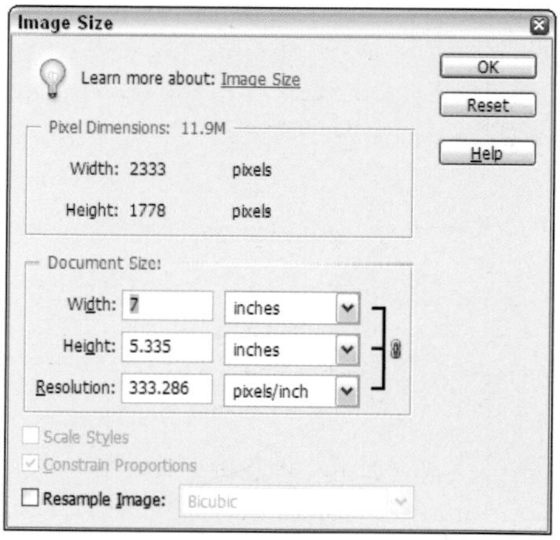

   The Pixel Dimensions area in the
   Image Size dialog box shows the
   file size (such as 11.9M). This
   number is the amount of space
   the image takes up on your hard
   drive. The width and height
   values are fixed unless you click
   the Resample Image check box
   at the bottom of the dialog box.

   Figure 3-2: Choose Image⇨Resize⇨Image
   Size to open the Image Size dialog box.

2. **In the Document Size area, you
   can redefine dimensions and resolution. The options are**

   - **Width:** Type a value in the text box to resize the image's width, and
     then press Tab to move out of the field to implement the change.
     From the drop-down menu to the right of the text box, you can
     choose a unit of measure: percent, inches, centimeters, millime-
     ters, points, picas, or columns.

   - **Height:** The Height options are the same as the Width options with
     the exception of no column setting. If you keep the sizing propor-
     tional, you typically edit either the Width or Height text box, but
     not both. As you size either width or height, the resolution sizes
     inversely.

   - **Resolution:** Edit the text box to change resolution and press the
     Tab key to change the value. As resolution is edited, the Width
     and Height values are changed inversely (when the Constrain
     Proportions check box is checked).

3. **If you're okay with resampling your image to get the desired size,
   select the Resample Image check box.**

   With this check box selected, you can change dimensions and pixels at
   the same time, which results in reducing or increasing the number of
   pixels. When the box is unchecked, the values for dimensions are linked.
   Changing one value automatically changes the other values.

   Before you resample your image, however, be sure to check out the section "Understanding the results of resampling," later in this chapter.

4. **If you select the Resample Image check box, you can choose a resampling method as well as other resample options.**

   In the drop-down list, you find choices for choosing a resampling method. See Table 3-1 for details. The two check boxes above the Resample Image check box become active when you select the Resample Image box. Here's what they do:

   - **Scale Styles:** Elements has a Styles palette from which you add a variety of different style effects to images. (See Chapter 11 for details.) When you apply a style, like a frame border, the border appears at a defined width. When you select the Scale Styles box and then resize the image, the Styles effect is also resized. Leaving the check box unselected keeps the style at the same size while the image is resized.

   - **Constrain Proportions:** By default, this check box is selected, and you want to keep it that way unless you want to intentionally distort an image.

5. **When you're done selecting your options, click OK to resize your image.**

Table 3-1		Resampling Methods
Method	*What It Does*	*Best Uses*
Nearest Neighbor	The method is faster, and the results produce a smaller file size.	This method is best used when you have large areas of the same color.
Bilinear	This method produces a medium-quality image.	You might use this option with grayscale images and line art.
Bicubic	This method is the default and provides a good-quality image.	Unless you find better results in using any of the other methods, leave the default at Bicubic.
Bicubic Smoother	This method improves on the Bicubic method, but you notice a little softening of the edges.	If sharpness isn't critical and you find Bicubic not quite doing the job, try this method.
Bicubic Sharper	This method produces good-quality images and sharpens the results.	Downsample high-resolution images that need to be output to screen resolutions and Web pages.

Understanding the results of resampling

As a general rule, reducing resolution is okay, but increasing resolution isn't. If you need a higher-resolution image and you can go back to the original source, like rescanning the image or reshooting a picture, always favor creating a new file using the resolution you want over resampling in Elements. In many cases, images being upsampled can be severely degraded.

If you take a picture with a digital camera and you want to add the picture to a Web page, the image needs to be sampled at 72 ppi. In most cases, you visit the Image Size dialog box, select the Resample Image check box, add a width or height value, and type **72** in the Resolution text box. What you end up with is an image that looks great on your Web page. In Figure 3-3, you can see an image that was downsampled in Elements from over 14 inches horizontal width.

Figure 3-3: Downsampling images most often produces satisfactory results.

If you start out with an image that was originally sampled for a Web page and you want to print a large poster, you can forget about using Elements or any other image editor. Upsampling low-resolution images often turns them to mush, as you can see in Figure 3-4.

You might wonder whether upsampling can be used for any purpose. In some cases, yes, you can upsample with some satisfactory results. You can experience better results

Figure 3-4: Upsampling low-resolution images often produces severely degraded results.

with higher resolutions of 300 ppi and more if the resample size isn't extraordinary. If all else fails, try applying a filter to a grainy, upsampled image to mask the problem. Chapter 11 has the details.

Choosing a Resolution for Print or On-Screen

The importance of resolution in your Elements work is paramount to printing files. Good ol' 72 ppi images can be forgiving, and you can get many of your large files scrunched down to 72 ppi for Web sites and slide shows. With output to printing devices, it's another matter. There are many different printing output devices, and their resolution requirements vary.

For your own desktop printer, plan to print a variety of test images at different resolutions. You can quickly determine the best file attributes by running tests. When you send files to service centers, ask the technicians what file attributes work best with their equipment.

For a starting point, look over the recommended resolutions for various output devices listed in Table 3-2.

Table 3-2	Resolutions and Printing	
Output Device	*Optimum Resolution*	*Acceptable Resolution*
Desktop color inkjets	300 ppi	180 ppi
Large-format inkjets	150 ppi	120 ppi
Professional photo lab printers	300 ppi	200 ppi
Desktop laser printers (black and white)	170 ppi	100 ppi
Magazine quality — offset press	300 ppi	225 ppi
Screen images (Web, slide shows, video)	72 ppi	72 ppi

Go Ahead — Make My Mode!

Regardless of what output you prepare your files for, you need to consider color mode and file format. In Chapter 2, we talk about RGB color mode. This color mode is what you use to prepare color files for printing on your desktop color printer or for preparing files for photo service centers.

You can also use color modes other than RGB. If you start with an RGB color image and you want to convert to a different color mode, you have menu options for converting color. Photoshop Elements uses an algorithm (a mathematical formula) to convert pixels from one mode to another. In some cases, the conversion that's made via a menu command produces good results, and in other cases, you can use some different options for converting modes.

In the following sections, we introduce the modes that are available in Elements and explain how to convert from RGB to the mode of your choice: bitmap, grayscale, or indexed color.

Another mode you may have heard of is CMYK. Although CMYK mode isn't available in Photoshop Elements, you should be aware of what it is and the purposes of CMYK images. CMYK, commonly referred to as *process color,* contains percentages of Cyan, Magenta, Yellow, and Black colors. This mode is used for commercial printing. If you design a magazine cover in Elements and send off the file to a print shop, the file is ultimately converted to CMYK.

Converting to bitmap mode

Bitmap mode is most commonly used in printing line art, such as black-and-white logos, illustrations, or black-and-white effects you create from your RGB images. Also, you can scan your analog signature as a bitmap image and import it into other programs, such as the Microsoft Office programs. If you're creative, you can combine bitmap images with RGB color to produce many interesting effects.

The Elements bitmap mode isn't the same as the Windows `.bmp` file format. In Elements, bitmap mode is a color mode. A `.bmp` file can be an RGB color mode image, a grayscale color mode image, or a bitmap color mode image.

One important thing to keep in mind is that, when you combine images into single documents, as we explain in Chapter 8, you need to convert bitmap files to grayscale or color if you want to merge the images with an RGB image. If you convert to grayscale, Elements takes care of converting grayscale to RGB mode.

As an example of an effect resulting from combining grayscale and color images, look over Figure 3-5. The original RGB image was converted to a bitmap and then saved as a different file. The bitmap was converted to grayscale and dropped on top of the RGB image. After adjusting the opacity, the result is a grainy effect with desaturated color.

Figure 3-5: You can create some interesting effects by combining the same image from a bitmap file and an RGB file.

You can acquire bitmap (.bmp) mode images directly in Elements when you scan images that are black and white. Illustrated art, logos, your signature, or a copy of a fax might be the kind of files you scan directly in bitmap mode. Additionally, you can convert your images to bitmap mode.

Converting RGB color to bitmap is a two-step process. You need to first convert to grayscale, and then convert from grayscale to bitmap. If you select the Bitmap menu command while in RGB color, Elements prompts you to convert to grayscale first.

To convert RGB mode to bitmap mode, do the following:

1. **Open an image that you want to convert to bitmap mode in either Standard Edit or Quick Fix mode.**

2. **Choose Image⇨Mode⇨Bitmap.**

   If you start in RGB mode, Elements prompts you to convert to grayscale.

3. **Click OK, and the Bitmap dialog box opens.**

   The Bitmap dialog box provides options for selecting the output resolution and a conversion method.

4. **Select a resolution.**

   By default, the Bitmap dialog box, shown in Figure 3-6, displays the current resolution. You can edit the text box and type a new resolution value or accept the default.

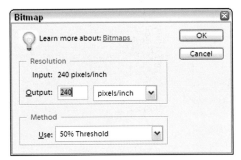

5. **From the Method drop-down menu, you can choose from these settings:**

   - 50% Threshold

   - Pattern Dither

   - Diffusion Dither

Figure 3-6: Type a resolution for your output and select the conversion method from the Use drop-down menu.

Look over Figure 3-7, and you can see a comparison of the different methods used in converting RGB images to bitmaps.

6. **Click OK to convert your image to Bitmap mode.**

RGB Image

50% Threshold

Pattern Dither

Diffusion Dither

Figure 3-7: An original RGB image converted to bitmap using 50% Threshold, Pattern Dither, and Diffusion Dither.

Converting to grayscale mode

Grayscale images have black and white pixels and any one of 256 levels of gray. By converting an RGB image to grayscale, you can make it look like a black-and-white photo.

You can convert an image to grayscale in one of three ways, but remember that one of these methods isn't as good as the others. We recommend that you avoid converting to grayscale by choosing Image➪Mode➪Grayscale. When Elements performs this conversion, it removes all the color from the pixels, so you lose some precious data during the conversion and can't regain the color after conversion. If you convert an image to grayscale, save the file, and delete the original from your hard drive or memory card, the color image is lost forever. You can save a secondary file, but this method can add a little confusion and require some more space on your hard drive.

As an alternative to using the menu command for converting images to grayscale, try this method:

1. **Open an RGB image in Elements.**

2. **Duplicate a layer.**

   The default Palette Bin contains the Layers palette. In this palette, you find a pop-up menu when you click More in the upper-right corner. From the menu commands, choose Duplicate Layer. (For more information on working with layers, see Chapter 8.)

3. **Choose Enhance⇨Adjust Color⇨Adjust Hue/Saturation (or press Ctrl+U) to open the Hue/Saturation dialog box.**

4. **Drag the Saturation slider to the far left, as shown in Figure 3-8, to desaturate the image.**

   All color disappears, but the brightness values of all the pixels remain unaffected. (For more information on using the Hue/Saturation dialog box and the other Adjust Color commands, see Chapter 10.)

5. **Turn off the color layer by clicking the eye icon.**

   In the Layers palette, you see two layers, as shown in Figure 3-9. You don't need to turn off the color layer to print the file in grayscale, but turning it off can help you remember which color layer you used the last time you printed or exported the file.

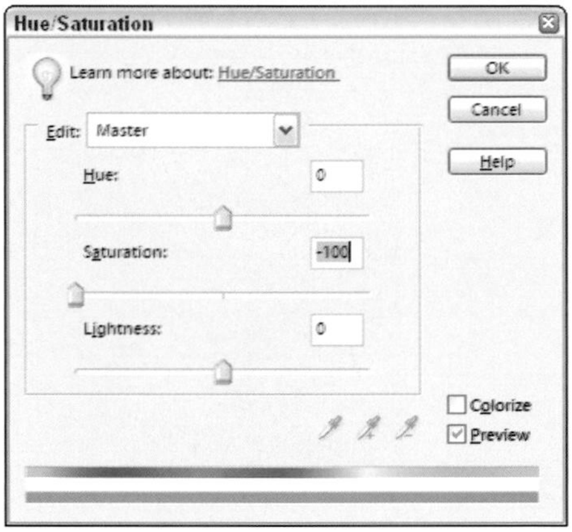

Figure 3-8: Open the Hue/Saturation dialog box and move the Saturation slider to the far left to eliminate color.

Figure 3-9: The Layers palette shows the grayscale and color layers. You can turn layers on or off by clicking the eye icon.

Following the preceding steps provides you with a file that contains both RGB and grayscale. If you want to print the color layer, you can turn off the grayscale layer. If you need to exchange files with graphic designers, you can send the layered file and then the design professional can use both the color image and the grayscale image.

The other advantage of converting RGB color to grayscale by using the Hue/Saturation dialog box is that you don't disturb any changes in the brightness values of the pixels. Moving the Saturation slider to desaturate the image affects only the color. The luminance and lightness values remain the same.

A new menu command has been introduced in Elements 5. Choose Enhance➪ Convert to Black and White in either Standard Edit mode or Quick Fix mode, and you see the Convert to Black and White dialog box, shown in Figure 3-10.

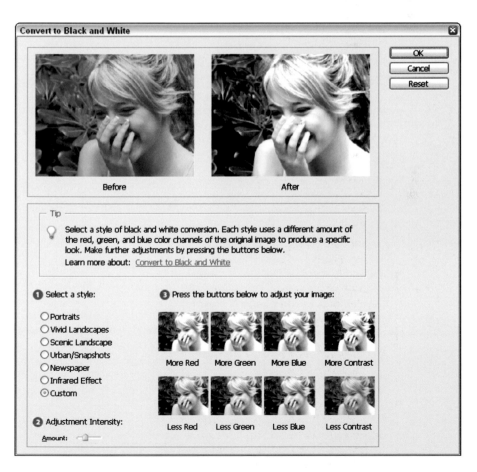

Figure 3-10: The new Photoshop Elements 5 Convert to Black and White dialog box.

This dialog box contains many controls for adjusting brightness and contrast in images you convert to grayscale. You select from some preset options by selecting the radio buttons under the Select a Style heading. You move the Amount slider in the Adjustment Intensity area and then fine-tune your adjustments by clicking thumbnail previews in the third area, where you see small image previews.

If you want to keep your original RGB image in the same file as the grayscale version, duplicate the background by choosing Duplicate Layer from the Layers palette More menu. Click the background and choose Enhance⇨ Convert to Black and White. The conversion is applied to only the background while leaving the Background copy layer in your original color mode.

Converting to indexed color mode

Indexed color is a mode you use occasionally with Web graphics, such as saving in GIF format. When saving indexed color images, you can, at times, create smaller file sizes than RGB that are ideal for using in Web site designs.

RGB images in 24-bit color (8 bits per channel) are capable of rendering colors from a palette of 16.7 million colors, as we explain in Chapter 2. An indexed color image is an 8-bit image with only a single channel. The total number of colors you get with indexed color can be no more than 256. When you convert RGB images to indexed color, you can choose to dither the color, which displays the image with a dithered effect much like you see with bitmapped images. This dithering effect makes the file appear as though it has more than 256 colors, and the transition between colors appears smoother than if no dithering were applied.

On occasion, indexed color images have an advantage over RGB images when hosting the images on Web servers: The fewer colors in a file, the smaller the file size. When you prepare images for Web hosting, you can choose to use indexed color or RGB color. Whether you choose one over the other really depends on how well the image appears on your monitor. If you have some photos that you want to show on Web pages, you should use RGB images and save them in a format appropriate for Web hosting, as we explain a little later in this chapter.

If you have files composed of artwork such as logos, illustrations, and drawings, you may find that the appearance of index colors is no different from viewing the same images as RGB. If that's the case, you can keep the index color image and use it for your Web pages.

To convert RGB images to indexed color, choose Image⇨Mode⇨Indexed Color; the Indexed Color dialog box opens. A number of different options are available to you, and, fortunately, you can preview the results as you make choices. Get in and poke around, and you can see the options applied in the image window.

Saving Files with Purpose

Photoshop Elements files are saved in a variety of different formats. Some format types require you to convert a color mode before the format can be used. Therefore, a relationship exists between file formats and saving files. Additionally, bit depths in images also relate to the kinds of file formats you can use in saving files.

Before you go too far in Elements, become familiar with file formats and the conversions that need to be made to save in one format or another. If you do nothing to an image in terms of converting modes or changing bit depth, you can save a file after editing in the same format in which the file was opened. In many circumstances, you open an image and prepare it for some form of output, which requires more thought about the kind of file format you use in saving the file.

Using the Save/Save As dialog box

In most any program, the Save (or Save As) dialog box is a familiar place where you make some choices about the file to be saved. Using Save As, you can save a duplicate copy of your image or a modified copy and retain the original file.

To use the Save (or Save As) dialog box, choose File⇨Save for files to be saved the first time, or choose File⇨Save As for any file, and a dialog box then opens.

The standard navigational tools you find in any Save dialog box appear in the Elements Save/Save As dialog box. Here are some standard options you find in the Elements Save/Save As dialog box:

- **File name:** This item is common to all Save dialog boxes. Type a name for your file in the text box.

- **Format:** From the drop-down menu, you select file formats. We explain the formats supported by Elements later in this chapter.

A few options make the Photoshop Elements Save/Save As dialog box different from other Save dialog boxes you might be accustomed to using. The Save Options area in the Save As dialog box provides these choices:

- **Include in the Organizer:** If you want the file added to the Organizer, select this check box. (For more information about using the Organizer, see Chapter 6.)

- **Save in Version Set with Original:** You can edit images and save a version of your image, but only in Quick Fix mode. When you save the file from Quick Fix mode, this check box is active. Select the box and a version of the original is saved and appears in the Organizer.

✔ **Color:** Check the box for ICC (International Color Consortium) Profile. Depending on which profile you're using, the option appears for sRGB or Adobe RGB (1998). When the check box is selected, the profile is embedded in the image. See Chapter 2 for more information on profiles.

✔ **Thumbnail:** This option relates to your Saving Files preferences, which we discuss in Chapter 2. If you save a file with a thumbnail, you can see a miniature representation of your image when viewing it in folders or on the desktop. If you select Ask When Saving in the Saving Files preferences, the check box can be enabled or disabled. If you're choosing an option for Never Save or Always Save in the Preferences dialog box, this box is enabled or disabled for you and is grayed out. You need to return to the Preferences dialog box if you want to change the option.

✔ **Use Lower Case Extension:** File extensions give you a clue to which file format was used when a file was saved. Elements automatically adds the extension to the filename for you. Your choices are to use uppercase or lowercase letters for the extension name. Select the check box for Use Lower Case Extension for lowercase, or deselect the check box if you want to use uppercase characters in the filename.

Saving files for the Web

You save files for Web hosting in a different dialog box than when you're saving files for other output. Choose File➪Save for Web, and the Save for Web dialog box opens. We explain all you need to know about how to use the Save for Web dialog box for saving Web images in Chapter 15.

Understanding file formats

When you save files from Elements, you need to pick a file format in the Format drop-down menu found in both the Save and Save As dialog boxes.

As you choose from the different format options, keep the following information in mind:

✔ File formats are especially important when you exchange files with other users. Each format has a purpose, and other programs can accept or reject files depending on the format you choose.

✔ Whether you can select one format or another when you save a file depends on the color mode and the bit depth and on whether layers are present. If a format isn't present in the Format drop-down menu when you attempt to save a file, return to one of the edit modes and perform some kind of edit, such as changing a color mode or flattening layers, in order to save the file in your chosen format.

For a glimpse at all the file formats available to you, open a standard RGB color image in Standard Edit mode, choose File⇨Save As, and click the down arrow to open the Format drop-down menu. As you can see in Figure 3-11, you have many options for choosing a format.

In the following sections, we explain most of the file formats supported by Elements and the purpose for each format.

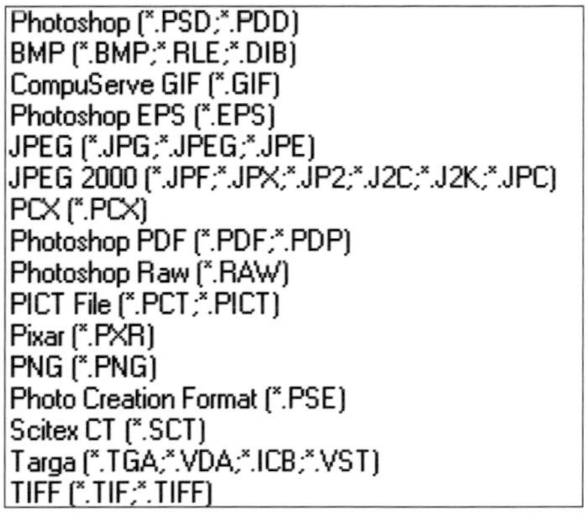

```
Photoshop (*.PSD;*.PDD)
BMP (*.BMP;*.RLE;*.DIB)
CompuServe GIF (*.GIF)
Photoshop EPS (*.EPS)
JPEG (*.JPG;*.JPEG;*.JPE)
JPEG 2000 (*.JPF;*.JPX;*.JP2;*.J2C;*.J2K;*.JPC)
PCX (*.PCX)
Photoshop PDF (*.PDF;*.PDP)
Photoshop Raw (*.RAW)
PICT File (*.PCT;*.PICT)
Pixar (*.PXR)
PNG (*.PNG)
Photo Creation Format (*.PSE)
Scitex CT (*.SCT)
Targa (*.TGA;*.VDA;*.ICB;*.VST)
TIFF (*.TIF;*.TIFF)
```

Figure 3-11: Open the Format drop-down menu in either the Save or Save As dialog box, and the formats supported by Elements appear.

Photoshop (*.PSD, *.PDD)

This format is the native file format for both Photoshop and Photoshop Elements. The format supports saving all color modes and bit depths, and you can preserve layers. Use this format when you want to save in a native format or exchange files with Photoshop users. Also use it for saving files that you need to return to for more editing. When you save layers, any text you add to layers can be edited when you return to the file. (See Chapter 13 for more information on adding text to an image.)

BMP (*.BMP, *.RLE, *.DIB)

The term *bitmap* can be a little confusing. You have both a file format type that's bitmap and a color mode that's also bitmap. Don't confuse the two. The bitmap *format* supports saving in all color modes and in all bit depths. The bitmap *color mode,* which we cover earlier in this chapter, is 1-bit black-and-white only.

Use the bitmap format when you want to add images to system resources, such as wallpaper for your desktop. Bitmap is also used with many different application programs. If you can't import images in other program documents, try to save them as BMP files.

CompuServe GIF (*.GIF)

Barb was a college coed, and Ted had a mustache and wore a green leisure suit when CompuServe was the host for our e-mail accounts. We exchanged files and mail on 300 baud modems. Later, in 1987, CompuServe developed GIF (Graphics Interchange Format) to exchange files between mainframe computers and the ever-growing number of users working on Osborne, Kaypro, Apple, and Radio Shack TRS-80 computers.

GIF is now a popular format for hosting Web graphics. GIF images can be indexed color or animated images and support the smallest file sizes. Use this format when you need fewer than 256 colors and when you want to create animation in your images.

Photoshop EPS (*.EPS)

Photoshop EPS (Encapsulated PostScript) files are sometimes used by graphic artists when they're designing jobs for commercial printing. The more popular format for creative professionals is TIFF, but Photoshop EPS has some advantages not found in other formats.

Depending on the color mode of your image, you have different options when you're using the Photoshop EPS file format. Select the format in the Save/Save As dialog box and click Save. If you're working on a bitmap image (1 bit), the EPS Options dialog box, shown in Figure 3-12, opens. It offers an option to save transparency wherever white appears in your document.

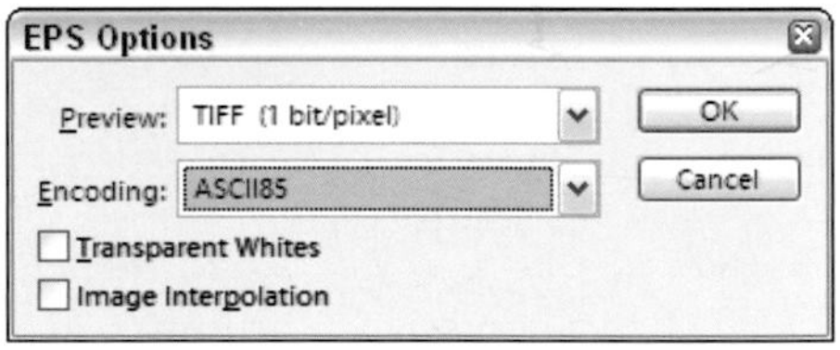

Figure 3-12: When you're working on 1-bit bitmap images, this dialog box offers an option to save transparency where white appears in the document.

Notice the Transparent Whites check box. You might have a circular logo for which you want the area around the circle to appear transparent. If you import the graphical image in another program, you can see the black in the image while all the white area is transparent and shows any background through what was white in the original bitmap image. If you save a file in a higher bit depth, the EPS Options dialog box doesn't provide an option for making whites transparent.

JPEG (*.JPG, *.JPEG, *.JPE)

JPEG (Joint Photographic Experts Group) is perhaps the most common file format now in use. JPEG files are used with e-mail attachments and by many photo labs for printing files, and they can be viewed in JPEG viewers and directly in Web browsers. Just about every program capable of importing images supports the JPEG format. Creative professionals wouldn't dream of using the JPEG format in design layouts, but everyone else uses the format for all kinds of documents.

You need to exercise some caution when you're using the JPEG format. JPEG files are compressed to reduce file size. You can scrunch an image of several megabytes into a few hundred kilobytes. When you save a file with JPEG compression, you experience data loss. You might not see this on your monitor, or it might appear noticeably on photo prints if you're using low compression while preserving higher quality. However, when you save with maximum compression, more pixels are tossed away, and you definitely notice image degradation.

As you save, open, and resave images in JPEG format, each new save degrades an image more. If you need to submit JPEG images to photo labs for printing your pictures, keep saving in Photoshop PSD file format until you're ready to save the final image. Save in JPEG format when you want to save the final file for printing, and use a low compression with high quality.

When you select JPEG for the format and click Save, the JPEG Options dialog box opens, as shown in Figure 3-13. You choose the amount of compression by typing a value in the Quality text box or by moving the slider below the Quality text box. The acceptable ranges are from 0 to 12, where 0 is the lowest quality and results in the highest compression, and 12 is the highest quality that results in the lowest amount of compression.

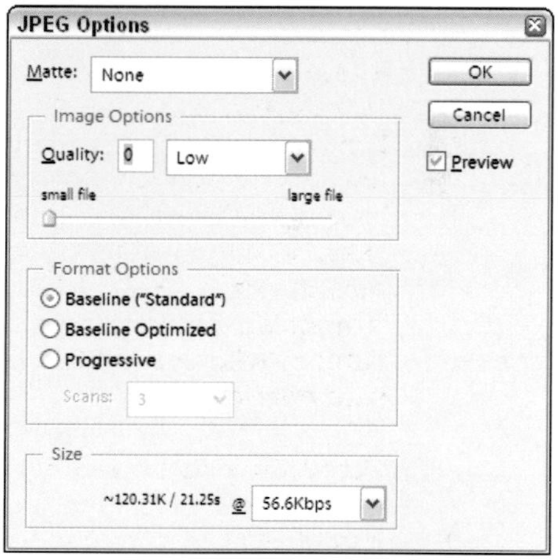

Notice that you also have choices in the Format area of the JPEG Options dialog box. The Progressive option creates a progressive JPEG file commonly used with Web browsers. This file type shows progressive quality

Figure 3-13: When saving in JPEG format, you make a choice for the amount of compression to apply to the saved image.

as the file downloads from a Web site. The image first appears in a low-quality view and shows higher-resolution views until the image appears at full resolution when it's completely downloaded in your browser window.

JPEG 2000 (*.JPF, *.JPX, *.JP2, *.J2K, *.JPC)
JPEG 2000 is a newer JPEG file format. This format offers you the same mode quality as the JPEG format and an option to save the file with compression without tossing away pixels, in which case you get *lossless compression*. The JPEG 2000 dialog box shows you, right in the dialog box and before you save the image, the results of the choices you make in terms of the resulting file size.

If you need to save images in JPEG format for your commercial photo lab, check with the technicians and ask whether they support JPEG 2000. If so, save your files in this format with a lossless compression. When files are compressed with lossless compression, you can expect to lose about two-thirds of the original file size. For example, a 6MB file can be reduced to about 2MB when it's saved as JPEG 2000 in a lossless-compression format. Note that if you save files in JPEG 2000 format for the Web, Web browsers need to have a plug-in to see the images.

PCX (*.PCX)

PCX is a native PC format first used with PC Paintbrush. Most programs now support newer file formats, and you're not likely to need to save in PCX format. If you have legacy files from years ago, you can open PCX files in Elements, edit them, and save them in a newer format.

Photoshop PDF (*.PDF, *.PDP)

Adobe PDF (Portable Document Format) was designed to maintain document integrity and exchange files between computers. PDF is one of the most popular formats and can be viewed in the free Adobe Reader program available for installation on your Elements CD installer or by downloading it from the Adobe Web site.

PDF is all over the place in Elements. When you jump into Organize mode and create slide presentations, cards, and calendars, for example, you can export your documents as PDF files. When you save in Photoshop PDF format, you can preserve layers and text. Text is recognizable in Adobe Reader (or other Acrobat viewers) and can be searched by using the Reader's Find and Search tools.

PDF files can be printed, hosted on Web sites, and exchanged with users of Windows, Macintosh, Unix, and Linux. All in all, this format is well suited for all the files you create in Elements that contain text, layers, and transparency, and for when you want to exchange files with users who don't have Elements or Photoshop.

Photoshop Raw (*.RAW)

This format is used to exchange files between Windows and Mac users and mainframe computers. Unless you prepare files to be viewed on mainframes, don't bother saving in this format.

PICT File (*.PCT, *.PICT)

PICT (Picture) format is Apple's answer to PCX on Windows. This format originated with the 1984 introduction of the Macintosh and the MacDraw program. PICT files are helpful for creating slides and video files on the Macintosh and for printing your images on film recorders that don't use PostScript. You might use the format when requested by a Mac user or when sending files that need to be printed as slides on a non-PostScript film recorder.

PNG (*.PNG)

PNG (Portable Network Graphics) is another format used with Web pages. PNG supports all color modes, 24-bit images, and transparency. Some browsers, however, may need a plug-in to see PNG files on Web pages. One disadvantage of using PNG is that color profiles can't be embedded in the images, as they can with JPEG.

Photo Creation Format

The Photo Creation Format is used to save multiple files to a single file format. Unlike conventional file formats for images that require you to open individual image files, the Photo Creation Format lets you create up to 30 pages at one time.

TIFF (*.TIF, *.TIFF)

TIFF (Tagged Image File Format) is the most common format used by graphic designers. TIFF is generally used for importing images in professional layout programs like Adobe InDesign and Adobe PageMaker and when commercial photo labs and print shops use equipment that supports downloading TIFF files directly to their devices. (*Note:* Direct downloads are used in lieu of opening a Print dialog box.)

Inasmuch as creative professionals have used TIFF for so long, a better choice for designers using a program like Adobe InDesign is saving in the native Photoshop PSD file format. This requires a creative professional to save only one file in native format without bothering to save both native and TIFF formats.

TIFF, along with Photoshop PSD and Photoshop PDF, supports saving layered files and works in all color modes. When you save in TIFF format, you can also compress files in several different compression schemes, and compression with TIFF files doesn't lose data, like it does with JPEG files.

When you select TIFF for the format and click Save in the Save/Save As dialog box, the TIFF Options dialog box opens, as shown in Figure 3-14.

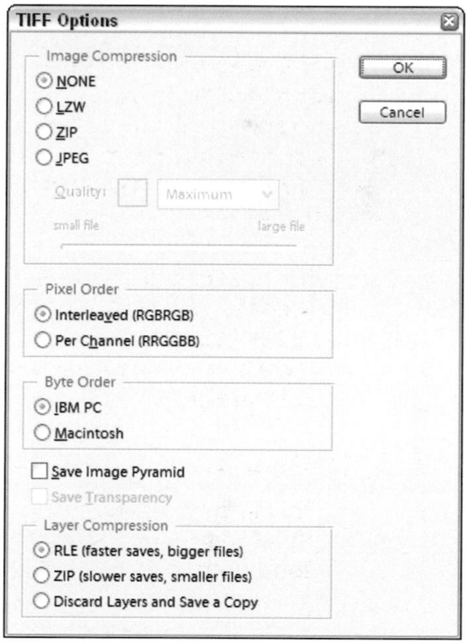

Figure 3-14: Choose TIFF from the Format drop-down menu and click Save to open the TIFF Options dialog box.

In the Image Compression area, you have these choices:

- **NONE:** Selecting this option results in no compression. You use this option when sending files to creative professionals for creating layouts in programs like Adobe InDesign. None of the compression schemes below is recommended for printing files to commercial printing devices.
- **LZW:** This lossless compression scheme results in much lower file sizes without destroying data.
- **ZIP:** ZIP is also a lossless compression scheme. You can favor ZIP compression over LZW when you have large areas of the same color in an image.
- **JPEG:** JPEG is lossy and results in the smallest file sizes. Use JPEG here the same as when you apply JPEG compression with files saved in the JPEG format.

File formats at a glance

We have been working with Photoshop, which saves in the same formats listed in this section, since 1989. At no time since then have we used all the formats available in Photoshop Elements. At most, you'll use maybe three or four of these formats.

You don't need to remember all the formats and what they do. Just pick the ones you use in your workflow, mark Table 3-3 for reference, and refer to it from time to time until you have a complete understanding of how files need to be prepared in order to save them in your desired formats. If you happen to receive a file from another user in one of the formats you don't use, come back to the description in this chapter when you need some detail on what the format is used for.

Table 3-3	File Format Attributes Supported by Photoshop Elements			
Format	**Color Modes Supported**	**Embed Profiles* Supported**	**Bit Depth Supported**	**Layers Supported**
Photoshop PSD, PDD	Bitmap, RGB, Index, Grayscale	Yes	1, 8, 24, H	Yes
BMP	Bitmap, RGB, Index, Grayscale	No	1, 8, 24, H	No

Format	Color Modes Supported	Embed Profiles* Supported	Bit Depth Supported	Layers Supported
CompuServe GIF**	Bitmap, RGB, Index, Grayscale	No	1, 8, 24	No
Photoshop EPS	Bitmap, RGB, Index, Grayscale	Yes	1, 8, 24	No
JPEG	RGB, Grayscale	Yes	8, 24	No
JPEG 2000	RGB, Grayscale	Yes	8, 24, H	No
PCX	Bitmap, RGB, Index, Grayscale	No	1, 8, 24	No
Photoshop PDF	Bitmap, RGB, Index, Grayscale	Yes	1, 8, 24, H	Yes
Photoshop RAW	RGB, Index, Grayscale	No	8, 24, H	No
PICT File	Bitmap, RGB, Index, Grayscale	Yes	1, 8, 24	No
Pixar	RGB, Grayscale	No	8, 24	No
PNG	Bitmap, RGB, Index, Grayscale	No	1, 8, 24, H	No
Photoshop Multiple Page Document	Bitmap, RGB, Index	No	1, 8, 24, H	No
Scitex CT	RGB, Grayscale	No	8, 24	No
Targa	RGB, Index, Grayscale	No	8, 24	No
TIFF	Bitmap, RGB, Index, Grayscale	Yes	8, 24, H	Yes

The letter H in Column 4 represents higher-bit modes, such as 16- and 32-bit images, which you might acquire from scanners and digital cameras. See Chapter 2 for more information on higher-bit images.

* Embedding profiles is limited to embedding either sRGB IEC61966-2.1 or AdobeRGB (1998).

** CompuServe GIF doesn't support saving layers, although it supports saving layers as frames. You use the frames when creating an animated GIF file used for Web pages.

Audio and video formats supported in Elements

In addition to the image formats listed in Table 3-3, Elements supports audio and video files. The support is limited to adding and viewing audio and video files in the Organizer and printing the first frame in a video file. Other kinds of edits made to audio and video files require special software for audio and video editing.

Audio files can be imported in slide shows, as we explain in Chapter 15. The acceptable file formats for audio files are MP3, WAV, QuickTime (Mac), and WMA. If you have audio files in another format, you need to convert the file format. For these kinds of conversions, you can search the Internet for a shareware audio-conversion program.

Video files can also be imported in slide shows, as we discuss in Chapter 15. Elements supports the WMV (Windows) video format. As with audio files, if videos are saved in other formats, such as Apple QuickTime (for Windows users), you need to convert the QT video format to WMV. Mac users can use QuickTime format. For video-conversion utilities, you can also find shareware programs to do the job. Search the Internet for a video converter.

Part II
Getting Organized

In this part . . .

The first thing you'll want to do after opening the Photoshop Elements program is to access your photos from a digital camera, from your hard drive, or from your scanner. In this part, we talk about how to access your pictures and get them into Elements for editing. We talk about organizing your pictures by using many impressive organizing features in the program as well as by searching for photos and labeling them and then creating different versions of the same picture. When it comes to organizing pictures, Elements is one of the best tools you can find to keep your precious photos neatly cataloged and accessible.

Getting Your Images

*Y*ou have many different sources to work with for getting a picture into Elements, where you can play with it, experiment on it, and edit it. If you have a digital camera, you're in the right place; we walk you through all kinds of different options for getting the shots you took with your camera into Elements.

If you have a digital scanner, you're in the right place, too! We talk about scanning photos as well. If you have some CDs, sources of files on the Internet, some massive collection of images written to a DVD, or even a picture or two that you took with your cell phone, you're still in the right place!

In previous chapters, we flirt with opening files. If you followed some of the steps in those chapters for opening images, you should have a feel for using the Open tool and Open command. But there's more to acquiring images than just using the Open command, as you find out in this chapter.

This chapter covers all you need to know about getting images into Elements from all kinds of sources. This chapter answers all your questions about how to move around the workspaces to get your files into Elements.

Digital Cameras versus Scanners and Film Cameras

If you don't have a digital camera, we encourage you to buy one as soon as you can. Digital cameras and Photoshop Elements were made to work together. If you've spent any time scanning images on a digital scanner, you'll appreciate the speed that a camera offers you compared to a scanner when the time comes to get your images into Elements.

"But I can do more with my scanner than with a digital camera," you say? "Not really," we say. Just for starters, here are some of the benefits you get with a digital camera:

- **Faster access to files:** Copying images from a digital camera media card is much faster than scanning images from prints and film.

- **Higher-quality images:** Considering the costs of medium- to higher-end scanners, you can shoot much better pictures with a good-quality SLR (single lens reflex) camera with a quality lens than you can scan film or prints with a good-quality consumer-grade scanner.

- **OCR and text recognition:** Unless you have industrial-strength needs for scanning reams of text documents that need to be interpreted by optical character recognition (OCR) software, which converts images to editable text, you'll do just fine with a digital camera. If you scan individual pages on a scanner, shooting pages with a camera is much faster and can produce the same results when pages need to be converted to text.

- **3-D objects:** With digital cameras, you can shoot 3-D objects. Try scanning a pair of shoes — well, maybe some other three-dimensional object — on a scanner bed sometime. The experiment isn't worth getting dirt all over your scanner.

- **Reduced costs:** With a digital camera, you eliminate film and film-processing costs. You can order photo prints in superstore outlets, at less than 10 cents apiece, that are printed on the same photo paper you get with prints from film. What's more, you can order prints of only the pictures you want to keep rather than develop an entire roll to have just that one good photograph.

- **Organizing and archiving:** Digital images can be saved to DVD-ROMs, where you can add information for every image to keep them easily organized, as we explain in Chapter 5. Searching a DVD is much faster than searching through photo books of slides, film, or prints. Archiving digital images is fast and easy, and you don't need to worry about scratches, faded colors, or damaged originals.

- **Control over image processing:** With film, you're stuck with the processing time and temperature that the photo lab uses to process your film. With some digital cameras, you can post-process images after shooting the image, as we explain in the last section of this chapter.

✓ **Video clips:** Many digital cameras provide a video-shooting mode so that you can shoot video.

These are some of the benefits you find with using a digital camera over using a scanner. Scanners do have their place, and some of the benefits you have with a scanner that you don't have with cameras involve

✓ **Auto document feeders:** You can buy scanners with automatic document feeders, where pages of documents can be scanned unattended. If you need to scan large volumes of pages to recognize text, this operation is much more practical than using a camera.

✓ **Legacy pictures:** You can shoot photo prints with digital cameras and, depending on the camera, produce images equal to or better than using a scanner. Filmstrips and slides are easily handled with scanners and adapters. However, you can also find attachments for your camera that enable you to shoot slides and negatives. For more information on shooting slides and negatives with a digital camera, check out *Color Correction For Digital Photographers Only* by Ted Padova and Don Mason (Wiley).

Grabbing Images from Your Camera

Copying photos from your digital camera to your computer so that you can work with them in Elements is simple if you're familiar with your camera and the tools at your disposal. In this section, you find some points to consider about choosing a resolution when you shoot your pictures as well as how to use the Microsoft Camera and Scanner Wizard and Adobe Photo Download Manager after you hook up your camera to your computer.

Choosing a file format

When you work with digital photos in Elements, the file format of your images is an important point to consider. You choose this format before you take your pictures, and the format is carried over to your computer when you pull images off your camera.

The most common file formats that digital cameras offer are JPEG and Camera Raw. Some cameras offer other options, but these two formats are the most common. Low-cost point-and-shoot cameras offer you only the JPEG format, and the more expensive cameras and the SLR types offer you both JPEG and Camera Raw.

✓ **JPEG:** Cameras that produce JPEG images process images with JPEG compression before saving them. It's as though your camera performs a darkroom method of film processing when the shot is taken.

We describe the JPEG file format in Chapter 3.

✔ **Camera Raw:** This format provides you with an optimum image for editing in Elements. When a Camera Raw image is saved to a media source, all the information the sensor captured is saved with the file. These images are post-processed when you open them. (See the "Everything You Want to Know about Camera Raw" section, later in this chapter, to find out about opening Camera Raw images.) For example, you can open a Camera Raw image and, before the image opens in Elements, adjust temperature, exposure, and a bunch of other settings. You can return to the original Camera Raw file and change the temperature or exposure, for example, to open the file with different settings. Just like chemical temperature and development time affect analog film processing, similar options affect post-processing Camera Raw images. The difference between analog film and Camera Raw is that after your analog film is processed, you can't change the processing attributes. With Camera Raw, you can go back and post-process the image a hundred times and change the processing attributes each time.

Camera Raw also supports higher-bit-depth images than JPEG files do.

If you have a choice between just JPEG and both JPEG and Camera Raw, always choose the latter. You have much more editing control over your images, and ultimately you get better results.

Using the Microsoft Scanner and Camera Wizard (Windows)

Microsoft Scanner and Camera Wizard may automatically be launched when your computer is connected to a media source. You can use the wizard to download images from your media source to your computer.

To copy images from a media source or when your camera is connected to your computer, follow these steps:

1. **Hook up the media to your computer.**

   Connect your computer and your camera or external media reader, or insert a media source into a port or drive on your computer. The methods available to you should be detailed in the user's guide that shipped with your camera.

   When you connect your media to your computer, a dialog box opens, providing options for how to handle the media.

2. **Select Copy Pictures to a Folder on My Computer Using Microsoft Scanner and Camera Wizard, and click OK.**

3. **Click Next in the opening pane in the wizard.**

   You see a pane in which you see thumbnail images of the pictures on your media source, as shown in Figure 4-1.

Figure 4-1: Click Next to see thumbnails of your images in a scrollable window.

4. **If you want to copy all images on the media source to your computer, click Next. If you want selected images copied to your hard drive, click the Clear All button to remove the check marks below each thumbnail. After the check marks are removed, select the pictures you want to copy and click Next.**

5. **In the next pane in the wizard, browse your hard drive to locate a folder where you want to copy your pictures. Then click OK.**

   The images are copied to the target folder.

Using Adobe Photo Download Manager

The Adobe Photo Download Manager (Photo Downloader) is installed with your Elements program. Photo Downloader acquires images from digital cameras connected to your computer, from card readers, and from card reader ports on your computer. Photo Downloader is an alternative application to Microsoft Scanner and Camera Wizard.

To use the Adobe Photo Download Manager:

1. **Hook up the media to your computer.**

2. **Click Cancel in the Microsoft Scanner and Camera Wizard.**

Because the wizard auto-launches, the opening pane appears when you make a connection between your camera media source and your computer. To bail out of the wizard, click Cancel.

3. **If you don't see the download launch automatically, choose Start⇨ All Programs⇨Adobe⇨Adobe Download Manager⇨Adobe Download Manager.**

Alternatively, you can launch Elements and click the View and Organize button in the Organizer or click the Photo Browser button in either Quick Fix or Standard Edit mode.

4. **Click Advanced in the Adobe Photoshop Elements – Photo Downloader.**

5. **Select photos to download.**

The Photo Downloader program displays thumbnail images, much like the Microsoft wizard. The Photo Downloader offers a few more options for acquiring your images, though, as shown in Figure 4-2.

Figure 4-2: The Photo Downloader enables you to suggest photo stacks, make group custom name tags, and fix red-eye.

6. **On the right, follow the steps to identify the source, browse for a location folder, add a subfolder if you like, and then rename the files, if desired.**

7. **Click the Get Photos button to commence copying files from the source to your hard drive.**

   When the photos complete the downloading process, a dialog box opens and asks whether you want to delete the original photos from your media source.

8. **Click Yes to delete or No to retain the originals.**

   Immediately after making your selection, the Organizer window opens. All the photos downloaded to your hard drive appear in a new Organizer window, as you see in Figure 4-3.

To simplify the process, stick with using one tool to acquire your digital camera images — either the Microsoft Wizard or the Adobe Photo Download Manager.

Figure 4-3: After downloading is complete, thumbnail images of the copied files appear in a new Organizer window.

Resizing images from digital cameras

Depending on your camera and the camera settings you use, you may need to resize your images after you download them.

Camera image resolution, which is measured in megapixels (millions of pixels), is a factor in image size. If you have a 6-megapixel camera, the full-resolution images from your camera are about 3000 x 2000 pixels. The file size for a 6-megapixel image is about 5.7MB.

On the screen, the resolution of all digital camera images is 72 ppi (pixels per inch). Using the 6-megapixel image as an example, the resolution at 72 ppi produces an image a little more than 41 x 27 inches. Regardless of whether your camera takes pictures at 3, 5, or 8 megapixels, the images are all captured at 72 ppi, but the dimensions vary according to the total number of pixels captured.

Invariably, you visit the Image Size dialog box, deselect Resample Image, and edit the resolution text box when you're preparing images for print. (See Chapter 3 for more information on using the Image Size dialog box.) If your color printer requires 150 ppi, changing a 6-megapixel image from 72 ppi at 41 x 27 inches produces an image of a little more than 20 x 13 inches.

Using a Scanner

Scanners connect through the same ports as cameras and card readers. Unless you have a SCSI (Small Computer Systems Interface) device, which is another type of connection port, you use either USB or FireWire. Most low-end scanners sold now are USB devices.

Even the lowest-end scanners provide 16-bit scans that help you get a little more data in the shadows and highlights. As with a digital camera, a scanner's price is normally in proportion with its quality.

Preparing before you scan

Just as you would clean a lens on a digital camera and set various menu selections before clicking the shutter button, you should prepare a few things ahead of time before scanning:

- **Connect the scanner properly.** Make sure that you have all connections made to your computer according to the user manual that came with your scanner. If you just purchased a scanner, check for any lock bolts and remove them according to the instructions.

- **Clean the scanner platen.** Use a lint-free cloth and some glass cleaner to remove all dust and particles on the glass. The more dust particles you remove, the easier job you have of editing your image in Elements.

✔ **Clean the source material.** Be certain that the print or film you want to scan is free from dust and spots.

If you have old negatives that are dirty or that have water spots or debris that you can't remove with a cloth and film cleaner, soak the film in photo flo (a liquid you can purchase at a photo reseller). Be certain that your hands are clean, and then run the filmstrip between two fingers to remove the excess liquid. Turn on your shower full force with hot water only and hang film nearby to dry it. Remove the film when it's dry and you should see a surprisingly clean filmstrip compared to your soiled original.

✔ **Get to know your scanner software.** When you scan in Elements, the software supplied with your scanner takes charge, and you use the options in this software before it finally drops into an Elements Image window.

✔ **Prepare the artwork.** If you plan on scanning pages in a book or pamphlet, remove the pages or try to make photocopies so that the piece you scan lies flat on the scanner platen. Make sure that you observe copyright laws if you're scanning printed works. For faxes and photocopies, try to improve originals by recopying them on a photocopier with darker settings.

✔ **Find the scanner's sweet spot.** Every scanner has an area where you can acquire the best scans. This area is often called the *sweet spot.* To find the scanner's sweet spot, scan a blank piece of paper. The sweet spot is the brightest area on the resultant scan. Other areas should be darker. The sweet spot is most often in the upper-left quadrant, the lower-right quadrant, or the middle of the page. Note the area and plan to place your source material within this area when scanning pictures.

Understanding image requirements

All scanning software provides you with options for determining resolution and color mode before you start a new scan. You should decide what output you intend to use and scan originals at target resolutions designed to accommodate a given output. Some considerations include

✔ **Scan the artwork or photo at the size and resolution for the final output.** If you have a 3-x-5 photo that needs to be 1.5 x 2.5 inches on a Web page, scan the original with a 50 percent reduction in size at 72 ppi. (See Chapter 3 for information about resizing images.)

✔ **Size images with the scanner software.** If you have a 4-x-6 photo that needs to be output for prepress and commercial printing at 8 x 12 inches, scan the photo at 4 x 6 inches at 600 ppi (enough to size to 200 percent for a 300 dpi image).

✔ **Scan properly for line art.** *Line art* is 1-bit black-and-white only. When you print line art on laser printers or prepare files for commercial printing, the line art resolution should match the device resolution. For example, printing to a 600 dpi (dots per inch) laser printer requires 600 ppi for a 1-bit line art image. When you're printing to an image setter at a print shop or it's going directly to plate or press, the resolution should be 1200 dpi.

✔ **Scan grayscale images in color.** In some cases, it doesn't matter, but with some images and scanners, you can get better results by scanning in RGB color and converting to grayscale using the Hue/Saturation dialog box, as we explain in Chapter 3.

✔ **Scan in high-bit depths.** If your scanner is capable of scanning in 16- or 32-bit, by all means scan at the higher bit depths to capture the most data. See Chapter 3 for more information about working with higher-bit images.

Using scanner plug-ins

Generally, when you install your scanner software, a stand-alone application and a plug-in are installed to control the scanning process. *Plug-ins* are designed to work inside other software programs, like Photoshop Elements. When you're using the plug-in, you can stay right in Elements to do all your scanning. Here's how it works:

1. **After installing a new scanner and the accompanying software, launch Elements and then open the Organizer by clicking View and Organize Photos in the Welcome screen.**

2. **From the Organizer, open the Preferences dialog box by pressing Ctrl+K.**

3. **Click Scanner in the left column and adjust the Scanner preferences, as we describe in Chapter 2.**

When the Preferences dialog box sees your scanner, you know that the connection is properly set up and you're ready to scan. Here's how to complete your scan:

1. **To open the scanner software from within Elements, choose File⇨Get Photos⇨From Scanner.**

   (You must be in the Organizer window to access this menu command).

   Elements may churn a bit, but eventually your scanner software appears atop the Organizer window, as you see in Figure 4-4. The window is the scanner software provided by your scanner manufacturer. (Your window will look different unless you use the same scanner we use.) Regardless of which software you use, you should have similar options for creating a preview; selecting resolution, color mode, and image size; scaling; and other options.

2. **Adjust the options according to your output requirements and recommendations made by your scanner manufacturer.**

3. **When everything is ready to go, click the Scan button.**

   The final image drops into an Elements Image window.

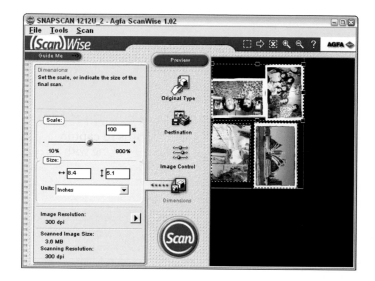

Figure 4-4: When you scan from within Elements, your scanner software loads on top of the Elements workspace.

Scanning many photos at a time

If you have several photos to scan, you can lay them out on the scanner platen and perform a single scan to acquire all images in one pass. Arrange the photos to scan on the glass, and set up all the options in the scanner window for your intended output. When you scan multiple images, they form a single scan, as you can see in Figure 4-5.

After you scan multiple images, Elements makes it easy for you to separate each image into its own Image window, where they can be saved as separate files. Choose Image➪Divide Scanned Pictures, and Elements magically opens each image in a separate window while your original scan remains intact. The images are neatly tucked away in the Photo Bin, where you can select them for editing, as shown in Figure 4-6.

Figure 4-5: You can scan multiple images with one pass.

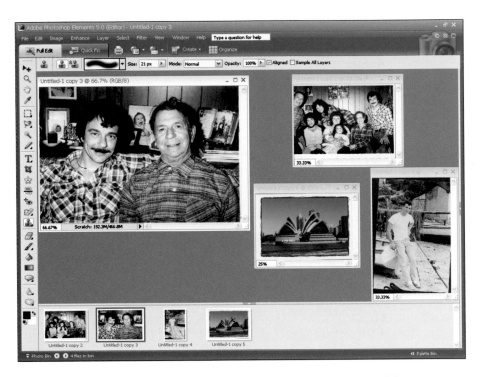

Figure 4-6: After you choose Image⇨Divide Scanned Pictures, the scan is split into separate Image windows.

Getting Files from Storage Media

When you acquire images in Elements from media sources such as CD-ROMs, DVDs, external hard drives, and your internal hard drive, the process is very similar to opening files from digital cameras, which we explain earlier in this chapter. Insert a CD or DVD into the CD/DVD drive, and the Windows Wizard opens just like when you insert a media cartridge or connect a cable from your camera to your computer.

Likewise, you can also open these files in the Organizer. Just cancel out of the wizard and follow these steps:

1. **Open the Organizer window from the Welcome screen or click Photo Browser from one of the editing modes.**

2. **When the Organizer window opens, choose File⇨Get Photos⇨From Files and Folders.**

   Alternatively, you can click the Open tool or press Ctrl+O. The Get Photos from Files and Folders dialog box opens.

3. **Open the source drive from the listed drives.**

   You see the photos stored on the media.

4. **Select images and click the Get Photos button to open them in the Organizer.**

   Now you can edit them in Elements or save them to your hard drive.

Using Online Services

Online printing and sharing services require you to set up an account with a service. You can access services provided by Adobe, Kodak, and other sources from the Preferences dialog box. To use a service, you begin by setting up an account with the Organize and Share Preference settings in the Organizer, as we explain in Chapter 2.

You can create digital photo albums from your images and share them with friends, family, and coworkers. To initiate a sharing service, you send an e-mail invitation to others. Each member of your sharing group needs to set up an account individually. After everyone has an account, you and your friends can then order prints that are mailed from the online service center. All the kinds of prints you might order from a local superstore or photo lab are available from online services, including specialty items, like calendars.

After setting up an account and adjusting your preferences, you handle sharing services by using the Share Photos drop-down menu on the Shortcuts bar, as we explain in Chapter 16.

Phoning In Your Images

At first blush, you might get excited by thinking that you can just hook up your phone to your computer, like you can hook up a digital camera, and import your camera photos directly in the Organizer. Unfortunately, this technology isn't available to Elements from all cell phones. You can use Bluetooth connections and USB cables that permit you to copy images to your hard drive, or you need to e-mail files to yourself and then use the File➪Get Photos➪From Files and Folders command.

To get photos from your cell phone, follow these steps:

1. **Copy photos from your phone to your computer either through a cable connection or via e-mail.**

   You use another utility, not Elements, to copy the pictures. Check your cell phone manual to find out how to transfer files from your phone to your computer.

Where Elements comes in is simply to identify the folder where you copy your mobile phone images.

2. **In the Organizer, open the Specify Mobile Phone Folder by choosing File⇨Get Photos⇨From Mobile Phone.**

   The Specify Mobile Phone Folder dialog box opens, as shown in Figure 4-7.

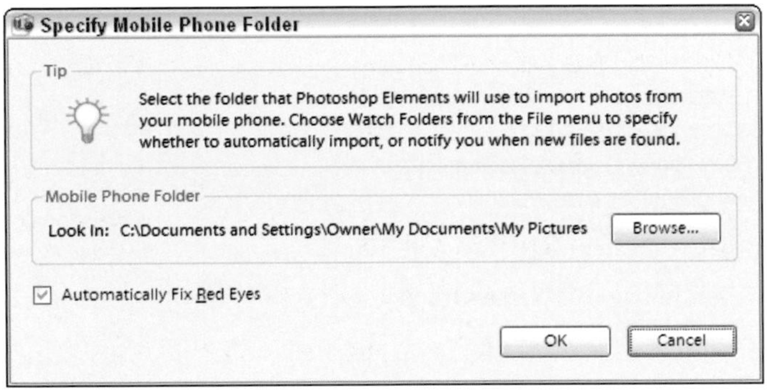

Specify Mobile Phone Folder ☒

Tip

Select the folder that Photoshop Elements will use to import photos from your mobile phone. Choose Watch Folders from the File menu to specify whether to automatically import, or notify you when new files are found.

Mobile Phone Folder

Look In: C:\Documents and Settings\Owner\My Documents\My Pictures   [Browse...]

☑ Automatically Fix Red Eyes

[OK]   [Cancel]

Figure 4-7: Choose File⇨Get Photos⇨From Mobile Phone in the Organizer.

3. **Click Browse and locate the folder where you copied your mobile phone images.**

   After you locate the folder, Elements loads all photos in the folder into a new Organizer window.

4. **From the folder, select images to edit and print.**

Creating Images from Scratch

You may want to start from scratch by creating a new document in Elements. New, blank pages have a number of uses. You can mix and merge images in a new document, as we explain in Chapter 8; create a canvas where you can draw and paint, as we explain in Chapter 12; or use the New dialog box to get some feedback on file sizes, dimensions, and resolution.

You can create new, blank documents by using one of several options. On the Welcome screen, which appears when you first launch Elements, click Start from Scratch. The New dialog box opens, in which you choose the document size, resolution, and other attributes. Likewise, you can create new files while working in either Full Edit or Standard Edit mode or in the Organizer.

Here's how you create a new document while working in any editing mode:

1. **Open Elements and select an editing mode.**

   Click either Quick Fix Photos or Edit and Enhance Photos in the Welcome screen or select View and Organize Photos to open the Organizer.

2. **Open the New dialog box by choosing File⇨New⇨Blank File in any workspace or pressing Ctrl+N (or ⌘+N on the Mac).**

   Either way, the New dialog box opens, as shown in Figure 4-8.

3. **Select the attributes for the new file.**

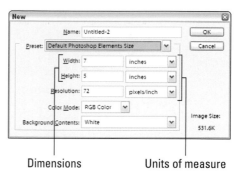

Dimensions   Units of measure

Figure 4-8: Regardless of the method used to create a new, blank document, the New dialog box opens.

You have several options from which to choose:

- *Name:* Type a name for your file.

- *Preset:* You can select a preset size from a long drop-down list. This is optional because you can change the file attributes in the other text boxes and drop-down menus.

- *Units:* Units come in handy when you want to examine dimensions in another unit of measure. If, for example, you have digital camera images at 3000 pixels by 2000 pixels, that number may not mean much. You can quickly select inches on either the Width or Height drop-down menu, and the values in the text boxes convert to inches.

- *Dimensions:* Values in the Width and Height text boxes are independent. Either box can be edited without affecting the other.

- *Resolution:* Resolution here is similar to editing the resolution value in the Image Size dialog box when the Resample check box is selected. The resolution is an independent value and isn't linked to the dimensions. If you want to know how resolution changes dimensions without resampling, create a new, blank file at the known values and click OK. Then choose Image⇨Resize⇨Image Size and change the values in the Image Size dialog box, which we discuss in Chapter 3.

- *Color Mode:* Your choices are bitmap, grayscale, and RGB. (See Chapter 3 for more information about color modes.)

- *Background Contents:* You have three choices: White, Background Color, and Transparent. The selection you make results in the color of the blank image. If you choose Background Color, the current background color assigned on the Tools palette is applied to the background. See Chapter 12 for information on changing background color. If you choose Transparent, the image is created as a layer, as we explain in Chapter 8.

- *Image Size:* This value dynamically changes as you change the Width, Height, and Resolution values. The reported value is how much file size is required to save the uncompressed file.

4. **Click OK after setting the file attributes to create the new document.**

In addition to creating new, blank files, the New dialog box can be a helpful source of information for all your work in Elements. Suppose that you want to know how many images you can copy to a 128MB USB storage device or how large your digital camera files will print with a 150 ppi resolution. All you have to do is press Ctrl/⌘+N to open the New dialog box, plug in the values, and read the Image Size number or examine the file dimensions. If your files will be converted to grayscale, choose Grayscale from the Color Mode drop-down menu and check out the Image Size number to see how much your file size is reduced. Because this number is *dynamic,* it changes with each change you make to the file attributes.

Another means for creating new documents has been introduced in Photoshop Elements 5. Rather than create a new, blank file, you can add pages to an existing file in the form of a project. Here's how to do it:

1. **Open an image in Standard Edit mode.**

2. **Open the Photo Bin by dragging the separator bar up or clicking the Photo Bin icon in the lower-left corner of the Elements window.**

3. **Right-click (Windows) or Ctrl+click (Mac) the photo thumbnail in the Photo Bin.**

   The context menu shown in Figure 4-9 appears.

4. **Choose either Add Blank Page (for adding a new, blank page) or Add Page Using Current Layout (to duplicate the current photo as a new page).**

5. **Save the file by choosing File⇨Save As and selecting Photoshop Multiple Project as your file format.**

   All the pages you add to a project are saved as separate files in a folder automatically created by Elements. When you open

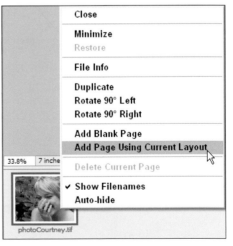

Figure 4-9: Open a context menu and choose an option for adding a page to the photo selected in the Photo Bin.

any one of the images, they appear stacked in the Photo Bin. To open the stack, just click the right-pointing arrow appearing adjacent to the first image thumbnail. All pages in your project are then displayed in the Photo Bin. Click any one of the thumbnails to view and edit that page.

In Figure 4-10, you can see thumbnails of a project where the original RGB image appears on the left followed by a grayscale image, a sepia-tone image, and a bitmap image — all contained in the same photo project.

Figure 4-10: Click the right-pointing arrow to open the project, and click a thumbnail to view that page in the Image window.

Everything You Want to Know about Camera Raw

We added this more elaborate description of Camera Raw in this part of the chapter after sharing with you all the other options you have for getting images in Elements. We recognize that not all of our readers have digital cameras capable of capturing Camera Raw images, so it may not be of much interest to you now.

If you don't have a camera capable of capturing Camera Raw images, you might want to look over this section to understand how this file format can benefit you. When you purchase a camera equipped with Camera Raw support, you'll have some understanding of the advantages of using this format.

Understanding Camera Raw

Camera Raw images enable you to post-process your pictures. When you take a picture with a digital camera in Camera Raw format, the camera's sensor records as much information as it can. When you open a Camera Raw file in Elements, you decide what part of that data is opened as a new image.

Suppose that your camera is set for exposure in tungsten lighting, which is used with tungsten flash photography in a studio. If you take this camera outside in daylight and shoot an image, all your images appear with a blue cast. This happens because tungsten lighting requires a cooler temperature than daylight. See Figure 4-14, later in this chapter, for an example of an image taken outdoors with settings for tungsten lighting.

If you acquire images that are saved in JPEG format, you need to do a lot of color correction after the image opens in Elements. If you shoot the image in Camera Raw format, you just process the image with a warmer temperature (consistent with conditions when the shot was taken), and your color correction in Elements is a fraction of what it would be to fix a JPEG image.

Post-processing Camera Raw images requires a plug-in that's installed with Photoshop Elements. When you open a Camera Raw image, the Camera Raw plug-in takes over and provides you with a huge set of options for post-processing the image before you open it in one of the Elements editors.

Acquiring Camera Raw images

If you read through the first part of this chapter, you know how to acquire images from your camera and copy them to your hard drive. We don't bother going through those steps again; we just assume that you have some Camera Raw images on your hard drive. That's where you want them, anyway. Opening files from your hard drive is much faster than working off media cards.

To open a Camera Raw image, follow these steps:

1. **Open the image by pressing Ctrl+O (or ⌘+O on the Mac) and selecting it in the Open dialog box.**

   If you want to select several images in a row, click the first image, hold down the Shift key, and then click the last image. If you want to select several nonadjacent images, Ctrl/⌘+click each image.

2. **Click Open in the Open dialog box.**

   If you're selecting multiple images, only one image appears in the Camera Raw dialog box. When you click Open, the next image opens in the Camera Raw dialog box, shown in Figure 4-11.

   As you can see, you can use a vast number of options to post-process your image before you drop it into Elements. This window is like a digital darkroom, where you can process the film and see what you're doing to the image before you accept the changes.

3. **Choose from the options to post-process your images.**

   If you have your monitor properly calibrated, as we explain in Chapter 2, all the adjustments you make for Camera Raw format are dynamically updated in the Image preview. Don't be shy. Poke around and adjust settings to see the results in the preview area. The more you play with the settings, the more you find out how to get the best out of Camera Raw.

Figure 4-11: Open a Camera Raw image, and the image opens in the Camera Raw plug-in window.

A large number of settings are in the Camera Raw window, as the following list describes; mark this section to refer to when you work with Camera Raw images:

- **Tools:** Five tools appear in the window:
  - *Zoom:* Zooms in and out of the image preview.
  - *Hand:* Moves the image around, like it does in the Elements image window.
  - *Eyedropper:* Samples color in the image. We cover using the Elements Eyedropper tools in Chapter 12, and that information also applies to using the Eyedropper in the Camera Raw window.
  - *Rotate Left:* Appears first.
  - *Rotate Right:* The last tool you see below the Title bar.

    (The last two rotation tools are self-explanatory.)

- **Image Preview:** The Image Preview shows you all the changes you make before you eventually open the image in an Elements editor.

✔ **Preview:** Notice the Adjust and Details tabs. All adjustments you make on the tabs can be previewed when this check box is selected. Deselecting the box shows you the image as you first opened it in the Camera Raw window.

✔ **Shadow/Highlight:** The Shadow and Highlight check boxes show clipping in the shadows (dark areas of the image) and highlights (light areas of the image). *Clipping* means that, in a certain area, some data and, ultimately, detail have been lost in an image. Think of clipping as something that you don't want to appear in your pictures. When you make adjustments with these two check boxes selected, shadow clipping is shown in blue and highlight clipping is shown in red in the image preview. Take a look at Figure 4-12, in which we exaggerate clipping to show how the clipping preview appears.

✔ **RGB values:** When you first open an image, you don't see any values in the RGB area. Click the Zoom tool, the Hand tool, or the Eyedropper tool, and move the cursor over the image preview. As you move any of these tools around the image, the RGB values corresponding to the point below the cursor are reported in this area.

✔ **Histogram:** This graph displays all three channels (red, green, and blue) in an image simultaneously. The histogram changes as you change other options in the Camera Raw window.

The histogram graphs how pixels in an image are distributed. The distribution includes the number of pixels at each color-intensity level (one of the 256 levels you find out about in Chapter 3).

If images have pixels concentrated in the shadows, you see the histogram skewed to the left. Conversely, images with pixels concentrated in the highlights reveal a histogram skewed to the right.

Figure 4-12: Shadow clipping appears in red, and highlight clipping appears in blue.

As you begin to understand histograms more, you can develop your skill to the point where a quick glance at the histogram provides you with a clue to what adjustments you need to make to improve images.

✔ **Settings:** From this drop-down menu, you have choices for applying settings to the open image. If you change any setting, the menu option changes to *Custom*. If you previously made settings choices on a Camera Raw image and you want to return to the shot as it was taken by the camera, open the image and select Camera Raw Defaults.

Another option you have is Previous Conversion. This selection is handy if you have a collection of images that all require the same settings. After adjusting the first image, open additional images and select Previous Conversion. The Camera Raw plug-in applies the last settings you made to a Camera Raw image to the current open file.

✔ **Adjust/Detail tabs:** In Figure 4-11, you can see the options on the Adjust tab. Click the Detail tab and the options change, as shown in Figure 4-13. Here, you have three items to adjust by either dragging the sliders or typing values in the text boxes.

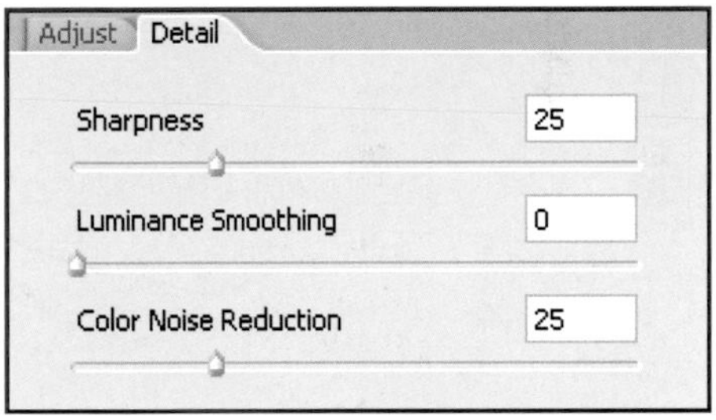

Sharpness sharpens images. You can choose to sharpen images in the Camera Raw window or in Elements. Try to avoid sharpening here and use the sharpening tools in Elements, as we explain in Chapter 9.

Figure 4-13: Click the Detail tab to open the options for sharpness and noise reduction.

Luminance Smoothing is a noise-reduction tool. You've probably seen images with a lot of noise. In extreme cases, they look like the pictures were printed on sandpaper. Noise in an image is okay if that's an effect you intentionally apply to a picture. However, if you want a smooth-looking image, you have to eliminate any noise introduced by the camera. Luminance Smoothing reduces grayscale noise. The next setting is Color Noise Reduction, which is used to reduce color noise.

✔ **White Balance:** White Balance settings are used to adjust the color balance of an image to reflect the lighting conditions under which the shot was originally taken. Think of the sensor in a digital camera capable of capturing the entire range of white balance the sensor can see. You make a choice not necessarily for what you see, but rather for the white balance for the shot you took. Therefore, if your camera is set for taking pictures under one set of lighting conditions and you move to another set of lighting conditions and forget to change the settings, you can let the Camera Raw plug-in make a correction for the white balance because the sensor picked up the entire range and the necessary data is contained in the file.

In Figure 4-14, you can see a picture taken with the camera set for tungsten lighting, but the shot was taken outdoors in daylight. The white balance options selected on the Settings drop-down menu are listed in the figure.

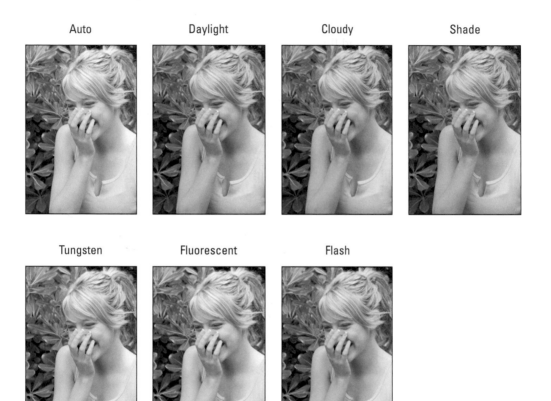

Figure 4-14: From the Settings drop-down menu, you have several choices for white balance.

> ✔ **Temperature:** If one of the preset White Balance options doesn't quite do the job, you can move the Temperature slider or edit the text box to settle on values between one White Balance choice and another. Use this item to fine-tune the White Balance.

> ✔ **Tint:** Tint is another fine-tuning adjustment affected by White Balance. This slider and text box are used to correct any green or magenta tints that might appear in a photo.

✓ **Brightness adjustments:** Several adjustment sliders and text boxes help you control the image brightness and tonal range. Notice the Exposure setting. This item lets you correct photos taken at the wrong exposure. In analog darkrooms, you might ask technicians to push or pull film during processing, which results in longer and shorter processing times. Changing exposure times compensates for under- and overexposing film. A nice advantage of using Camera Raw is that you can change the exposure for one image and then later open the original raw image and change to a different exposure value. Analog film can't be reprocessed, but with Camera Raw, you can reprocess over and over again.

Other options for the brightness and tonal controls are similar to the choices you have in the Elements Standard Editing mode. For more information on these adjustments, see Chapter 10.

✓ **Cancel/Reset:** When you open the Camera Raw window, the button you see by default is Cancel. Press the Alt key, and the button changes to Reset. If you want to scrub all the settings you made and start over, press Alt and click Reset.

✓ **Open/Update/Skip:** This single button has three different purposes:

   • *Open:* This button is the default. Click Open after you choose all your settings to process the photo and open it in Elements.

   • *Update:* Press the Alt/Option key, and the button changes to Update. If you click Update and then cancel out of the dialog box, the next time you open the file in the Camera Raw window, you seethe changes you made before the Update button was clicked. This action lets you change a bunch of settings on several images that you intend to open and edit later in Elements.

   • *Skip:* Press the Shift key to see this button. If you open several images at a time, press Shift, and click Skip, the current active window is dismissed and you move to the next document.

✓ **Save:** Clicking Save merely saves your current settings. You can eliminate the settings saved with the file by selecting Camera Raw Defaults in the Settings drop-down menu.

✓ **Help:** Clicking this button opens a Help document to assist you in understanding more about Camera Raw.

✓ **Bit Depth:** If your camera is capable of shooting higher bit depths, they're listed here. If you want to convert to 8-bit images for printing, you can select the option from the drop-down menu.

✓ **Zoom:** From this drop-down menu, you can choose from several zoom presets. You can also edit the text box or click the minus (–) button to zoom out or the plus (+) button to zoom in. Using any option zooms the Image preview.

All we can hope to provide in this book is a simple cursory view for using Camera Raw. Several entire books have been written exclusively covering the Camera Raw format and how to open files in the Camera Raw plug-in window. For a more detailed look at using Camera Raw, see *Color Management For Digital Photographers For Dummies* by Ted Padova and Don Mason (Wiley).

Viewing and Finding Your Images

*T*he *Organizer* is a powerful tool that helps you locate files and keeps your photos arranged and organized. You can easily access the Organizer by clicking the Photo Browser button on the Shortcuts bar while you're in one of the editing modes. Or, when you open the Welcome screen, click the View and Organize Photos button.

In this chapter, you discover how to view and organize your pictures in the Organizer and the Image window and how the many options help speed up your work in Photoshop Elements.

The Many Faces of the Organizer

The default Organizer view is like a slide sorter, and this view is one you're likely to use in all your Elements work sessions. The Organizer makes accessing photos an efficient means for opening a picture in one of the editors. Just double-click a photo in the Organizer, and you see the image zoom in size to fill an Organizer window. You can carefully examine the photo to be certain that it's the one you want and then just select which editor you want to use from the Edit drop-down list on the Shortcuts bar or from the top-level Edit menu.

In addition to the default view in the Organizer, you have some other opportunities for examining your pictures. You can view pictures in a slide show, or you can view pictures side-by-side to compare them.

Adding files to the default Organizer view

Before you explore alternative viewing options in the Organizer, take a look at how you add photos to the thumbnail images you see in the Organizer window.

After copying the photos to your hard drive, as we explain in Chapter 4, here's how you go about adding those files to an existing group of images in the Organizer:

1. **View photos to add to the Organizer window.**

   Be certain that you have photos in the Organizer window.

2. **In the Organizer, choose File⇨Get Photos⇨From Files and Folders.**

   The Get Photos from Files and Folders dialog box opens, as shown in Figure 5-1.

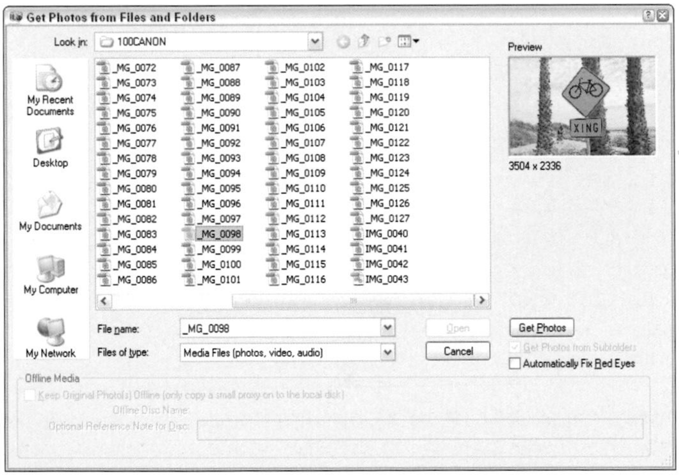

Figure 5-1: The Get Photos from Files and Folders dialog box.

3. **In the Get Photos from Files and Folders dialog box, choose Thumbnails from the View menu (the icon with the down arrow, to the far right of the Look In drop-down list).**

   In Thumbnails view, thumbnail images of most of your files appear in a scrollable window. (***Note:*** You might not see Camera Raw files and some files saved in different formats.) This view makes it easy to locate the files you want to add to the Organizer.

4. **Select files to add to the Organizer window.**

   Click a thumbnail and use either the Shift key or the Ctrl/⌘ key to select additional photos. When you hold down Shift and click, all photos between the first thumbnail and the thumbnail you Shift+click are selected. When you Ctrl/⌘+click, you can select a series of noncontiguous photos.

5. **Click Get Photos to add the selected photos to the Organizer window.**

6. **Add the new photos to the Organizer window you originally opened by clicking the Back button on the Shortcuts bar.**

   The photos you add to the Organizer may appear out of order when you're viewing the Organizer. Depending on the sort order, which we explain later in this chapter, the additional photos you added to the Organizer can appear before or after or integrated within the original photos. Use the scroll bar in the Organizer to view the added photos.

Viewing photos in a slideshow (Full Screen view)

Are you ready for some exciting viewing in Photoshop Elements? To take an alternative view of your Organizer files, you can see your pictures in a self-running slide show (in Full Screen view), complete with transition effects and background music. Full Screen view takes you to a slide show view. For the purposes of clarity, think of Full Screen view and viewing a slide show as the same thing. Full-screen viewing temporarily hides the Elements tools and menus and gives you the most viewing area on your monitor to see your pictures.

Viewing files in slide show mode can be helpful for quickly previewing the files you want to edit for all kinds of output as well as for previewing photos that you might use for an exported slide show, which we explain in Chapter 15.

Setting up your images for viewing

To set up your slide show and/or enter Full Screen view, follow these steps:

1. **Click the Photo Browser button to open the Organizer and navigate to a folder of images you want to view.**

2. **Select individual images to see in a slide show, or use all the images in the Organizer for your slide show.**

   If no images are selected when you enter Full Screen view, all photos in the Organizer window are shown in Full Screen view.

3. **Choose View⇨View Photos in Full Screen.**

   The Full Screen View Options dialog box, shown in Figure 5-2, opens.

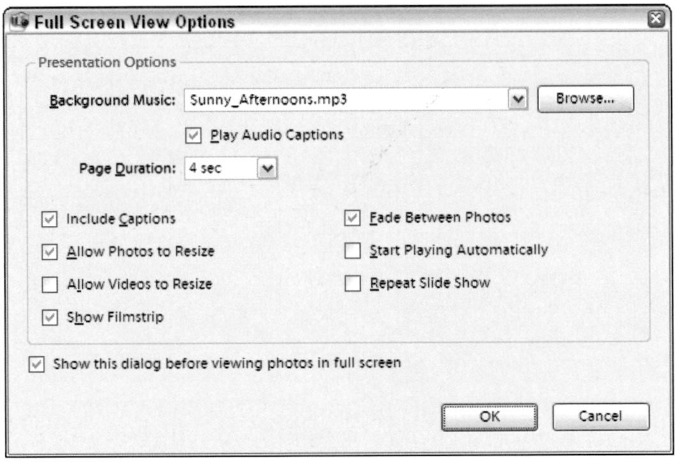

Figure 5-2: Choose View⇨View Photos in Full Screen to open the Full Screen View Options dialog box, where full-screen viewing options are selected.

4. **Choose the options for your slide show in the dialog box.**

   The Full Screen View Options dialog box offers a number of choices for viewing a slide show in Full Screen view. Table 5-1 explains each option.

5. **After you determine the attributes for full-screen viewing, click OK.**

   You enter full-screen mode. For a moment, the Full Screen View toolbar appears at the top of the window. This toolbar hides automatically after a few seconds. We explain in Table 5-1 how, if you select the Show Filmstrip check box, Full Screen view appears, as shown in Figure 5-3.

Figure 5-3: When Show Filmstrip is selected, the full-screen view shows, on the right side of the Image window, thumbnail images of the files selected for viewing.

Table 5-1	Using the Full Screen View Options Dialog Box
Option	*What It Does*
Background Music	You can select a preinstalled sound file from the drop-down list or click the Browse button to locate sound files stored on your computer. The sound file formats you can use with Elements are `.mp3`, `.wav`, and `.wma`. You can add sound files to the Organizer by choosing File⇨Get Photos⇨From Files and Folders and selecting sound files.
Play Audio Captions	You can add audio captions to images, as we explain in Bonus Chapter 1 on the Web. Select this check box to play these captions.
Page Duration	You can specify the duration of each slide before it advances to the next slide. The text box accepts durations ranging from 1 to 3600 seconds.

(continued)

Table 5-1 *(continued)*

Option	What It Does
Include Captions	You can add text captions to images, as we explain in Chapter 6. If you want to see the text captions, select this check box.
Allow Photos to Resize	Images appear at full-screen size when you select this check box. Be certain that the resolution is sufficient before resizing the images to fit the screen. Image resolution is optimal at 72 ppi at 100 percent size, as we point out in Chapter 3.
Allow Videos to Resize	Any video clips you add to the Organizer can be played in the slide show. If you select this check box, the video frames are sized to full-screen size. You also need to be certain that the video supports a resolution sufficient to clearly see the video frames. When in doubt, just test a movie clip in Full Screen view to see whether the quality is satisfactory.
Show Filmstrip	When this check box is selected and you open the files in Full Screen view, a filmstrip appears along the right side of the full-screen window. Click the thumbnails in the filmstrip to jump to the selected slide.
Fade Between Photos	This option adds a fade transition between slides.
Start Playing Automatically	Select this check box, and the slide show moves into play mode automatically. If you don't check the box, you must click a tool in Full Screen view to start the play manually.
Repeat Slide Show	Select this check box to create a continuous loop. You could use this option for a self-running kiosk.
Show This Dialog Before Viewing in Full Screen	If you want to dismiss the Full Screen View Options dialog box keep it from appearing each time you enter Full Screen view, deselect this box. To bring back this dialog box whenever you enter full-screen view, press Ctrl/⌘+K to open the General Preferences dialog box and click the Reset All Warning Dialogs button. If you want to keep the dialog box from opening but access it after entering Full Screen view, choose Full Screen View Options from the Action drop-down menu on the Full Screen toolbar. See the next section for details on using the toolbar.

Working with the toolbar

While in Full Screen view, you can play the slide show and move back and forth between slides. These options and more are available to you on the toolbar that opens when you first enter full-screen viewing. After the toolbar disappears, you can bring it back by simply moving the mouse.

The toolbar shown in Figure 5-4 contains tools for the following:

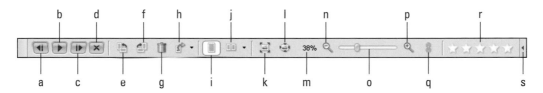

Figure 5-4: The Full Screen View toolbar.

a **Previous Photo (left-arrow key):** Click this button to view the previous slide, or press the shortcut left-arrow key.

b **Play/Pause (spacebar):** Click this button to pause play. When play is paused, the icon changes and you can click the new icon to resume play.

c **Next Photo (right-arrow key):** Click this button to view the next slide, or press the shortcut right-arrow key.

d **Exit (Esc):** Click this button or press Esc to exit Full Screen view.

e **Rotate 90 Degrees Left (Ctrl/⌘+left-arrow key):** Click this button to rotate the photo in the Image window and in the Organizer default window.

f **Rotate 90 Degrees Right (Ctrl/⌘+right-arrow key):** This button works the same as the button in the preceding bullet, but rotates to the right.

g **Delete (Del):** Press this key to delete the photo in the Image window from the slide show and the Organizer.

h **Action Menu:** The commands on this drop-down menu, shown in Figure 5-5, provide options for editing images, printing, and organizing files. For more information on the editing options, see Chapter 9. For information on printing, see Chapter 14. For information on organizing, see Chapter 6.

Figure 5-5: The Action drop-down menu.

i **Full Screen View (F11):** When you enter Full Screen view, this tool is selected.

j **Side by Side/Above and Below (F12):** From this drop-down menu, you can choose to show two slides horizontally or vertically. The selected slide in the filmstrip is compared to the next slide in the filmstrip. Additionally, you can click a slide and Ctrl/⌘+click to compare two selected slides. To return to the default view, click the Full Screen View tool.

k **Fit in Window (Ctrl/⌘+0):** This tool zooms the view as large as needed to fill in the Image window.

l **Actual Pixels (Ctrl/⌘+Alt/Option+0):** Use this tool to see images at actual sizes.

m **Current Zoom Percentage:** Shows you the zoom level of the image in the Image window. You can't edit this readout.

n **Zoom Out (Ctrl/⌘+–):** Click this tool to zoom out.

o **Specify zoom level:** Move the slider left to zoom out and right to zoom in.

p **Zoom In (Ctrl/⌘++):** Click this tool to zoom in on the image.

q **Sync Pan and Zoom in side-by-side view:** Panning and zooming are synchronized by default. When two slides are compared and appear side by side or one above the other, both images are sized together as you change the zoom level. Click the chain link icon to desynchronize the view.

r **Specify a favorites ranking for this photo:** Click one of the five stars to specify a favorites ranking.

s **Show Only Navigation Controls:** You can collapse the toolbar to show only the first four tools (and this one). When the toolbar is collapsed, click the arrow again to expand to the default toolbar.

Moving Around the Image Window

When you edit images in either Quick Fix or Standard Edit mode, you continually interact with the Image window. Whether you're zooming in and out of a single window or viewing multiple windows, you need to work comfortably in this area for all your editing tasks. To help you move around the Image window, Elements provides a rich set of tools. If you become familiar with the many viewing options and keyboard shortcuts available in Elements, all your editing jobs will be much easier. The tools, menu commands, and palettes described in this section are essential for just about everything you do in Elements.

Zooming in and out of images

Zooming in and out of images is a task you perform routinely while editing images in the Image window and also when working in other windows, such as the Camera Raw window and the Full Screen View window. Zooming in is necessary when you want to precisely edit a section of an image or examine detail in a small area. You then need to zoom out to see the edits as they compare to the entire image.

Zoom by clicking

The Zoom tool appears on the Tools palette. To use the tool for zooming in and out, take a look at how it all works:

1. **Click the Zoom tool on the Tools palette to select it (or simply press Z).**

2. **Move the cursor, now loaded with the Zoom tool, to the Image window and click the place where you want to zoom.**

   To zoom in more, click again; keep clicking until you zoom in far enough.

3. **To zoom out of an image, keep the Zoom tool selected, hold down the Alt/Option key, and click.**

   The cursor changes to a magnifying glass tool with a minus (–) symbol when you hold down the Alt/Option key.

Zoom to a selection

Another way to change a view is to zoom to a target area in an image. Here's how:

1. **Click the Zoom tool on the Tools palette.**

2. **Drag a box around the area you want to zoom.**

   A dashed rectangle marquee appears, as shown in Figure 5-6.

Figure 5-6: Click the Zoom tool on the Tools palette and drag around an area you want to zoom.

3. **Move the rectangle marquee if you need to adjust the selection.**

   Now it's time to get fancy. If you have a marquee drawn with the Zoom tool and the size appears just right but you want to move just the rectangle, press the spacebar while you keep the mouse button pressed. You can drag the marquee rectangle anywhere in the image to zoom to the area defined by the rectangle boundary.

4. **Release the mouse button.**

   The view zooms to fit the space defined by the marquee rectangle.

Using the Options bar

Above the Image window and below the Shortcuts bar you find the Options bar. The Options bar is ever-changing, offering different options as you select different tools on the Tools palette. When you click the Zoom tool, the Options bar changes, as shown in Figure 5-7. You have many similar choices for zooming in and out of images and a few options unique to the Options bar:

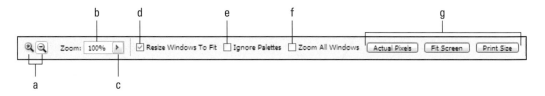

Figure 5-7: Click the Zoom tool on the Tools palette, and the Options bar changes to reflect choices for zooming in and out of images.

a **Zoom In/Zoom Out tools:** You can choose Zoom In or Zoom Out as separate tools to avoid using the Alt/Option key to toggle between the two.

b **Zoom percentage:** This figure shows you the current zoom level as a percentage. You can edit the text by typing values between 1 and 1600.

c **Zoom slider:** Click the right-pointing arrow, and a slider bar opens. Drag the slider left to zoom out or right to zoom in.

d **Resize Windows To Fit:** Select this check box to resize the window along with the image zoom. Deselect the box to zoom in and out of an image while the Image window remains at a fixed size.

e **Ignore Palettes:** This check box is selected when you select the Resize Windows to Fit check box. Selecting this box ignores palettes when you're using the Zoom tool, so you can zoom to an area covered by the palettes. If you deselect the box, you can't zoom to an area beneath the Palette Bin.

f **Zoom All Windows:** If you have multiple images open and select this check box, zooming with the Zoom tool zooms all open documents simultaneously.

g **Actual Pixels/Fit Screen/Print Size:** The same options are available as discussed earlier in this chapter, in the "Working with the toolbar" section.

Viewing multiple documents

When you need to view two or more images at one time, choose Window⇨ Images to open a submenu of viewing options used for viewing multiple files. The Window menu also provides a list of all your open documents. Here's a list of options you find on the submenu:

- **Maximize Mode:** In Maximize mode, you see only one Image window and lose the option for resizing the window by dragging the lower-right corner in or out. If you want to bring back the title bar and the resizing options, choose the Window⇨Images⇨Maximize Mode command again. Notice the Maximize Mode check box; click it to remove the check mark on the submenu and minimize the Image window.

- **Tile:** Tiling images reduces Image window sizes to a size that accommodates viewing all images in scrollable windows within the Elements workspace. Choose Window⇨Images⇨Tile when multiple images are open to get a view similar to the one shown to Figure 5-8.

- **Cascade:** Choose Window⇨Images⇨Cascade, and the Image windows overlap each other in a cascading view.

- **Match Zoom:** Set the zoom level for one of several images open in Elements and choose Window⇨Images⇨Match Zoom. All open documents are zoomed to the same level as the foreground image.

- **Match Location:** If you zoom into, for example, the upper-right corner and then select Match Location, all open images zoom to the same location in the respective photos.

- **Bring Image to Foreground:** As you open photos, the open documents are listed by name on the Window menu. The active document is the foreground image. If you want to edit another image, choose Window and select the image you want to edit. That image comes to the foreground as the active image.

Although you can use a menu command to bring images to the foreground and make them active, you can perform the same action by clicking an image thumbnail in the Photo Bin.

Figure 5-8: Open several images in one of the editing modes and choose Window⇨Images⇨Tile to show all Image windows.

Using Pan and Zoom

When you zoom in on a document larger than the Image window can accommodate, scroll bars provide a means for moving the image inside the window. Moving the image around a window is *panning* the image.

You can also use the Hand tool to pan the image. Zoom into an image and click the Hand tool. Click and drag the image around the window. If you want to zoom in or out while the Hand tool is selected, hold down the Ctrl/⌘ key, and the Hand tool temporarily changes to the Zoom In tool. Hold down Ctrl+Alt (or ⌘+Option) and the Hand tool temporarily changes to the Zoom Out tool.

Using the Navigator palette

The Navigator palette affords you several different options for both zooming and panning an image.

To open the Navigator palette, choose Window⇨Navigator. The Navigator palette, shown in Figure 5-9, opens as a floating palette in the Elements workspace. (For more information on floating palettes, see Chapter 1.)

While you select options for zooming on the Navigator palette, the image preview in the Palette window stays fixed to show you the entire image. As you zoom in and out inside the palette, the corresponding zoom is applied to the active document.

Figure 5-9: The Navigator palette.

TIP Either use the zoom tools on the palette or drag the slider left and right to zoom in and out. If you place the cursor inside the image preview thumbnail, you can drag a rectangle and zoom into the image.

TIP Using the Navigator palette can be particularly helpful if you use two monitors. Just drag the Navigator palette to your second monitor, where you can change zoom levels without having the palette obscure the background image.

Sorting Your Photos

With all the Photoshop Elements modes and workspaces, you need a consistent starting place to handle all your editing tasks. Think of the Organizer as Grand Central Station, and from this central location you can take the Long Island Railroad to any destination you desire. In Elements terms, rather than head out to Port Washington, you travel to an editing mode. Rather than go to the Hamptons, you journey through all the creation areas. In short, the Organizer is the central depot on the Photoshop Elements map.

In addition to being a tool to navigate to other workspaces, the Organizer is a management tool you can use to organize, sort, search, and describe photos with identity information. In terms of sorting and organizing files, Elements provides many different options, and we cover them all in the following sections.

Using sort commands

In the lower-left corner of the Organizer window is a pop-up menu that provides some sorting options, as shown in Figure 5-10. Alternatively, you can choose View➪Arrangement, and a sub-menu providing the same commands opens.

Date (Newest First)	Ctrl+Alt+0
Date (Oldest First)	Ctrl+Alt+1
Import Batch	Ctrl+Alt+2
✓ Folder Location	Ctrl+Alt+3

Figure 5-10: The Organizer's sort options.

The sorting options available to you are

- ✔ **Date (Newest First):** Select this option to view images according to the date you took the photos, beginning with the most recent date.

- ✔ **Date (Oldest First):** This option displays photos in chronological order, starting with the oldest file.

- ✔ **Import Batch:** You might import a batch of photos in one Photoshop Elements session and import another batch in the same session or in another session. When you select Import Batch, the images appear organized in groups, according to the date the batch was created. In Figure 5-11, you can see several batches imported and added as collections, which we describe in Chapter 6.

- ✔ **Folder Location:** Click Folder Location and you see an Explorer pane on the left side of the Organizer window. You can browse your hard drive for folder locations and select a folder containing images you imported into the Organizer.

Sorting media types

Photos can also be sorted according to media type. Elements supports viewing photos, video files, audio files, creations, and PDF files. To select different media types, choose View➪Media Types, and the Items Shown dialog box opens. Check the boxes for the media types you want to display in the Organizer window.

Figure 5-11: When you're importing photos in batches, you can sort files according to batch-import dates.

Using Search Options

The Organizer's Find menu is devoted entirely to searching photos. From the Find menu, you can locate photos in collections, catalogs, and the Organizer window according to a variety of different search criteria.

To use the commands on the Find menu, you need to have photos loaded in the Organizer window or create collections or catalogs, which we explain in Chapter 6. The categories in the following sections can be searched in the Organizer.

Searching by date

When you have a number of different files in an Organizer window from photos shot on different dates, you can narrow your search to find photos, and all other types of files supported by Elements, through a date search. To search files by date, do the following:

1. **Open files in the Organizer by choosing File➪Get Photos and then choosing a submenu command for acquiring files.**

   To open files stored on your hard drive, choose the From Files and Folders submenu command.

2. **Select a date range by choosing Find➪Set Date Range.**

   The Set Date Range dialog box, shown in Figure 5-12, opens.

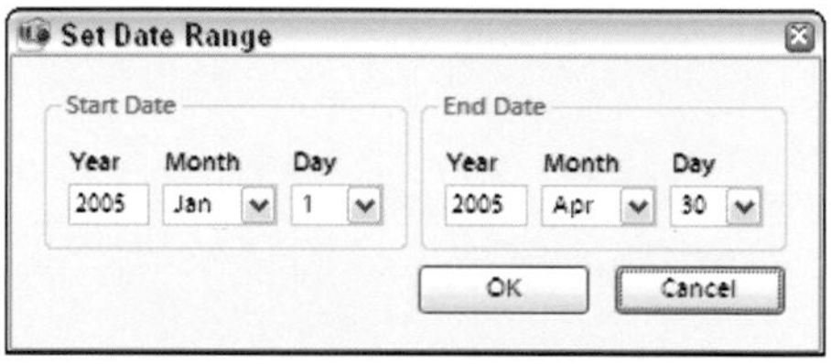

3. **Specify the dates.**

   Type a year in the Start Date Year text box. Select the month and day from the Month and Day drop-down lists. Repeat the same selections for the end date.

Figure 5-12: Open the Set Date Range dialog box and specify the start and end dates.

4. **Click OK.**

   The thumbnails shown in the Organizer window include only files created within the specified date range.

Searching for untagged items

You can tag files with a number of different criteria, as we explain in Chapter 6. When tags are added to images, you can sort files according to tag labels. We cover sorting by tag labels in Chapter 6, too. For now, take a look at the Find menu and notice the Untagged Items command. If you haven't added tags to some items and you want to show only the untagged files so that you can begin to add tags, choose Find➪Untagged Items or press Ctrl+Shift+Q. Elements displays all files without tags in the Organizer window.

Searching collections

Collections are among many items we address in Chapter 6. You can create collections and then select a collection on the Collections palette. Selecting a collection is like having a first level of sorting. You can then search by date or other sort options discussed here to narrow the choices.

Searching captions and notes

In Chapter 6, we talk about adding captions and notes to your files. When captions or notes are added to files, you can search on the caption name, contents of a note, or both. To search caption names and notes, do the following:

1. **Open files in the Organizer by choosing File➪Get Photos and then choosing a submenu command for acquiring files.**

   If you're opening files stored on your hard drive, choose the From Files and Folders submenu command.

2. **Choose Find➪By Caption or Note.**

   The Find by Caption or Note dialog box opens, as shown in Figure 5-13.

   Options in the dialog box are

   • *Find Items with Caption or Note:* In the text box, type the words you want to search.

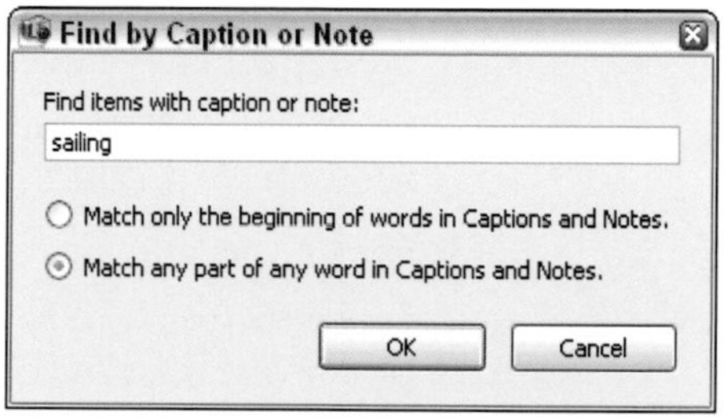

Figure 5-13: Choose Find➪By Caption or Note to open the dialog box in which search criteria for captions and notes are specified.

   • *Match Only the Beginning of Words in Captions and Notes:* Click this radio button when you know that your caption or note begins with words you type in the text box.

   • *Match Any Part of Any Word in Captions or Notes:* Click this radio button if you're not sure whether the text typed in the box is used at the beginning of a caption or note or whether it's contained within the caption name or note text.

3. **Click OK.**

   The Results appear in the Organizer window.

Searching by history

Elements keeps track of what you do with your photos, such as printing, e-mailing, sharing, and performing a number of other tasks. You can search for files based on the file history by choosing Find➪By History. Selecting options on the By History submenu reports files found on date searches meeting the history criteria.

Searching metadata

Metadata includes both information about your images that is supplied by digital cameras and custom data you add to a file. *Metadata* contains descriptions of the image, such as your camera name, the camera settings you used to take a picture, copyright information, and much more.

Searching metadata is easy. Just choose Find⇨By Details (Metadata) in the Organizer. The Find by Details (Metadata) dialog box opens, as shown in Figure 5-14. The first two columns in the dialog box offer a number of different choices for search criteria and options according to the criteria. In the third column, you specify exactly what you want to search by typing search criteria in the text box. Clicking the plus button adds new lines to add more criteria to the search, and clicking the minus button deletes a line.

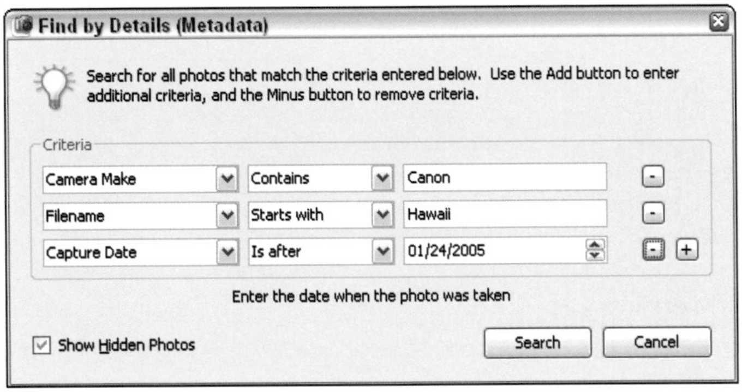

Find by Details (Metadata)

Search for all photos that match the criteria entered below. Use the Add button to enter additional criteria, and the Minus button to remove criteria.

Criteria

Camera Make	Contains	Canon	[-]
Filename	Starts with	Hawaii	[-]
Capture Date	Is after	01/24/2005	[-] [+]

Enter the date when the photo was taken

☑ Show Hidden Photos   [Search]   [Cancel]

Figure 5-14: Choose Find⇨By Details (Metadata) in the Organizer to open the dialog box in which metadata are specified.

Searching faces

If a magical method is available to you for searching files in Elements, it has to be searching for faces. When you choose Find⇨Find Faces for Tagging, Elements searches through files you select in the Organizer window and examines each image for a face — *Homo sapiens* faces, to be exact.

Note that you should first select image thumbnails in the Organizer window and then choose Find⇨Find Faces for Tagging. If you don't select files, Elements searches the entire catalog. Be aware that if you search through a large catalog, Elements takes some time to complete the search.

The results of the search magically include all photos containing faces in a new Organizer window. Although the command is intended to identify images you can tag, you can use the command for invoking a search and choose to view all files containing faces.

Organizing and Managing Your Photos

Downloading a bunch of media cards filled with photos and leaving them in folders distributed all over your hard drive is like having a messy office with papers stacked all over your desk. Trying to find a file, even with all the great search capabilities we cover in Chapter 5, can take you as much time as sorting through piles of papers. What you need is a good file-management system.

In this chapter, we talk about organizing and anno-tating files and the important task of backing up files. Be certain to take a little time to understand the organization methods that Elements provides and keep your files organized as you copy them to your hard drive and back up files to CD-ROMs or DVDs. The time you invest in organizing your pictures helps you quickly locate files when you need them.

Organizing Groups of Images with Collections

Elements provides you with a great opportunity for organizing files, in the form of collections. After you acquire your images in the Organizer, as we discuss in Chapter 4, you should sort them out and add them to some permanent collections according to the dates you took the pictures, the subject matter, or some other categorical arrangement.

In the Organizer window, two palettes help you sort your pictures and keep them well organized. You use the Tags palette, which we talk about in the section "Tag — You're It!" later in this chapter, to identify individual images by using a limitless number of options for categorizing your pictures. On the Collections palette, you can create collections and collection groups to neatly organize files.

Collections are handy when you want to use the many different creation options we explain in Chapter 16. You create a collection from files stored in various folders on your hard drive and preview the images to be used in a creation. Select the images you want to use in creating slide shows and photo albums, for example. When you finish with the creations, go back and delete the collection.

In the following sections, you find out how to create and manage collections.

Creating a new collection

To create a new collection and add photos to the collection, do the following:

1. **Open photos in the Organizer.**

   Open the Organizer window by clicking the Photo Browser button in an editing mode or selecting View and Organize Photos on the Welcome screen. Choose File⇨Get Photos⇨From Files and Folders. Note that you should have copied some photos to your hard drive, as we explain in Chapter 4.

2. **If you don't see the Collections tab in the Organize Bin, choose Window⇨Organize Bin.**

   By default, the Organize Bin should be open to the Collections tab.

3. **To create a new Collection, choose New⇨ New Collection on the Collections tab.**

   The Edit Collection dialog box opens, as shown in Figure 6-1.

Figure 6-1: The Edit Collection dialog box.

4. **Type a name for the collection in the Name text box, and add a note to describe the collection.**

   You might use the location where you took the photos, the subject matter, or other descriptive information.

5. **Click OK in the Edit Collection dialog box.**

   You return to the Organizer window.

6. **In the Organizer window, select the photos you want to add to your collection.**

   Click a photo and Shift+click another photo to select photos in a group. Click a photo and Ctrl+click different photos scattered around the Organizer window to select photos in a nonconsecutive order.

7. **To add the selected photos to the new collection, click one of the selected photos in the Organizer window and drag the photo thumbnail to the New Collection icon in the Organize Bin.**

   When you release the mouse button, the photos are added to the new collection.

8. **Repeat Steps 3 through 7 to create collections for all the images you want to organize.**

9. **To view one or more collections, click the empty squares adjacent to a collection icon to show the photos within that collection in the Organizer window.**

Figure 6-2: Click the empty square adjacent to the collection icon.

   When you click the empty square, an icon in the shape of a pair of binoculars appears inside the square, as shown in Figure 6-2.

Working with collections

You can manage collections by using menu commands from the New drop-down menu and other commands from a context menu that you open by right-clicking a collection on the Collections tab.

From the New drop-down menu, you have these commands:

- **New Collection:** Create a new collection, as described in the steps in the preceding section.

- **New Collection Group:** You can group several collections in a collection group and share your files with a sharing service. Select multiple collections and click the New button in the Collections palette. From the drop-down menu, select New Collection Group to open the Create Collection Group dialog box.

✔ **Save Collections to a File:** You can save collections to a file that can be retrieved using the From File command. This option is handy when you open a different catalog file and you want to import the same collection names created in one catalog file to another catalog file. (See the section "Cataloging Files," later in this chapter.)

✔ **From File:** Import a saved collection.

Right-click the mouse button on a collection name, and the following menu commands appear:

✔ **Edit <collection name> Collection:** Choose Edit <Collection Name> Collection, and the Edit Collection dialog box opens (refer to Figure 6-1). You can use this command to rename a collection or change the note. Alternatively, you can click the Pencil tool on the palette to open the same dialog box.

✔ **Delete <collection name> Collection:** Select a collection and click this menu option to delete a collection. Alternatively, click the Trash icon on the palette to delete a collection. Note that deleting a collection doesn't delete files.

✔ **Find Items in <collection name> Collection:** Opening a context menu on a collection that's not visible in the Organizer window and choosing this command is the same as clicking the empty square adjacent to a collection icon. All the photos in the collection appear in the Organizer window.

✔ **Add <number selected > Items to <collection name> Collection:** If you select one photo in the organizer, the number is one. Selecting more than one photo changes the number to the total number of selected images. When you open a context menu, the selected images are added to the collection where the context menu is opened.

Collections are automatically saved with the catalog you work with. By default, Elements creates a catalog and auto-saves your work to it. If you happen to create another catalog, as we explain in the next section, your collections disappear. You need to be aware of which catalog is open when you create collections in order to return to them.

Cataloging Files

As you open files in the Organizer, all your files are automatically saved to a catalog. The files themselves aren't really saved to the catalog, but rather links from the catalog to the individual files are saved. *Links* are like pointers that tell the catalog where to look for a file. As you add and delete files, the catalog is continually updated.

As you open more files in the Organizer, the default catalog file grows, and the maximum size of the catalog file is limited only by your available hard drive space. Working with a single catalog file has some disadvantages. For example, if your catalog file becomes corrupted and unrecoverable, you lose all the work you've done organizing files into collections. If you work with many files, the Organizer performance slows down.

Rather than work with a single catalog file, you can fine-tune your file organization by creating several catalogs. You might want to organize files according to subject matter, dates, locations, or some other division of categories and create separate catalogs for each category. You find all the details in the sections that follow.

Splitting a big catalog into smaller catalogs

Here's how you go about breaking up a large catalog into a smaller one:

1. **Open files in the Organizer.**

   If you have a large collection of files (100 images or more) open in an Organizer window, you can start with your open files. If you don't yet have files open, choose the File⇨Get Photos menu command and get photos from one of the submenu commands to load up the Organizer window.

2. **Open the Catalog dialog box, shown in Figure 6-3, by choosing File⇨Catalog.**

   Here's something to keep in mind when working with catalogs: You don't create or access catalogs by using menu commands. All the aspects of working with a catalog are handled in the Catalog dialog box.

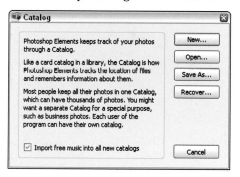

Figure 6-3: Choose File⇨Catalog to open the Catalog dialog box.

3. **Duplicate the catalog file by clicking the Save As button in the Catalog dialog box.**

   The Save Catalog As dialog box opens. By using Save As, you duplicate the current Organizer window and save it as a new catalog file.

4. **Type a descriptive name for the catalog in the File Name text box and click OK.**

   When you're done, you return to the Organizer window.

5. **Add and delete files in the Organizer.**

   You can delete files that don't belong to your newly created catalog topic and add files by choosing the File⇨Get Photos menu command.

Furthermore, you can add or delete collections, as described in the preceding section in this chapter. The view you create in the Organizer is automatically saved to your new catalog file.

When you delete a file from a catalog, Elements prompts you in a dialog box to confirm the deletion. Also in the dialog box is a check box for deleting files from your hard disk. If you click the box, the file is deleted from your hard disk. Be certain to exercise caution so that you don't inadvertently delete your only copy of a photo.

Importing photos to a new catalog

To keep your photos organized and your catalog files smaller, you can start a completely new catalog before you import photos. Follow these steps:

1. **Choose File➪Catalog and click New in the Catalog dialog box.**

2. **When the New Catalog dialog box opens, type a name for the new catalog in the File Name text box and click Save.**

3. **If you want to add free music files installed with Elements, click the check box for Import Free Music into All New Catalogs.**

4. **You can choose the File➪Get Photos menu commands to add files to the new catalog.**

   When the Get Photos from Files and Folders dialog box opens, a list of media files appears in the dialog box when the Import Free Music into All New Catalogs check box is selected. You can select the free music files to add to your collection; then navigate your hard drive and select the photos you want to add. After you identify all the files, click Open; the selected music files and photos are added to your new collection.

Switching to a different catalog

When you need to open a different catalog file, choose File➪Catalog and click Open. All your catalogs appear in the default folder where the catalogs are saved. Select a catalog and click Open, and the Organizer window changes to reflect files contained in the respective catalog.

Notice the Recover button in Figure 6-3. If you can't see thumbnail previews of images or open them in one of the editing modes, your catalog file might be corrupted. Click the Recover button to try to fix the problem.

Tag — You're It!

If you want to sort files into subcategories, Elements provides tags for identifying common files.

Think of a catalog as a parent item and collections as its children. Within collections, you can sort files according to date by using the sort options discussed in Chapter 5. If you still have a number of files in an Organizer window that are hard to manage, you can create tags that form subcategories within the collections. These tags can be

- ✔ Ratings, such as one to five stars, you assign to files in the Favorites area of the Tags palette

- ✔ Groups, like family, friends, and places

- ✔ Other custom categories you want to define by tagging files with these items

After creating tags and applying the tags to files in a catalog, clicking the box adjacent to a tag name on the Tags palette in the Organize Bin shows you all files assigned to the given tag. You can further sort the tagged files according to date, as described in Chapter 5.

Tags are handled with menu commands from the New drop-down menu on the Tags palette that's shown when you're working in the Organizer window. Click the Tags tab in the Organize Bin and click the down arrow adjacent to the New button to open the menu. These menu options are associated with tags:

- ✔ **New Tag:** Choose this menu command to open the Create Tag dialog box, where new tags are added to the Tags palette.

- ✔ **New Subcategory:** Choose this menu command to create a new subcategory.

- ✔ **New Category:** Choose this menu command to create a new tag category.

- ✔ **From File:** Choose this menu command to load tags that were saved using the Save Tags to File command.

- ✔ **Save Tags to File:** Choose this menu command to save tags to an XML (eXtensible Markup Language) file. XML files can be exported and imported in various ways in Elements, such as when you're using collections and tags. You can then open a different catalog and use the From File command so that all the new tags created in another catalog are imported into the current open catalog. This feature can save you a lot of time organizing files.

  Suppose that you're a wedding photographer and you create catalogs for each individual wedding you shoot. (If you combine a few weddings in one catalog, you can create separate collections for each individual wedding.) You can create tags for the pre-ceremony shots of the bride dressing and the groom dressing, another set of tags for the ceremony, and another set of tags for the reception. After you create your first catalog and identify the tags, export the file by using the Save Tags to File command. Each time you shoot a new wedding, you load the tags into a new catalog file by using the From File menu command.

Creating new tags

New tags can be added as subsets to existing tags. You can create new tags, add icons for the appearance of tags, and assign tags to selected files in a catalog file. Here's how you go about creating tags:

1. **Choose File⇨Catalog and open a catalog you created for a particular category.**

   If you haven't created a catalog, use files you open in the Organizer window.

2. **On the Tags tab in the Organize Bin, choose New⇨New Tag.**

   The Create Tag dialog box opens.

3. **To add an icon appearance, click the Edit Icon button.**

   The icon you add appears on the Tags palette to help you easily identify tags. The Edit Tag Icon dialog box, shown in Figure 6-4, opens.

4. **Click the Import button.**

   The Import Image for Tag Icon dialog box opens.

   Figure 6-4: Click Edit Icon in the Create Tag dialog box to open the Edit Tag Icon dialog box.

5. **Locate an image you want to use, select it, and click Open.**

   You can use any photo saved in `.jpg`, `.bmp`, `.png`, or `.gif` format. (See Chapter 3 for more information on file formats.) When the image is imported, an image preview is displayed in the dialog box (refer to Figure 6-5).

6. **Locate the place on a map where you shot the photo. Then click the Place on Map button in the Create Tag dialog box.**

   The Tag Location on Map dialog box opens.

7. **Type a location in the dialog box, such as city and country or city and state. Click the Find button and the Look Up Address dialog opens with a location listed. Click OK.**

   You return to the Edit Tag Icon dialog box with a Yahoo map showing the location you specified as shown in Figure 6-5.

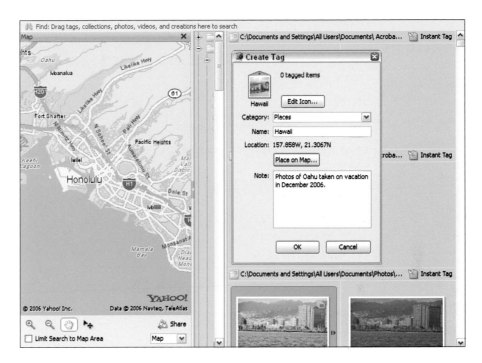

Figure 6-5: The Create Tag dialog box with an identified map location.

8. **The Category drop-down list identifies all the categories now on the Tags palette. Select the category where you want your new tag to appear as a child to the category.**

9. **Type a name for your tag in the Name text box.**

10. **Add a note to describe the tag and then click OK.**

   Your new tag is added to the Tags palette.

Creating new categories

In the Create Tag dialog box, the categories in the Category drop-down menu come from the category list on the Tags palette. If you want to use a category not available among the default tags, you can create your own new custom category by following these steps:

1. **Choose File⇨Catalog and open a catalog you created for a particular category.**

   If you haven't created a catalog, use files you open in the Organizer window.

2. **On the Tags palette, choose New⇨New Category.**

   The Create Category dialog box, shown in Figure 6-6, opens.

3. **Click the Choose Color button in the Create Category dialog box and select a color from the color palette that opens.**

4. **Type a name for the category in the Category Name text box.**

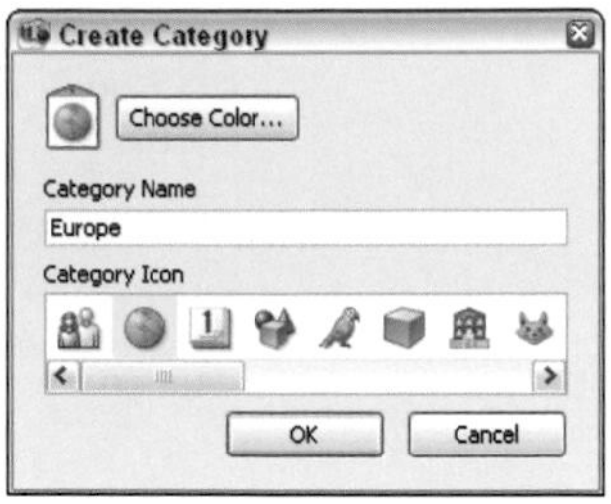

5. **Select an icon in the Category Icon list by clicking it.**

   You can scroll the list of icons by dragging the slider bar back and forth or click the left and right arrows. All icons you can assign to a category are available from this list. Elements doesn't provide an option for creating custom icons for categories.

6. **Click OK.**

   The category is added to the Tags palette.

Figure 6-6: The Create Category dialog box.

Creating new subcategories

When you open the Organizer and click the Tags palette, you see several tag categories that Elements provides by default. Categories such as Hidden, People, Places, Events, and Other are tags that always appear when you create any new collection. If you want to add custom subcategories to these default tags, Elements offers you a menu command to do so.

Do the following to create a subcategory:

1. **In the Organizer window, open a catalog in which you created a custom category.**

2. **On the Tags palette, choose New⇨ New Sub-Category.**

   The Create Sub-Category dialog box opens, as shown in Figure 6-7.

   Alternatively, you can right-click (Windows) a tag on the Tags palette and choose Create New Sub-Category in <category or subcategory name> Category.

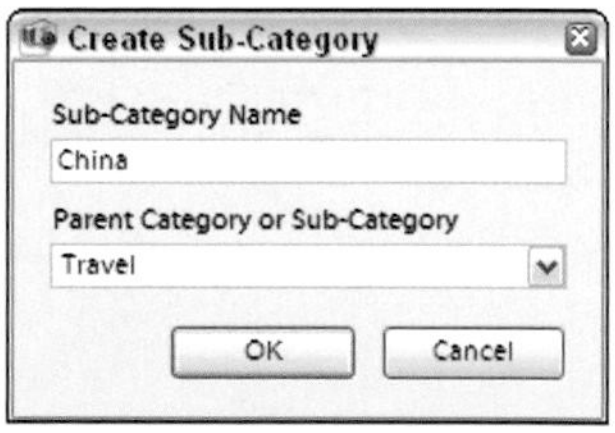

3. **Type a name for the subcategory in the Sub-Category Name text box.**

4. **Select a parent category from the Parent Category or Sub-Category drop-down list.**

Figure 6-7: The Create Sub-Category dialog box.

Subcategories appear as children below parent categories or below other subcategories. You can see all the categories and subcategories created in the open catalog.

5. Click OK.

The subcategory is added below the category or subcategory on the Tags palette.

Assigning and managing tags

After creating categories and subcategories on the Tags palette, you should assign tags to files. After the tags are assigned, you can further manage the tags.

To assign tags to a file, do any of the following:

- **Drag and drop files to a tag.** You can drag one or more files shown in the Organizer window and drop the files on top of a tag on the Tags palette. The files are then tagged.

- **Drag and drop a tag to a file.** You can tag files by dragging and dropping a tag from the Tags palette to a file in the Organizer window or to a group of selected files.

- **Tag categories.** Drag a file to a category name or drag the category name on the Tags palette to the selected files. The tag appears at the root of a category and doesn't appear in any subcategories.

- **Tag subcategories.** Drag a file to a subcategory name or drag the subcategory name on the Tags palette to the selected files. The tag appears in the subcategory and doesn't appear in the root category.

- **Use a menu command.** Select a file or files in the Organizer and then right-click a category or subcategory name. From the context menu that appears, choose Attach <category name> to <number> Selected Item(s).

When you use a context menu that you open by right-clicking (Windows) or Ctrl+clicking (Macintosh) a category or subcategory, you see menu options for managing files. The menu commands include the name of the category from which you open the context menu. The commands on the context menu are

- **Change <category name> to a Sub-Category:** Choose this command to change a category to a subcategory.

- **Edit <category name> Category:** Choose this command when you want to edit a category name, an icon's appearance, or a parent or subcategory.

- **Share <category name> tag through:** Choose this menu option to share photos.

- **Delete <category name> Category:** Select a category or subcategory and choose this menu command to delete it. Alternatively, you can click the Trash icon on the Tags palette.

    ✓ **New Search Using <category name> Category:** Choosing this menu item results in the same view as when you're clicking the square on the Tags palette adjacent to a tag name. Only files with the selected tag are viewed in the Organizer.

    ✓ **Add Photos with <category name> Category to Search Results:** You can search for photos in the Organizer by using the search options discussed in Chapter 5. Use this menu item to add tagged files to the search results.

    ✓ **Exclude Photos with <category name> Category from Search Results:** Use this command to exclude tagged items from search results.

    ✓ **Attach <category name> tag to X Selected Items:** Where X represents the number of selected items in the Organizer window, choose this command to attach the selected tag to the selected photo thumbnails.

Note that if you open a context menu on a category name versus opening a context menu on a subcategory name, the menu items change. If you don't see an option that's listed here when you open a context menu on a category, open a context menu on a subcategory and you'll find the command.

Hiding Files That Get in the Way

Elements offers a few ways to hide files so that you can keep your images organized and easy to find.

The hidden tag is on the Tags palette. This tag hides files in the Organizer window. You might use the hidden tag to hide similar images or one image with different variations while keeping only one image in view in the Organizer window. (You can tag files with the hidden tag by using any of the methods for tagging files that we discuss in the preceding section.) Files remain hidden when you click the check box adjacent to the Hidden tag.

Other ways to hide images are to create stacks and versions. Again, when working with an image with several different variations or versions, you can create a stack in which the best image is displayed in the Organizer window and all members of the stack group are hidden behind that foreground image. Additionally, you can create a *version set,* in which different versions of the same image are hidden while one version remains in view in the Organizer. In the following sections, we explain in more detail how you create stacks and versions.

Stack 'em up

Think of stacks like a stack of cards that are face-up. You see only the front card, and all the other cards are hidden behind that card. Stacks work the same way: You hide different images behind a foreground image. At any time, you can sort the images or display all images in the stack in the Organizer window.

To create a stack, follow these steps:

1. **In the Organizer, select several photos.**

   You can select any number of photos. You cannot stack audio or movie files.

2. **Choose Edit⇨Stack⇨Stack Selected Photos.**

   Elements stacks your photos. The first image you select remains in view in the Organizer window. In the upper-right area, an icon that looks like a stack of cards appears on the image thumbnail, as shown in Figure 6-8. The thumbnail itself appears as though it sits atop a stack of other thumbnails.

Figure 6-8: An image thumbnail.

After you stack a group of images, you can use the Stack submenu commands to manage the photos. Click a stack to select it and then choose Edit⇨Stack. The submenu commands that are available include

- **Automatically Suggest Photo Stacks:** Select this command, and Elements searches the photos in the Organizer window for visually similar appearances. Those photos having visually similar appearances are opened in a separate window where you select photos you want to stack. Make a selection of two or more photos and select Stack Selected Photos.

- **Stack Selected Photos:** This command remains grayed out unless you have several photos selected to create a stack.

- **Unstack Photos:** Click a stack in the Organizer and choose this command to return all images to the Organizer window and eliminate the stack.

- **Expand Photos in Stack:** This command expands the stack to show all thumbnail images in the Organizer window.

- **Collapse Photos in Stack:** This command collapses a stack to show only the top photo in the Organizer window.

- **Flatten Stack:** After you stack some photos, this command becomes available.

  Be careful with this command. When you flatten a stack, all photos except for the top photo are deleted from the catalog (not from your hard disk).

- **Remove Photo From Stack:** Choosing this command removes the selected photos from the stack. The menu item is available only after you choose Reveal Photos in Stack. In the new Organizer window that appears, you can then choose this menu command.

- **Set As Top Photo:** You also need to first choose Expand Photos in Stack before accessing this command. If you don't like the topmost photo, select another and choose this menu command to move the selected photo to the top of the stack.

If you want to view all stacks in an Organizer window in expanded form, choose View⇨Expand All Stacks. Using this command doesn't require you to individually select stacks in the Organizer before expanding them.

Creating versions

Versions are similar to stacks, but you create versions from only one file. You can edit an image and save the edited version and the original as a version set. Additional edits can be made in either editing mode and saved to a version set. To create a version set, do the following:

1. **Select an image by clicking it in the Organizer window.**

2. **Apply an edit.**

   For example, right in the Organizer, you can correct some brightness in your image. Choose Edit⇨Auto Smart Fix to adjust contrast and brightness. See Chapter 10 for more details on adjusting contrast and brightness.

3. **View the items in the version set by clicking the image in the Organizer and choosing Edit⇨Version Set⇨Expand Items in Version Set.**

   Elements automatically creates a version set for you when you apply the Auto Smart Fix to the file. A new Organizer window opens and shows two thumbnail images — one representing the original image and the other representing the edited version.

4. **To open the original in Standard Edit mode, select the original image and choose Edit⇨Go to Standard Edit from the drop-down menu on the Organizer Shortcuts bar.**

5. **Edit the image in Standard Edit mode.**

   You can choose from many different menu commands to edit the image. As an example, change the color mode to Indexed Color by choosing Image⇨Mode⇨Indexed Color, as we explain in Chapter 3.

6. **Save a version by choosing File⇨Save As.**

7. **In the Save Options area of the Save As dialog box, select the check boxes labeled Include in the Organizer and Save in Version Set with Original.**

8. **Click Save.**

   The edit made in Standard Edit mode is saved as another version in your version set.

When you have a version set, you can open the Edit⇨Version Set submenu and choose menu commands that are similar to commands available with stacks. (See the preceding section for details.)

Sticking Digital Notes on Your Photos

A way to identify your files beyond the tagging capabilities discussed earlier in this chapter is to add captions and notes. When you add a caption or note, you can search captions or notes by choosing the Find⇨By Caption or Note menu command. Captions and notes are also helpful when you create different collections — like slide presentations and photo albums — by using the Create command, as we explain in Chapter 16.

Text captions are easy to create. Although you can select a thumbnail image in the Organizer window and choose Edit⇨Add Caption, a better way is to use the Properties palette. Just follow these steps:

1. **To open the palette, select a thumbnail image in the Organizer, right-click it, and choose Show Properties from the context menu that appears.**

   Alternatively, you can choose Window⇨ Properties. In either case, the Properties palette opens, as shown in Figure 6-9.

2. **Type a caption by adding text to the Caption text box.**

3. **Type text in the Notes area on the palette to add a note.**

   That's all there is to it. You can also record audio notes about an image.

Figure 6-9: The Properties palette, docked in the Organize Bin.

Automating Your Organization

If you have a number of common edits you want to make on a collection of photos, Elements lets you perform common changes to multiple files.

With a single menu command, you can change file formats, change file attributes, and add common file base names. File renaming can be part of the Export command, or you can use a menu option for renaming files in the Organizer.

Automating common tasks when you export

You might use the Export Selected Items dialog box frequently when you're acquiring images from digital cameras. What you may not know is that this dialog box can automate other common tasks, too:

✔ Add common base names for the filenames (for example, change names like `DSC000001`, `DSC000002`, and so on to more descriptive filenames, like `Budapest 001` and `Budapest 002`).

✔ Change the file format.

✔ Change file size and quality.

Here's how you go about using options in the Export dialog box:

1. **Select files and open the Export New Items dialog box by choosing File⇨Export⇨To Computer.**

   The Export New Files dialog box opens, as shown in Figure 6-10.

Figure 6-10: The Export New Files dialog box permits you to rename and change formats for batches of files.

You don't have to select files beforehand. You can identify files in another dialog box that's accessible from within the Export New Files dialog box. If you know ahead of time which files you want to export, go ahead and select them in the Organizer window.

2. **Select a file type.**

   From the File Type options, select the format you want to use for the exported images. For more information on file formats, see Chapter 3.

3. Select a size and quality.

If you select Use Original Format, resizing options are grayed out. You use this setting when you want to retain the original sizes when you rename files. If you select JPEG, you can move the quality slider, as we explain in Chapter 3, for setting the image quality of JPEG images. None of the other format options provides a quality option.

For sizing images, select commands from the Photo Size drop-down list, where you find several fixed dimensions and an option for using a custom size.

4. Select a target location for the new files by clicking the Browse button and selecting a folder.

If you want to create a new folder, you can click the Make New Folder button in the Browse for Folder dialog box, which opens after you click the Browse button.

5. If you want to keep the original filenames, click the Original Names radio button. If you want to rename files with a common base name, select Common Base Name and type a name in the text box.

The resultant files are named `<base name>001.extension`, `<base name>002.extension`, `<base name>003.extension`, and so on.

6. If you want to add files to the list for exporting, click the plus (+) symbol in the lower-left corner.

This step opens the Add Photos dialog box, shown in Figure 6-11, which offers a number of different options for selecting files to export.

Among your choices in this dialog box are

- *Photos Currently in Browser:* Click this button when you want to export all files shown in the Organizer window.

- *Entire Catalog:* Click this button if you're viewing a catalog, tagged files, or a sorted group in which some files are temporarily hidden. When you select this option, all hidden files are included in the export.

- *Collection:* Click the Collection radio button and select from the drop-down list a collection you want to export.

- *Tag:* Click the Tag radio button and select a tag from the drop-down list. All files with the same tag are exported.

- *Photo Bin:* Click this radio button to select files in the Photo Bin. (See Chapter 4 for more information on using the Photo Bin.)

- *Show Favorites Only:* Favorites are those files you tag with stars. Select Favorites and all files tagged with one or more stars are exported.

- *Show Hidden Photos:* Any file that might be hidden in the Organizer can be made visible in the file list and included in the export.

- *Select All:* As you add files to the list window, you can choose to export all files from the selected category. Click the Select All button and all the files are marked for export.

- *Deselect All:* If you want some files from the list window exported while others remain behind, click the Deselect All button and then individually click the check boxes for all files you want to export.

- *Add Selected Photos:* When you add photos by using the options found in the Add Photos From area in the dialog box, the thumbnails for the images appear in a scrollable window inside the dialog box. You can choose individual photos by checking the boxes adjacent to each photo to be included in the export. After checking the photos you want to include, click this button. The button action doesn't dismiss the dialog box; it merely marks the files for inclusion.

- *Done:* Click this button to return to the Export Selected Items dialog box.

7. **Select any images you don't want included in the export by selecting the check boxes adjacent to the thumbnails and then clicking the minus (–) button.**

8. **Click Export.**

   Elements automatically exports the images to the selected folder.

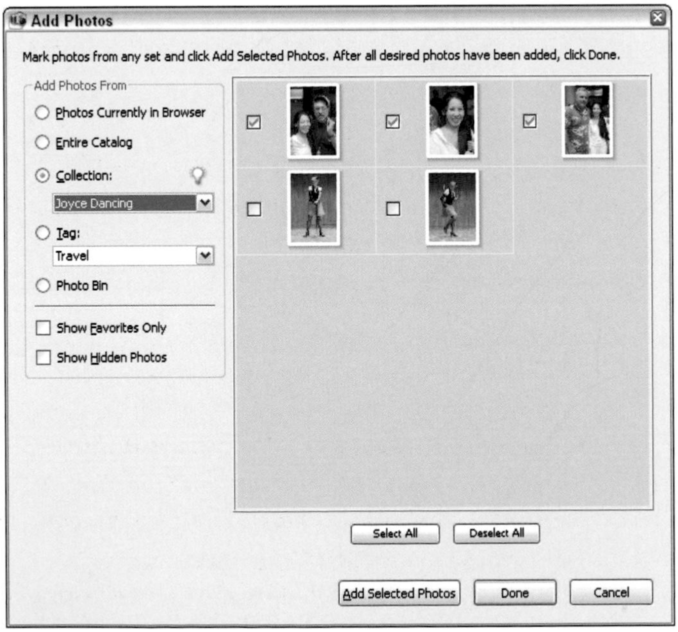

Figure 6-11: The Add Photos dialog box offers a number of options for exporting photos.

Renaming files

If you load up an Organizer window and you want to rename files, you don't need to use the Export command and wade through the options in the Export Selected Files dialog box. Just select the files you want to rename and then choose File⇨Rename. The Rename dialog box opens. In the text box, type a base name for the files and click OK. The selected files are renamed using a common base name. You'll find this a quick and easy way to rename those digital camera images.

Protecting Your Photos

The lesson most often learned the hard way by computer users is backing up a hard drive and the precious data you spent time creating and editing. We can save you some aggravation right now, before you spend any more time editing your photos in Elements.

We authors are so paranoid when we're writing a book that we back up our chapters on multiple drives, CDs, and DVDs as chapters are written. The standard rule is that if you spend sufficient time working on a project and it gets to the point at which redoing your work would be a major aggravation, it's time to back up files.

With files stored all over your hard drive, manually copying files to a second hard drive, CD-ROM, or DVD would take quite a bit of time. Fortunately, Elements makes the pain of finding files to back up a breeze.

Here's how you can use Elements to create a backup of your precious data:

1. **Choose File⇨Backup to open the Burn/Backup Wizard.**

   This wizard has three panes that Elements walks you through to painlessly create a backup of your files.

2. **Select the source to back up.**

   The first pane in the Burn/Backup Wizard offers two options:

   - *Full Backup:* Click this radio button to perform your first backup or when you're writing files to a new media source.

   - *Incremental Backup:* Use this option if you have already performed at least one backup and you want to update the backed-up files.

3. **Click Next and select a target location for your backed-up files.**

   Active drives, including CD/DVD drives attached to your computer, appear in the Select Destination Drive list, as shown in Figure 6-12. Select a drive, and Elements automatically assesses the write speed and identifies a previous backup file if one was created. The total size of the files to copy is reported in the wizard. This information is helpful so that you know whether more than one CD or DVD is needed to complete the backup.

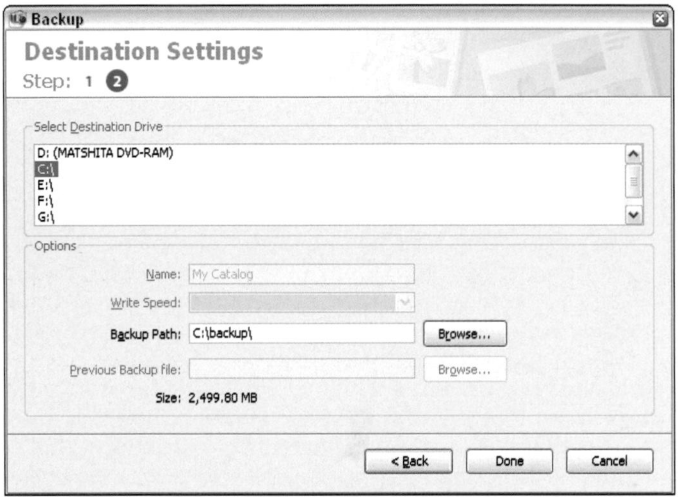

Figure 6-12: Step 2 in the wizard provides options for selecting the destination media for the backup.

4. **If you intend to copy files to your hard drive or to another hard drive attached to your computer, click the Browse button and identify the path.**

   If you use a media source, such as a CD or DVD, Elements prompts you to insert a disc and readies the media for writing.

5. **Click Done, and the backup commences.**

   Be certain to not interrupt the backup. It might take some time, so just let Elements work away until you're notified that the backup is complete.

Part III
Selecting and Correcting Photos

The 5th Wave   By Rich Tennant

@RKHTENNANT

"Hey— let's put scanned photos of ourselves through a ripple filter and see if we can make ourselves look weird."

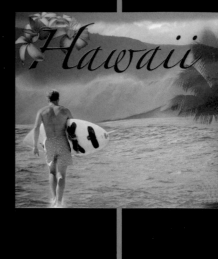

In this part . . .

The wide array of editing features in Elements permit you to change, optimize, perfect, and combine images into composite designs. In this part, you learn how to select image content and then alter that content for a variety of purposes, such as correcting color, changing the appearance, and extracting the content so that you can introduce it in other photos. Because photos are composed of many thousands of tiny pixels, you need to develop some skill in selecting just the pixels you want to use for any given editing task.

In addition to describing how to create image selections, this part covers photo correction for image contrast and brightness; color correction; and color conversions from one color mode to another. Rarely will you encounter digital images that don't require some kind of correction. In the chapters ahead, you find out how to quickly master some powerful correction techniques.

Making and Modifying Selections

In This Chapter

▶ Creating selections with the Lasso tools, Magic Wand, and more

▶ Using the Cookie Cutter tool

▶ Eliminating with the Eraser tools

▶ Using the Magic Extractor command

▶ Saving and loading selections

*I*f all you want to do is use your photos in all their unedited glory, feel free to skip this chapter and move on to other topics. But if you want to occasionally pluck an element out of its environment and stick it in another or apply an adjustment on just a portion of your image, this chapter is for you.

Finding out how to make accurate selections is one of those skills that is well worth the time you invest. In this chapter, we cover all the various selection tools and techniques. We give you tips on which tools are better for which kinds of selections. But remember that you usually have several ways to achieve the same result. Which road you choose is ultimately up to you.

Defining Selections

Before you dig in and get serious about selecting, let us clarify for the record what we mean by defining a selection. When you *define* a selection, you specify which part of an image you want to work with. Everything within a selection is considered selected. Everything outside the selection is unselected. After you have a selection, you can then adjust just that portion, and the unselected portion remains unchanged. Or, you can copy the selected area into another image altogether. Want to transport yourself out of your background and onto a white sandy beach instead? Select yourself out of that backyard BBQ photo, get a stock photo of the tropical paradise of your choice, and drag and drop yourself onto your tropics photo with the Move tool. It's that easy.

When you make a selection, a dotted outline — variously called a *selection border,* an *outline,* or a *marquee* — appears around the selected area. Elements, sophisticated imaging program that it is, also allows you to partially select pixels, which allows for soft-edged selections. You create soft-edged selections by feathering or anti-aliasing the selection or by using a mask. Don't worry: We cover these techniques later in this chapter.

For all the selection techniques described in this chapter, be sure that your image is in the Editor, in Full Edit mode (Standard Edit mode on the Mac), and not in Quick Fix mode or in the Organizer.

Creating Rectangular and Elliptical Selections

If you can drag a mouse, you can master the Rectangular and Elliptical Marquee tools. These two tools are the easiest selection tools to use, so if your desired element is rectangular or elliptical, by all means grab one of these tools.

The Rectangular Marquee tool, as its moniker states, is designed to select rectangular or square selections. This tool is great to use if you want to home in on the pertinent portion of your photo and eliminate unnecessary background.

Here's how to make a selection with this tool:

1. **Select the Rectangular Marquee tool from the Tools palette.**

   It looks like a dotted square. You can also press M to access the tool.

2. **Drag from one corner of the area you want to select to the opposite corner.**

   As you drag, the selection border appears. The marquee follows the movement of your mouse cursor.

3. **Release your mouse button.**

   You now have a completed rectangular selection, as shown in Figure 7-1.

Figure 7-1: Use the Rectangular Marquee tool to create rectangular selections.

The Elliptical Marquee tool, which shares the same flyout menu as the Rectangular Marquee tool, is designed for elliptical or circular selections. This tool is perfect for selecting balloons, clocks, and other rotund elements.

Here's how to use the Elliptical Marquee:

1. **Select the Elliptical Marquee tool from the Marquee flyout menu on the Tools palette.**

   Again, you can also use the keyboard shortcut. If the Rectangular Marquee is still visible, you need to press Shift+M. If the Elliptical Marquee tool is showing, press M.

2. **Position the crosshair near the area you want to select and then drag around your desired element.**

   With this tool, you don't drag from corner to corner. Instead, you drag from a given point on the ellipse. As you drag, the selection border appears.

3. **When you're satisfied with your selection, release the mouse button.**

   Your elliptical selection is done, as shown in Figure 7-2. If your selection isn't quite centered around your element, simply move the selection border by dragging inside the border.

Flat Earth

Figure 7-2: The Elliptical Marquee is perfect for selecting round objects.

TIP

You can move a selection while you're making it with either of the Marquee tools by pressing the spacebar while you're dragging.

Perfecting squares and circles with Shift and Alt (Option)

Sometimes you need to create a perfectly square or circular selection. To do so, simply press the Shift key after you begin dragging. After you make your selection, release the mouse button first and then release the Shift key.

When you're making an elliptical selection, making the selection from the center outward is often easier. To draw from the center, first click the mouse button and then, before you move the mouse, press Alt (Option on the Mac) and drag. When you make your selection, release the mouse button first and then release the Alt key (Option key on the Mac).

If you want to draw from the center outward *and* create a perfect circle or square, press the Shift key as well. After you make your selection, release the mouse button and then release the Shift+Alt keys (Option key on the Mac).

Applying marquee options

The Marquee tools offer additional options when you need to make precise selections at specific measurements. You also find options for making your selections soft around the edges.

The only thing to remember is that you must select the options on the Options bar, shown in Figure 7-3, before you make your selection with the Marquee tools. They cannot be applied after the selection has already been made. The exception is that you can feather a selection after the fact by choosing Select⇨Feather.

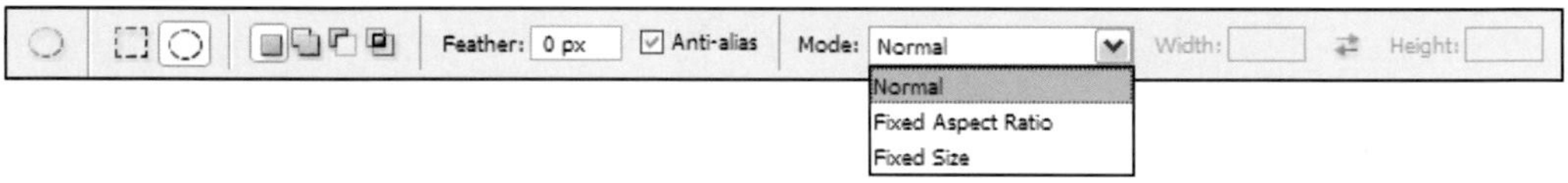

Figure 7-3: Apply marquee settings in the Options bar.

Here are the various marquee options available to you:

- **Feather:** Feathering creates soft edges around your selection. The amount of softness depends on the value, from 0 to 250 pixels, you enter. The higher the value, the softer the edges, as shown in Figure 7-4. Very small amounts of feathering can be used to create subtle transitions between selected elements in a collage. Larger amounts are often used when you're combining multiple layers so that one image gradually fades into another. If you just want a selected element to have a soft edge without the background, simply choose Select⇨Inverse and delete the background. See more on inversing selections in the "Modifying Your Selections" section, later in this chapter. For more on layers, see Chapter 8.

    Don't forget that those soft edges represent partially selected pixels.

- **Anti-alias:** Anti-aliasing barely softens the edge of an elliptical or irregularly shaped selection so that the jagged edges aren't quite so obvious. An anti-aliased edge is always only 1 pixel wide. We recommend leaving this option checked for your selections. It can help to create natural transitions between multiple selections when you're creating collages.

- **Mode:** The Mode drop-down list contains three settings:

    - *Normal* is the default setting, which allows you to freely drag a selection of any size.

- *Fixed Aspect Ratio* lets you specify a fixed ratio of width to height. For example, if you enter 3 for width and 1 for height, you get a selection that's three times as wide as it is high, no matter what the size.

- *Fixed Size* lets you specify desired values for the width and height. This setting can be useful when you need to make several selections that must be the same size.

✔ **Width and Height:** When you select Fixed Aspect Ratio or Fixed Size from the Mode drop-down list, you must also enter your desired values in the Width and Height text boxes. To swap the Width and Height values, click the double-headed arrow button between the two measurements.

The default unit of measurement in the Width and Height text boxes is pixels (px), but that doesn't mean that you're stuck with it. You can enter any unit of measurement that Elements recognizes — pixels, inches, centimeters, millimeters, points, picas, or percents. Type your value and then type the word or abbreviation of your unit of measurement.

Feather 6 pixels   Feather 50 pixels

Corbis Digital Stock

Figure 7-4: Feathering creates soft-edged selections.

Making Freeform Selections with the Lasso Tools

As we all know, you can't select everything with a rectangle or an ellipse. Life is just way too freeform for that. Most animate, and many inanimate, objects have undulations of varying sorts. Luckily, Elements anticipated the need to capture these and provided the Lasso tools.

The Lasso tools enable you to make any freehand selection you can think of. Elements generously provides three types of lasso tools:

- Lasso
- Polygonal
- Magnetic

Although all three tools are designed to make freeform selections, they differ slightly in their methodology, as we explain in the sections that follow.

To use these tools, all that's really required is a steady hand. You'll find that the more you use the Lasso tools, the better you become at your tracing technique. Don't worry if your initial lasso selection isn't super accurate. You can always go back and make corrections by adding and deleting from your selection. To find out how, see "Modifying Your Selections," later in this chapter.

If you find that you really love the Lasso tools, you may want to invest in a digital drawing tablet and stylus. This device makes tracing, and also drawing and painting, on the computer more comfortable. It better mimics pen and paper, and many users swear that they will never go back to a mouse after trying it out.

Selecting with the Lasso tool

Using the Lasso tool is the digital version of tracing an outline around an object on a piece of paper. It's that easy. And you have only two choices on the Options bar — Feather and Anti-alias. To find out more about these options, see "Applying marquee options," earlier in this chapter.

Here's how to make a selection with the Lasso tool:

1. **Select the Lasso tool from the Tools palette.**

   It's the sixth tool from the top and looks like a rope. You can also just press the L key.

2. **Position the cursor anywhere along the edge of the object you want to select.**

The leading point of the cursor is the protruding end of the rope, as shown in Figure 7-5. Don't be afraid to zoom into your object if you need to see the edge more distinctly. In this figure, we started at the upper-left corner of the butterfly's wing.

3. **Hold down the mouse button and trace around your desired object. Try to include only what you want to select.**

   As you trace around your object, an outline follows the mouse cursor.

   Try not to release the mouse button until you return to your starting point. When you release the mouse button, Elements assumes that you're done and closes the selection from wherever you released the mouse button to your starting point, creating a diagonal line across your image.

4. **Continue tracing around the object and return to your starting point; release the mouse button to close the selection.**

   You see a selection border that matches your lasso line.

Lasso cursor

Corbis Digital Stock
Figure 7-5: The Lasso tool makes freeform selections.

Getting straight with the Polygonal Lasso tool

The Polygonal Lasso tool has a specific mission in life: to select any element whose sides are straight. Think pyramids, stairways, skyscrapers, barns — you get the idea. It also works a tad differently from the Lasso tool. You don't drag around the element with the Polygonal Lasso. Instead, you click and release the mouse button at the corners of the element you're selecting. The Polygonal Lasso tool acts like a stretchy rubber band.

Follow these steps to select with the Polygonal Lasso tool:

1. **Select the Polygonal Lasso tool from the Tools palette.**

   You can also press the L key and then press Shift+L until you get the Polygonal Lasso tool.

2. **Click and release at any point to start the Polygonal Lasso selection line.**

   We usually start at a corner.

3. **Move (don't drag) the mouse and click at the next corner of the object. Continue clicking and moving to each corner of your element.**

   Notice how the line stretches out from each point you click.

4. **Return to your starting point and click to close the selection.**

   Be on the lookout for a small circle that appears next to your lasso cursor when you return to your starting point. This circle is an indication that you're indeed closing the selection at the right spot.

   Note that you can also double-click at any point and Elements closes the selection from that point to the starting point.

   After you close the polygonal lasso line, a selection border should appear, as shown in Figure 7-6.

Corbis Digital Stock

Figure 7-6: After closing the lasso line, Elements creates a selection border.

Snapping with the Magnetic Lasso tool

The third member of the Lasso team is the Magnetic Lasso. We aren't huge fans of this Lasso tool, which sometimes can be hard to work with. But we show you how it works so that you can decide for yourself whether to use it. The Magnetic Lasso tool works by defining the areas of the most contrast in an image and then snapping to the edge between those areas, as though the edge has a magnetic pull.

You have the most success using the Magnetic Lasso tool on an image that has a well-defined foreground object and high contrast between that element and the background — for example, a dark mountain range against a light sky.

The Magnetic Lasso tool also has some unique settings, which you can adjust on the Options bar before you start selecting:

- **Width:** Determines how close to the edge (between 1 and 256 pixels) you have to move your mouse before the Magnetic Lasso tool snaps to that edge. Use a lower value if the edge has lots of detail or if the contrast in the image is low. Use a higher value for high-contrast images or smoother edges.

- **Edge Contrast:** Specifies the percentage of contrast (from 1 percent to 100 percent) that is required before the Magnetic Lasso snaps to an edge. Use a higher percentage if your image has good contrast between your desired element and the background.

- **Frequency:** Specifies how many points (from 1 to 100) to place on the selection line. The higher the value, the greater number of points. As a general rule, if the element you want to select has a smooth edge, keep the value low. If the edge has a lot of detail, try a higher value.

- **Tablet Pressure (pen icon):** If you're the proud owner of a pressure-sensitive drawing tablet, select this option to make an increase in stylus pressure cause the edge width to decrease.

Follow these steps to use the Magnetic Lasso tool:

1. **Select the Magnetic Lasso tool from the Tools palette.**

   You can also press the L key and then press Shift+L until you select the Magnetic Lasso tool. The tool looks like a straight-sided lasso with a little magnet on it.

2. **Click the edge of the object you want to select to place the first fastening point.**

   Fastening points anchor the selection line, as shown in Figure 7-7. You can start anywhere; just be sure to click the edge between the element you want and the background you don't want.

Corbis Digital Stock

Figure 7-7: The Magnetic Lasso tool snaps to the edge of your element and places fastening points to anchor the selection.

3. Continue to move your cursor around the object, without clicking.

As the selection line gets pinned down with fastening points, only the newest portion of the selection line remains active.

If the Magnetic Lasso tool starts veering off the desired edge of your object, back up your mouse and click to force down a fastening point. Conversely, if the Magnetic Lasso tool adds a fastening point where you don't want one, press your Backspace key to delete it.

If the Magnetic Lasso isn't cooperating, you can temporarily switch to the other Lasso tools. To select the Lasso tool, press Alt (Option on the Mac), and then press the mouse button and drag. To select the Polygonal Lasso tool, press Alt (Option on the Mac) and click.

4. Return to your starting point and click the mouse button to close the selection.

You see a small circle next to your cursor indicating that you're at the right spot to close the selection. You can also double-click, whereby Elements closes the selection from where you double-clicked to your starting point. The selection border appears when the selection is closed.

Working Wizardry with the Magic Wand

The Magic Wand tool is one of the oldest tools in the world of digital imaging. This beloved tool has been around since both Photoshop and Elements were in their infancies. It's extremely easy to use, but a little harder to predict what selection results it will present.

Here's how it works: You click inside the image, and the Magic Wand tool makes a selection. This selection is based on the color of the pixel you clicked. If other pixels are similar in color to your target pixel, Elements includes them in the selection. What's sometimes hard to predict, however, is how to determine how *similar* the color has to be to get the Magic Wand tool to select it. Fortunately, that's where the *Tolerance* setting comes in. In the sections that follow, we first introduce you to this setting and then explain how to put the Magic Wand to work.

Talking about tolerance

The Tolerance setting determines the range of color that the Magic Wand tool selects. It's based on brightness levels that range from 0 to 255. That being said:

- Setting the Tolerance to 0 selects one color only.
- Setting the Tolerance to 255 selects all colors, or the whole image.

The default setting is 32, so whenever you click a pixel, Elements analyzes the value of that base color and then selects all pixels whose brightness levels are between 16 levels lighter and 16 levels darker.

What if an image contains a few shades of the same color? It's not a huge problem. You can make multiple clicks of the Magic Wand to pick up additional pixels that you want to include in the selection. You can find out how in the section "Modifying Your Selections," later in this chapter. Or, you can try a higher Tolerance setting. Conversely, if your wand selects too much, you can also lower your Tolerance setting.

So you can see by our talk on tolerance that the Magic Wand tool works best when you have high-contrast images or images with a limited number of colors. For example, the optimum image for the Wand would be a solid black object on a white background. Skip the wand if the image has a ton of colors and no real definitive contrast between your desired element and the background.

Wielding the wand to select

To use the Magic Wand tool to adjust Tolerance settings, follow these steps:

1. **Select the Magic Wand tool from the Tools palette.**

   You can't miss it. It looks like a wand, or maybe a fuzzy lollipop. You can also just press W.

2. **Click anywhere on your desired element, using the default Tolerance setting of 32.**

   Remember that the pixel you click determines the base color.

   If the pixel gods are with you and you selected everything you want on the first click, you're done. If your selection needs further tweaking, like the top image shown in Figure 7-8, continue to Step 3.

3. **Specify a new Tolerance setting on the Options bar.**

   If the Magic Wand selects more than you want, lower the Tolerance setting. If the wand didn't select enough, increase the value. While you're poking around the Options bar, here are a couple more options to get familiar with:

Tolerance 32

Tolerance 80

Corbis Digital Stock

Figure 7-8: The Magic Wand selects pixels based on a specified Tolerance setting.

- *Contiguous:* Forces the Magic Wand to select only pixels that are adjacent to each other. Without this option, the tool selects all pixels within the range of tolerance, whether or not they're adjacent to each other.

- *Sample All Layers:* If you have multiple layers and enable this option, the Magic Wand selects pixels from all visible layers. Without this option, the tool selects pixels from the active layer only. For more on layers, see Chapter 8.

4. **Click your desired element again.**

   Unfortunately, the Magic Wand tool isn't magical enough to modify your first selection automatically. Instead, it deselects the current selection and makes a new selection based on your new Tolerance setting. If it still isn't right, you can adjust the Tolerance setting again. Try, try again.

Modifying Your Selections

It's time for a seventh-inning stretch in this chapter on selection tools. In this section, you find out how to refine that Marquee, Lasso, or Magic Wand selection to perfection. Although these tools do an okay job of capturing the bulk of your selection, if you take the time to add or subtract a bit from your selection border, you can ensure that you get only what you really want.

You're not limited to the manual methods described in this section, or even to keyboard shortcuts. You can also use the four selection option buttons on the right side of the Options bar to create a new selection (the default), add to a selection, subtract from a selection, or intersect one selection with another. Just choose your desired selection tool, click the selection option button you want, and drag (or click if you're using the Magic Wand or Polygonal Lasso tool). The Add to Selection and Subtract from Selection buttons are also available when you're using the Selection Brush. When you're adding to a selection, a small plus sign appears next to your cursor. When you're subtracting from a selection, a small minus sign (–) appears. When you're intersecting two selections, a small multiplication sign appears.

Adding to a selection

If your selection doesn't quite contain all the elements you want to capture, you need to add those portions to your current selection border. To add to a current selection, simply press the Shift key and drag around the area you want to include. If you're using the Polygonal Lasso, click around the area. And, if you're wielding the Magic Wand, just press the Shift key and click the area you want.

You don't have to use the same tool to add to your selection as you used to create the original selection. Feel free to use whatever selection tool you think can get the job done. For example, it's very common to start off with the Magic Wand and fine-tune with the Lasso tool.

Subtracting from a selection

Got too much? To subtract from a current selection, press the Alt key (Option key on the Mac) and drag around the pixels you want to subtract. With the Alt key (Option key on the Mac), use the same method for the Magic Wand and Polygonal Lasso as you do for adding to a selection.

Intersecting two selections

Get your fingers in shape. To intersect your existing selection with a second selection, press the Shift and Alt keys together (or press the Option key on the Mac) and drag with the Lasso tool. Or, if you're using the Magic Wand or Polygonal Lasso, press and click rather than drag.

Avoiding key collisions

If you read the beginning of this chapter, you found out that by pressing the Shift key, you get a perfectly square or circular selection. We just told you that if you want to add to a selection, you press the Shift key. What if you want to create a perfect square while adding to the selection? Or, what if you want to delete part of a selection while also drawing from the center outward? Both require the use of the Alt key (or the Option key on the Mac). How in the heck does Elements know what you want? Here are a few tips to avoid keyboard collisions — grab your desired Marquee tool:

- **To add a square or circular selection, press Shift and drag.** As you drag, keep the mouse button pressed, release the Shift key for just a second, and then press it again. Your added selection area suddenly snaps into a square or circle. You must then release the mouse button first and then release the Shift key last.

- **To delete from an existing selection while drawing from the center outward, press Alt (Option on the Mac) and drag.** As you drag, keep the mouse button pressed, release the Alt key (the Option key on the Mac) for just a second, and then press it down again. You're now drawing from the center outward. Again, release the mouse button first, and then release the Alt key (the Option key on the Mac) last.

Painting with the Selection Brush

If you like the more organic feel of painting on a canvas, you'll appreciate the Selection Brush. Using two different modes, you can either paint over areas of an image that you want to select or paint over areas you don't want to select. This great tool also lets you make a basic, rudimentary selection with another tool, such as the Lasso, and then fine-tune the selection by brushing additional pixels into or out of the selection.

Here's the step-by-step process of selecting with the Selection Brush:

1. **Select the Selection Brush from the Tools palette, or simply press the A key.**

   This tool works in either Full Edit (Standard Edit on the Mac) or Quick Fix mode.

2. **Specify your Selection Brush options on the Options bar.**

   Here's the rundown on each option:

   - *Brush Presets:* Choose a brush from the presets drop-down palette. To load additional brushes, click the downward-pointing arrow to the left of Default Brushes and choose the preset library of your choice. You can select the Load Brushes command from the palette pop-up menu.

   - *Brush Size:* Specify a brush size, from 1 to 2500 pixels. Enter the value or drag the slider.

   - *Mode:* Choose between Selection and *Mask.* Choose Selection to add to your selection, and choose Mask to subtract from your selection. If you choose Mask mode, you must choose some additional overlay options. An *overlay* is a layer of color (that shows on-screen only) that hovers over your image, indicating protected or unselected areas. You must also choose an overlay opacity between 1 and 100 percent (described in a Tip paragraph at the end of this section). You can also choose to change the overlay color from the default red to another color. This option can be helpful if your image contains a lot of red.

   - *Hardness:* Set the hardness of the brush tip, from 1 to 100 percent.

3. **If your mode is set to Selection, paint over the areas you want to select.**

   You see a selection border. Each stroke adds to the selection. If you inadvertently add something you don't want, simply press the Alt key (Option key on the Mac) and paint over the undesired area. After you finish painting what you want, your selection is ready to go.

4. **If your mode is set to Mask, paint over the areas that you *do not* want to select.**

   This mode does the opposite of Selection mode. When you're done painting your mask, choose Selection from the Mode drop-down list, or simply choose another tool from the Tools palette, in order to convert your mask into a selection border.

As you paint, you see the color of your overlay. Each stroke adds more to the overlay area, as shown in Figure 7-9. When working in Mask mode, you're essentially covering up, or *masking,* the areas you want to protect from manipulation. That manipulation can be selecting, adjusting color, or performing any other Elements command. Again, if you want to remove parts of the masked area, press Alt (Option on the Mac) and paint.

If you painted your selection in Mask mode, your selection border is around what you *don't* want. To switch to what you do want, choose Select⇨Inverse.

Which mode should you choose? Well, it's up to you. But one advantage to working in Mask mode is that you can partially select areas. By painting with soft brushes, you create soft-edged selections. These soft edges result in partially selected pixels. If you set the overlay opacity to a lower percentage, your pixels are even less opaque, or "less selected." If this "partially selected" business sounds vaguely familiar, it's because this is also what happens when you feather selections, as we discuss earlier in this chapter.

Corbis Digital Stock
Figure 7-9: The Selection Brush allows you to make a selection (right) by creating a mask (left).

Painting with the Magic Selection Brush

The word *Magic* in front of any noun usually makes us think that we're in for an especially beneficial payoff. So, when you see the *Magic* Selection Brush, you're probably thinking, "Whoa, Nelly, it's new, it's magic — this has gotta be good." Theoretically speaking, this tool makes a selection when you simply draw, scribble, add a brush dot, or otherwise casually mar the area you want to select. What's more, theoretically speaking, you don't even have to precisely trace the object. Elements selects the object you want based on your brush stroke!

Okay, we'll cut the sarcasm and get to the point. Although this tool has some potential, it really works best when you provide it with as much data as possible. Rather than just add a dot or scribble on your desired element, for example, if you take a few seconds longer to paint at least a rudimentary outline around the element, you end up with a more accurate selection. By making a decent outline, you provide data for the tool's algorithm to figure out what it is you want to select. Similarly, if you further refine that initial selection by deleting and adding areas, you provide even more data, and the tool rewards you with an even more accurate selection. Unlike the Magic Wand, which allows you to add to and delete from an existing selection incrementally, the Magic Selection Brush redraws your selection from scratch each time you modify it. It also differs from the Magic Wand in that it not only analyzes color to make the selection, but also relies even more on texture.

By the way, this tool works in either Full Edit (Standard Edit on the Mac) or Quick Fix mode.

Now that you understand the mechanical reasoning behind the Magic Selection Brush, here's how to select with this new tool:

1. **Select the Magic Selection Brush tool from the Tools palette.**

   You can also press the F key.

2. **Specify the options on the Options bar. Here's a description of the options:**

   - *New Selection:* The default option enables you to create a new selection.

   - *Indicate Foreground (+ icon):* This option allows you to add to an existing selection.

   - *Indicate Background (– icon):* This option enables you to subtract from an existing selection.

   - *Overlay Color:* As with the Selection brush, you can change the color of your overlay from the default red to the color of your choice.

   - *Brush Size:* Choose a brush size, from 1 to 100 pixels, from the Size menu. If you want to try to make a more precise outline, we suggest using a smaller brush.

3. **Select an area by clicking it with your mouse, dragging a brush stroke around it, or painting over it, as shown on the left side in Figure 7-10. When you're done, release the mouse button.**

   After you release the mouse, the selection border should appear. If the Magic Selection Brush gave you what you want, you're done. If your selection needs refinement, go to Step 4. (Most likely, we'll see you at Step 4.)

Corbis Digital Stock

Figure 7-10: The Magic Selection Brush analyzes color and texture to determine your desired selection.

4. **To add to your existing selection, activate the Indicate Foreground option on the Options bar. Click, drag, or paint over the areas you want to add. To delete from your existing selection, activate the Indicate Background option on the Options bar. Click, drag, or paint over the areas you want to remove from your existing selection.**

   Note that if your object is fairly detailed, like our Lacy Seahorse, you may even need to break out the Lasso or another selection tool to make some final clean-ups. Eventually, you should arrive at a selection you're happy with, as shown on the right in Figure 7-10.

Working with the Cookie Cutter Tool

The Cookie Cutter tool is a cute name for a pretty powerful tool. You can think of it as a Custom Shape tool for images. But, although the Custom Shape tool creates a mask and just hides everything outside the shape, the Cookie Cutter crops away everything outside the shape. The preset libraries offer you a large variety of interesting shapes, from talk bubbles to Swiss cheese. (We're not being funny here — check out the food library.)

Here's the lowdown on using the Cookie Cutter:

1. **Choose the Cookie Cutter tool from the Tools palette.**

   There's no missing it; it looks like a star. You can also press the Q key.

2. **Specify your options on the Options bar. Here's the list:**

   - *Shape:* Choose a shape from the preset library. To load other libraries, click the palette pop-up menu and choose one from the submenu.

   - *Shape Options:* These options let you draw your shape with certain parameters:

     Unconstrained, the default, enables you to draw freely.

     Defined Proportions enables you to keep the height and width proportional.

     Defined Size crops the image to the original, fixed size of the shape you choose. You can't make it bigger or smaller.

     Fixed Size allows you to enter your desired width and height.

     From Center allows you to draw the shape from the center outward.

   - *Feather:* This option creates a soft-edged selection. See "Applying marquee options," earlier in this chapter, for more details.

   - *Crop:* Click this option to crop the image into the shape. Figure 7-11 shows an image cropped to the shape of an elephant.

Figure 7-11: Crop your photo into interesting shapes with the Cookie Cutter.

3. **Drag your mouse on the image to create your desired shape. Size the shape by dragging one of the handles of the bounding box. Position the shape by placing the mouse cursor inside the box and dragging.**

   You can also perform other types of transformations, such as rotating and skewing. For more on transformations, see Chapter 9.

4. **Click the Commit button on the Options bar or press Enter to finish the cropping.**

   If you want to bail out of the bounding box and not crop, you can always press the Cancel button on the Options bar or press Esc.

Eliminating with the Eraser Tools

The Eraser tools let you erase areas of your image. Elements has three eraser tools: the regular Eraser, the Magic Eraser, and the Background Eraser. The Eraser tools look like those pink erasers you used in grade school, so you can't miss them. If you can't locate them, you can always press E and then Shift+E to toggle through the three tools.

WARNING!

When you erase pixels, those pixels are history — they're gone. So, before using the Eraser tools, you should probably have a backup of your image stored somewhere. Think of it as a cheap insurance policy in case things go awry.

The Eraser tool

The Eraser tool enables you to erase areas on your image either to your background color or, if you're working on a layer, to a transparent background, as shown in Figure 7-12. For more on layers, check out Chapter 8.

To use this tool, simply select it and drag through the desired area on your image, and you're done. Because it isn't the most accurate tool on the planet, remember to zoom way in and use smaller brush tips to do some accurate erasing.

Corbis Digital Stock

Figure 7-12: Erase either to your background color (left) or to transparency (right).

You have several Eraser options to specify on the Options bar:

- ✔ **Brush Presets:** Click the drop-down palette to access the Brush presets. Choose the brush of your choice. Again, additional brush libraries are available from the Brushes pop-up menu.

- ✔ **Mode:** Select from Brush, Pencil, and Block. When you select Block, you're stuck with one size (a 16-x-16-pixel tip) and cannot select other preset brushes.

- ✔ **Opacity:** Specify a percentage of transparency for your erased areas. The lower the Opacity setting, the less it erases. Opacity isn't available in Block mode.

The Background Eraser tool

The Background Eraser tool, which is more savvy than the Eraser tool, erases the background from an image while being mindful of leaving the foreground untouched. The Background Eraser tool erases to transparency on a layer. If you drag an image with only a background, Elements converts the background into a layer.

TIP

The key to using the Background Eraser is to carefully keep the *hot spot,* the crosshair at the center of the brush, on the background pixels as you drag. The hot spot samples the color of the pixels and deletes that color whenever it falls inside the brush circumference. But, if you accidentally touch a foreground pixel with the hot spot, it's erased as well. And the tool isn't even sorry about it! This tool works better with images that have good contrast in color between the background and foreground objects, as shown in Figure 7-13. Also, if your image has very detailed or wispy edges (such as hair or fur), you're better off using the Magic Extractor command, described in the next section.

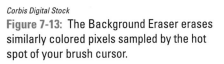

Corbis Digital Stock

Figure 7-13: The Background Eraser erases similarly colored pixels sampled by the hot spot of your brush cursor.

Here's the rundown on the Background Eraser options:

- ✔ **Brush Preset picker:** Provides settings to customize the size and appearance of your brush tip. The size and Tolerance settings at the bottom are for pressure-sensitive drawing tablets.

- ✔ **Limits:** *Discontiguous* erases all similarly colored pixels wherever they appear in the image. *Contiguous* erases all similarly colored pixels that are adjacent to those under the hot spot.

- ✔ **Tolerance:** Like the Magic Wand and the Magic Eraser, the Background Eraser uses a Tolerance setting. The value determines how similar the colors have to be to that of the color under the hot spot before Elements erases them. A higher value picks up more colors, whereas a lower value picks up fewer colors. See "Talking about tolerance," earlier in this chapter, for more details.

The Magic Eraser tool

You can think of the Magic Eraser tool as a combination Eraser and Magic Wand tool. It selects *and* erases similarly colored pixels simultaneously. Unless you're working on a layer with the transparency locked (see Chapter 8 for more on locking), the pixels are erased to transparency. If you're working on an image with just a background, Elements converts the background into a layer.

The Magic Eraser shares most of the same options with the other erasers. Here are the unique options:

- **Anti-alias:** Creates a slightly soft edge around the transparent area.

- **Sample All Layers:** Samples colors using data from all visible layers, but erases pixels on the active layer only.

Using the Magic Extractor Command

The last selection tool in the Elements repertoire is the Magic Extractor command. This command enables you to make selections based on your identification of the foreground and background portions of your image. This command is similar in methodology to the Magic Selection Brush tool. You specify your foreground and background by simply clicking these areas with the brush tool and "marking" them. Click the magic OK button, and your object or objects are neatly and painlessly extracted.

Though it isn't mandatory, you can make a rough selection first before selecting the Magic Extractor command. This technique obviously restricts what is extracted and can result in a more accurate selection.

Follow these steps to magically extract your element:

1. **Choose Image⇨Magic Extractor.**

   The huge Magic Extractor dialog box appears.

2. **Grab the Foreground Brush tool and click or drag to mark your *foreground* areas — or the areas you want to select.**

   The default color of the Foreground Brush is red.

   Again, as with the Selection brush, the more accurate the data you provide to the command's algorithm, the more accurate your extraction. Be sure to use the Zoom and Hand tools to help magnify and move around your image as needed. For more on these tools, see Chapter 5.

   You can also change the size of your brush tip (from 1 to 100 pixels) in the Tool Options area on the right side of the dialog box. If necessary, change the color of your foreground and background colors by clicking the swatch and choosing a new color from the Color Picker.

3. **Select the Background Brush tool and click or drag to mark the background area or the portions you don't want to select.**

   The default color of the Background Brush is blue, as shown in Figure 7-14.

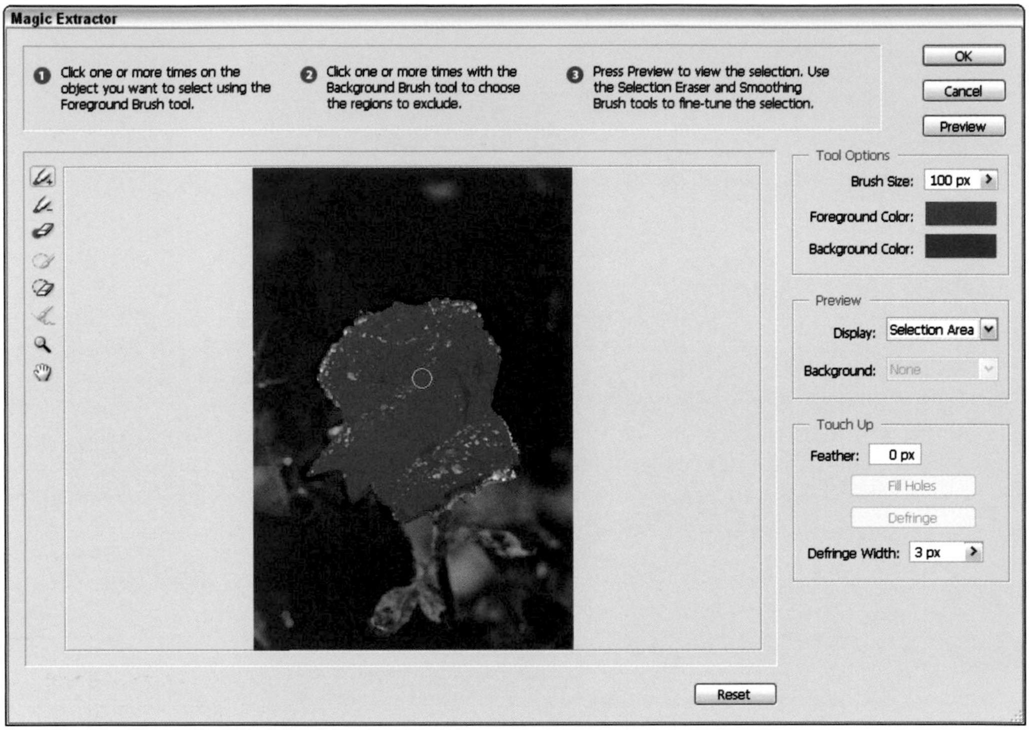

PhotoDisc/Getty Images

Figure 7-14: The Magic Extractor allows you to identify foreground and background areas.

4. **Click Preview to view your extraction.**

   Elements churns for a few seconds before presenting you with a look at your extraction. You can change the preview by choosing either Selection Area or Original Photo from the Display pop-up list.

   If you want to see your selection against a different background, choose one, such as black matte for a black background, from the Background pop-up list.

5. **If you aren't happy with the preview of your selection, you can refine the selection:**

   • *To erase any markings:* Select the Point Eraser tool and click or drag over the offending areas.

   • *To add areas to the selection:* Click or drag over your desired areas with the Add to Selection tool.

- *To delete areas from the selection:* Drag with the Remove from Selection tool.

- *To smooth the edges of your foreground selection:* Drag over the edges with the Smoothing Brush tool.

- *To soften the edges of your selection:* Enter a value in the Feather box. **Remember:** The higher the value, the softer the edge.

- *To fill a hole:* Click the aptly named Fill Holes button.

- *To remove the halo of pixels between the foreground and background areas:* Click Defringe. Enter a value in the Defringe Width box.

If things start to get messy, you can always start over by clicking Reset at the bottom of the dialog box.

6. **When you're pleased with the results, click OK to finish the selection process, as shown in Figure 7-15, and close the Magic Extractor dialog box.**

Your newly extracted image appears as a new file.

Figure 7-15: A rose selected with the Magic Extractor.

Using the Select Menu

In this section, we breeze through the Select menu. Along with the methods we describe in the "Modifying Your Selections" section, earlier in this chapter, you can use this menu to further modify selections by expanding, contracting, smoothing, softening, inversing, growing, and grabbing similarly colored pixels. If that doesn't satisfy your selection needs, nothing will.

Selecting all or nothing

The Select All and Deselect commands are no-brainers. To select everything in your image, choose Select⇨All or press Ctrl+A (⌘+A). To deselect everything, choose Select⇨Deselect or press Ctrl+D (⌘+D). Remember that you usually don't have to Select All. If you don't have a selection border in your image, Elements assumes that the whole image is fair game for any manipulation.

Reselecting a selection

If you sacrifice that second cup of coffee to steady your hand and take the time to carefully lasso around your desired object, you don't want to lose your selection before you have a chance to perform your next move. But all it takes is a mere inadvertent click of your mouse while you have an active selection border to obliterate your selection. Fortunately, Elements anticipated such a circumstance and offers a solution. If you choose Select⇨Reselect, Elements retrieves your last selection.

One caveat: The Reselect command works only for the last selection you made, so don't plan to reselect a selection you made last Tuesday, or even just 5 minutes ago, if you selected something else after that selection. If you want to reuse a selection for the long term, you need to save it, as we explain in "Saving and loading selections," later in this chapter.

Inversing a selection

You know the old song lyric: If you can't be with the one you love, love the one you're with. Well, Elements is kind of like that. Sometimes it's just easier to select what you don't want rather than what you do want. For example, if you're trying to select your beloved in his or her senior photo, it's probably easier to just click the studio backdrop with the Magic Wand and then inverse the selection by choosing Select⇨Inverse.

Feathering a selection

In the "Applying marquee options" section, earlier in this chapter, we describe how to feather a selection when using the Lasso and Marquee tools by entering a value in the Feather box on the Options bar. Remember that this method of feathering requires that you set the Feather value *before* you create your selection. What we didn't tell you is that there's a way to apply a feather *after* you make a selection.

Choose Select⇨Feather and enter your desired amount from .2 to 250 pixels. Your selection is subsequently softened around the edges.

This method is actually a better way to go. Make your selection and fine-tune it by using the methods described earlier in this chapter. Then apply your feather. The problem with applying the feather before you make a selection happens when you want to modify your initial selection. When you make a selection with a feather, the marquee outline of the selection adjusts to take into account the amount of the feather. That means that the resulting marquee outline doesn't resemble your precise mouse movement, making it harder to modify that selection.

Using the Modify commands

Although the commands on the Modify submenu definitely won't win any popularity contests, they may occasionally come in handy. Here's the scoop on each command:

Corbis Digital Stock

Figure 7-16: Fill a border with color to create a stroke around your object.

- **Border:** Selects the area, from 1 to 200 pixels, around the edge of the selection border. By choosing Edit⇨Fill Selection, you can fill the border with color, as shown in Figure 7-16.

- **Smooth:** Rounds off any jagged, raggedy edges. Enter a value from 1 to 100 pixels, and Elements looks at each selected pixel and then includes or deselects the pixels in your selection based on your chosen value. Start with a low number, like 1, 2, or 3 pixels. Otherwise, it may make your selection worse.

- **Expand:** Enables you to increase the size of your selection by a given number of pixels, from 1 to 100. This command is especially useful if you just barely missed getting the edge of an elliptical selection and need it to be a little larger.

- **Contract:** Decreases your selection border by 1 to 100 pixels. When you're compositing multiple images, you often benefit by slightly contracting your selection if you plan on applying a feather. That way, you avoid picking up a fringe of background pixels around your selection.

Applying the Grow and Similar commands

The Grow and Similar commands are often used in tandem with the Magic Wand tool. If you made an initial selection with the Magic Wand but didn't quite get everything you want, try choosing Select⇨Grow. The Grow command increases the size of the selection by including adjacent pixels that fall within the range of tolerance. The Similar command is like Grow, except that the pixels don't have to be adjacent to be selected. The command searches throughout the image and picks up pixels within the tolerance range.

These commands don't have their own tolerance options. They use whatever Tolerance value is displayed on the Options bar when the Magic Wand tool is selected. You can adjust that Tolerance setting to include more or fewer colors.

Saving and loading selections

Finally, there may be times when you toil so long over a complex selection that you really want to save it for future use. Saving it is not only possible, but also highly recommended. It's also a piece a cake. Here's how:

1. **After you perfect your selection, choose Select⇨Save Selection.**

2. **In the Save Selection dialog box, leave the Selection option set to New and enter a name for your selection, as shown in Figure 7-17.**

   The operation is automatically set to New Selection.

3. **Click OK.**

4. **When you want to access the selection again, choose Select⇨Load Selection and choose a selection from the Selection drop-down list.**

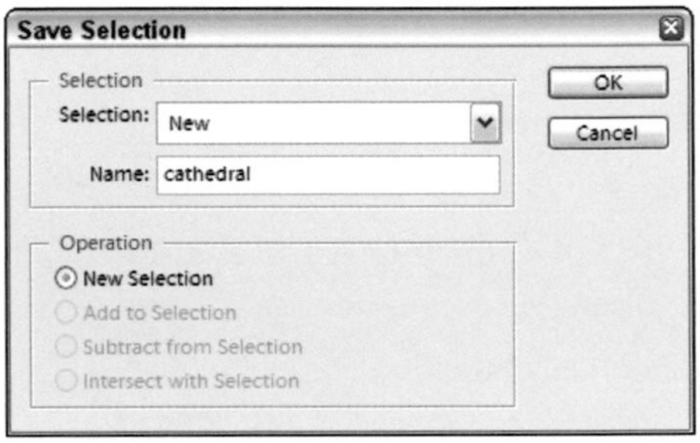

Figure 7-17: Save your selection for later use to save time and effort.

To inverse your selection, click the Invert box. Notice that you now have available options to add to, subtract from, or intersect with your selection. These can come in handy if you want to modify your existing selection. For example, you may select the center and petals of a flower but not the stem and leaves. You later decide that you really need the whole flower. Rather than make a whole new selection, you can select just the stem and leaves and then choose Add to Selection, and you've got your whole flower. If you want, you can then save the flower as a new selection for later use.

Working with Layers

*U*sing Elements without ever using layers would be like typing a book on an old IBM Selectric typewriter: Sure, you could do it, but it wouldn't be fun. An even bigger issue would occur when it came time to edit that book and make changes. Correction tape, Wite-Out, and erasers would make that task downright tedious, not to mention messy. The benefit of using layers is that you have tremendous flexibility. You can quickly make as many edits as you want for as long as you want, as long as you keep your composite image in layers. Layers make working in Elements a lot more productive. Don't give a darn about productivity? Well, let's just say that layers also make it a breeze for you to dabble in your more artsy side. This chapter gives you everything you need to know about layers. After you try them out, you'll wonder how you ever lived without them.

Getting to Know Layers

Think of layers as sheets of acetate or clear transparency film. You have drawings or photographs on individual sheets. What you place on each sheet doesn't affect any of the other sheets. Any area on the sheet that doesn't have an image on it is transparent. You can stack these sheets on top of the others to create a combined image, or *composite* (or *collage,* if you prefer). You can reshuffle the order of the sheets, add new sheets, and delete old sheets.

In Elements, layers are essentially a digital version of these clear acetate sheets. You can place elements such as images, type, or shapes on separate layers and create a composite, as shown in Figure 8-1. You can hide, add, delete, or rearrange layers. Because layers are digital, of course, they have some added functionality. You can adjust how opaque or transparent the element on the layer is. You can also add special effects and change how the colors interact between layers.

When you create a new file with background contents of white or a background color, scan an image into Elements, or open a file from a CD or your digital camera, you basically have a file with just a *background.* There are no layers yet.

An image contains only one background, and you can't do much to it besides paint on it and make basic adjustments. You can't move the background or change its transparency or blend mode. How do you get around all these limitations? Convert your background into a layer by following these easy steps:

Corbis, PhotoDisc/Getty Images
Figure 8-1: Layers enable you to easily create composite images.

1. **Choose Window⇨Layers to display the Layers palette.**

   The Layers palette is explained in detail in the next section.

2. **Double-click Background on the Layers palette.**

   Or, choose Layer⇨New⇨Layer from Background.

3. **Name the layer or leave it at the default name of Layer 0.**

   You can also adjust the blend mode and opacity of the layer in this dialog box. You can also do it via the Layers palette commands later.

4. **Click OK.**

   Elements converts your background into a layer, known also as an *image layer.*

   When you create a new image with transparent background contents, the image doesn't contain a background but instead is created with a single layer.

Anatomy of a Layers palette

Elements keeps layers controlled on their own palette named, not surprisingly, the *Layers palette.* To display the Layers palette, shown in Figure 8-2, choose Window⇨Layers in the Editor in Full Edit mode (Standard Edit mode on the Mac).

The order of the layers on the Layers palette represents the order in the image. We refer to this concept in the computer graphics world as the *stacking order.* The top layer on the palette is the top layer in your image, and so on. Depending on what you're doing, you can work either on a single layer or on multiple layers at one time. Here are some tips for working with the Layers palette:

- ✔ **Select a layer.** Click a layer name or its thumbnail. Elements highlights the *active layer* on the palette.

- ✔ **Select multiple contiguous layers.** Click your first layer and then Shift+click your last layer.

- ✔ **Select multiple noncontiguous layers.** Ctrl+click (⌘+click on the Mac) your desired layers.

- ✔ **View and hide layers.** To hide the layer, click the eye icon for that layer so that the eye disappears. To redisplay the layer, click the blank space in the eye column. You can also hide all the layers except one by selecting your desired layer and Alt+clicking (Option+clicking on the Mac) the eye icon for that layer. Redisplay all layers by Alt+clicking (Option+clicking on the Mac) the eye icon again. Hiding all the layers except the one you want to edit can be helpful in allowing you to focus without the distraction of all the other imagery.

Create a New Layer

Create Adjustment Layer

Delete Layer   Lock Transparent Pixels

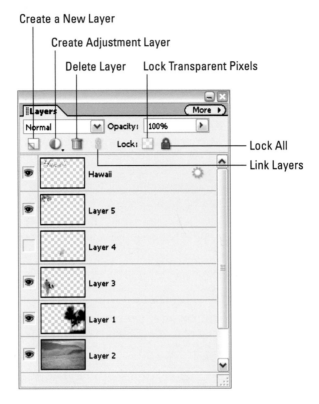

Lock All

Link Layers

Figure 8-2: The Layers palette controls layers in your image.

REMEMBER

Only layers that are visible are printed. This can be useful if you want to have several versions of an image (each on a separate layer) for a project within the same file.

✔ **Select the actual element (the nontransparent pixels) on the layer.** Ctrl+click (⌘+click) the layer's thumbnail (not the name) on the palette.

✔ **Create a new blank layer.** Click the Create a New Layer icon at the top of the palette.

✔ **Create an adjustment layer.** Click the Create Adjustment Layer icon at the top of the palette. *Adjustment* layers are special layers that correct contrast and color in your image. You can also add *fill* layers — layers containing color, gradients, or patterns — by using this command. We give you more details on adjustment and fill layers in upcoming sections.

✔ **Duplicate an existing layer.** Drag the layer to the Create a New Layer icon at the top of the palette.

✔ **Rearrange layers.** To move a layer to another position in the stacking order, drag the layer up or down on the Layers palette. As you drag, you see a fist icon. Release the mouse button when a highlighted line appears where you want to insert the layer.

If your image has a background, it always remains the bottommost layer. If you need to move the background, convert it to a layer by double-clicking the name on the Layers palette. Enter a name for the layer and click OK.

✔ **Rename a layer.** When you create a new layer, Elements provides default layer names (Layer 1, Layer 2, and so on). If you want to rename a layer, double-click the layer name on the Layers palette and enter the name directly on the Layers palette.

✔ **Adjust the interaction between colors on layers and adjust the transparency of layers.** You can use the blend modes and the opacity options at the top of the palette to mix the colors between layers and adjust the transparency of the layers, as shown in Figure 8-3.

✔ **Link layers.** Sometimes you want your layers to stay grouped as a unit to make your editing tasks easier. If so, link your layers by selecting the layers on the palette and then clicking the Link Layers icon at the top of the palette. A link icon appears to the right of the layer name. To remove the link, click the Link Layers icon again.

Corbis Digital Stock

Figure 8-3: We created this effect by using blend modes and opacity options.

✔ **Lock layers.** Select your desired layer and then click one of the two lock icons at the top of the palette. The checkerboard square icon locks all transparent areas of your layers. This prevents you from painting or editing any transparent areas on the layers. The lock icon locks your entire layer and prevents it from being changed in any way, including moving or transforming the elements on the layer. You can, however, still make selections on the layer. To unlock the layer, simply click the icon again to toggle off the lock.

By default, the background is locked and cannot be unlocked until you convert the background into a layer by choosing Layer➪New➪Layer from Background.

✔ **Delete a layer.** Drag it to the trash can icon.

Using the Layer and Select menus

As with many features in Elements, you usually have more than one way to do something. This is especially true when it comes to working with layers. Besides the commands on the Layers palette, you have two layer menus — the Layers menu and the Select menu, both of which you can find on the main menu bar at the top of the application window.

The Layers menu

Much of what you can do with the Layers palette icons you can also do by using the Layers menu on the Menu bar and the Layers palette pop-up menu connected to the Layers palette (click the More button in the upper-right corner). Commands such as New, Duplicate, Delete, and Rename are omnipresent throughout. But you find commands that are exclusive to the palette, the main Layers menu, and the Layers pop-up menu. So, if you can't find what you're looking for in one area, just go to another. Some commands require an expanded explanation and are described in sections that follow. Here's a quick description of most of the commands:

✔ **Delete Linked Layers and Delete Hidden Layers:** These commands delete only those layers that have been linked or hidden from display on the Layers palette.

✔ **Layer Style:** These commands manage the styles, or special effects, you apply to your layers. Find more on layer styles in an upcoming section.

✔ **Change Layer Content:** Depending on the type of layer you have selected, this command enables you to change or adjust the contents of your layer. For example, you can change the contents of a shape layer from a solid color into a pattern.

✔ **Arrange:** Enables you to shuffle your layer stacking order with commands like Bring to Front and Send to Back. Reverse, a new command, switches the order of your layers if you have two or more layers selected.

✔ **Group with Previous and Ungroup:** The Group command creates a *clipping group,* in which a group of layers is constrained to the boundaries of a base layer. Find more details in an upcoming section.

✔ **Type:** The commands on the Type menu control the display of type layers. For more on type, see Chapter 13.

✔ **Rename Layer:** Enables you to give a layer a new name. You can also simply double-click the name on the Layers palette.

✔ **Simplify:** This command converts a type layer, shape layer, or fill layer into a regular image layer. Briefly, a *shape layer* contains a vector object, whereas a *fill layer* contains a solid color, a gradient, or a pattern.

✔ **Merge and Flatten:** The various merge and flatten commands combine multiple layers into a single layer or, in the case of flattening, combine all your layers into a single background.

✔ **Palette Options:** You can choose display options and choose to use a layer mask on your adjustment layers. Leave this option selected and read more about it in the upcoming section.

The Select menu

Although the Select menu's main duties are to assist you in making and refining your selections, it offers a few handy layer commands, all of which are new additions to the menu. Here's a quick introduction to each command:

✔ **Select All Layers:** Want to quickly get everything in your file? Choose Select⇨All Layers.

✔ **Select Layers of Similar Type:** This command is helpful if you have different types of layers in your document, such as regular layers, type layers, shape layers, and adjustment layers, and you want to select just one type. Select one of your layers and then choose Select⇨Similar Layers. For details on different types of layers, see the upcoming section.

✔ **Deselect All Layers:** Choose Select⇨Deselect Layers.

Working with Different Layer Types

Layer life exists beyond just converting an existing background into a layer, which we describe earlier. In fact, Elements offers five kinds of layers. You'll probably spend most of your time creating image layers, but just so that you're familiar with all types, the following sections describe each one.

Image layers

The *image layer,* usually just referred to as a layer, is the type of layer we're referring to when we give the analogy of acetate sheets earlier in this chapter. You can create blank layers and add images to them, or you can create layers from images themselves. You can have as many image layers as your computer's memory allows. Just keep in mind that the more layers you have, the larger your file size and the slower your computer responds.

Each layer in an image can be edited without affecting the other layers. You can move, paint, size, or apply a filter, for example, without disturbing a single pixel on any other layer, or on the background, for that matter. And, when an element is on a layer, you no longer have to make a selection to select it (see Chapter 7 for selection info). Just drag the element with the Move tool.

We tell you more about how to work with image layers later in this chapter.

Adjustment layers

An *adjustment layer* is a special kind of layer used for correcting color and contrast. The advantage of using adjustment layers for your corrections, rather than applying them directly on the image layer, is that you can apply the corrections without permanently affecting the pixels. They're totally nondestructive. And, because the correction is on a layer, you can edit, or even delete, the adjustment at any time. Adjustment layers, shown in Figure 8-4, apply the correction only to all the layers below them, without affecting any of the layers above them.

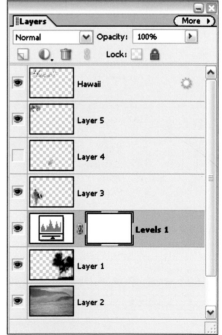

Corbis, PhotoDisc/Getty Images

Figure 8-4: Adjustment layers correct color and contrast in your image.

TECHNICAL STUFF

Another unique feature of adjustment layers is that when you create one, you also create a *layer mask* on that layer at the same time. A layer mask is like a second sheet of acetate that hovers over the underlying layers. The layer mask allows you to selectively apply the adjustment to the layers below it by applying shades of gray — from white to black — on the mask. For example, by default, the mask is completely white. This allows the adjustment to be fully applied to the layers. If you paint on a layer mask with black, the areas under those black areas don't show the adjustment. If you paint with a shade of gray, those areas partially show the adjustment. The darker the shade of gray, the less it shows the adjustment, as shown in Figure 8-5. Note that if you have an active selection border in your image before you add an adjustment layer, the adjustment is applied to only that area within the selection border. The resulting layer mask also reflects that selection: The selected areas are white, and the unselected areas are black.

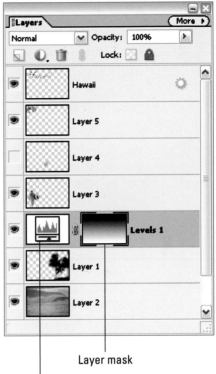

You can also use just the layer mask to creatively blend two layers. Create an adjustment layer and just don't make any adjustment settings. Then use the layer mask to blend two layers. Be sure to sandwich the layer mask between the two layers. Then select the topmost layer and choose Layer⇨Group with Previous. Paint on your layer mask, as described earlier in this section, to selectively hide and show portions of your topmost layer.

Layer mask

Adjustment layer

Elements has eight kinds of adjustment layers, and you can use as many as you want. These adjustments are the same adjustments you find on the Enhance⇨Adjust Lighting and Adjust Color and Filter⇨Adjustments submenus. For specifics on each adjustment, see Chapters 9 and 10. Here's how to create an adjustment layer:

Corbis, PhotoDisc/Getty Images

Figure 8-5: Layer masks control the amount of adjustment applied to your layers.

1. **Open an image that needs a little contrast or color correction.**

   Note that you don't need to convert your background into a layer to apply an adjustment layer.

2. **Click the Create Adjustment Layer icon on the Layers palette.**

3. **From the drop-down list at the top of the Layers palette, choose your desired adjustment.**

   The dialog box specific to your adjustment appears.

4. **Make necessary corrections and click OK.**

   After you close the dialog box, the adjustment layer appears on the Layers palette. The Adjustment Layer icon and a thumbnail appear on the adjustment layer. The thumbnail represents the layer mask we just described.

You can paint on the layer mask to selectively allow only portions of your image to receive the adjustment. Use the Brush or Pencil tool to paint. Or, you can also make a selection and fill that selection with any shade of gray, from white to black. Finally, you can use the Gradient tool on the mask to create a gradual application of the adjustment.

As with image layers, you can adjust the opacity and blend modes of an adjustment layer. Reducing the opacity of an adjustment layer reduces the effect of the adjustment on the underlying layers.

Here are a few more tips on using adjustment layers:

- ✔ **To view your image without the adjustment,** click the eye icon in the left column of the Layers palette to hide the adjustment layer.

- ✔ **To delete the adjustment layer,** drag it to the trash can icon on the Layers palette.

- ✔ **To edit an adjustment layer,** simply double-click the adjustment layer on the Layers palette. You can also choose Layer⇨Layer Content Options. In the dialog box that appears, make any edits and then click OK. The only adjustment layer that you cannot edit is the Invert adjustment. It's either on or off.

- ✔ **To switch to a different adjustment layer,** choose Layer⇨Change Layer Content and choose a different adjustment layer from the submenu.

Fill layers

A *fill layer* lets you add a layer of solid color, a gradient, or a pattern. Like adjustment layers, fill layers also include layer masks. You can edit, rearrange, duplicate, delete, and merge fill layers similarly to adjustment layers. You can blend fill layers with other layers by using the opacity and blend mode options on the Layers palette. Finally, you can restrict the fill layer to just a portion of your image by either making a selection first or painting on the mask later.

Follow these steps to create a fill layer:

1. **Open an image.**

    Use an image that will look good with a frame or border of some kind. Remember that if you don't have a selection, the fill layer covers your whole image.

2. **Click the Create Adjustment Layer icon on the Layers palette. From the drop-down list, choose a fill of a solid color, gradient, or pattern.**

    The dialog box specific to your type of fill appears.

3. **Specify your options, depending on the fill type you chose in Step 2:**

   - *Solid Color:* Choose your desired color from the Color Picker. See Chapter 12 for details on choosing colors and also gradients and patterns.

   - *Gradient:* Click the downward-pointing arrow to choose a preset gradient from the drop-down palette or click the gradient preview to display the Gradient Editor and create your own gradient.

   - *Pattern:* Select a pattern from the drop-down palette. Enter a value to scale your pattern if you want. Click Snap to Origin to make the origin of the pattern the same as the origin of the document. Select the Link with Layer option to specify that the pattern moves with the fill layer if you move it.

4. **Click OK.**

   The fill layer appears on the Layers palette, as shown in Figure 8-6. Notice the layer mask that was created on the fill layer.

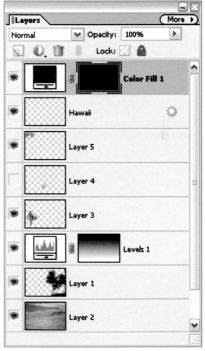

Corbis, PhotoDisc/Getty Images

Figure 8-6: Add a frame or border with a fill layer.

Shape layers

If you haven't made your way to Chapter 12 yet, you may be surprised to discover that Elements also lets you draw shapes with six different drawing tools. These shapes also have the bonus of being *vector*-based. This term means that the shapes are defined by mathematical equations, which create points and paths, rather than by pixels. The advantage of vector-based objects is that you can freely size these objects without causing degradation. In addition, they're always printed with smooth edges, not with the jaggies you're familiar with seeing in pixel-based elements.

To create a shape layer, grab a shape tool from the Tools palette and drag it on your canvas. When you create a shape, it resides on its own, unique shape layer, as shown in Figure 8-7. As with other types of layers, you can adjust the blend modes and opacity of a shape layer. You can edit, move, and transform the actual shapes. However, to apply filters, you must first *simplify* the shape layer. This process converts the vector paths to pixels.

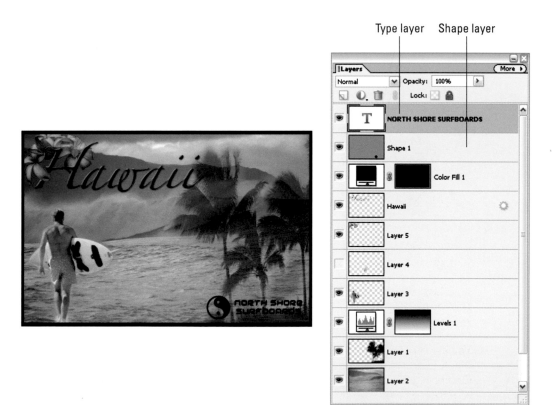

Type layer   Shape layer

Corbis, PhotoDisc/Getty Images

Figure 8-7: Shape layers are vector-based, allowing for smooth edges and optimum print quality.

Type layers

To add words to your images, as shown in Figure 8-7, click your canvas with the Type tool and just type. It's really as easy as that. Well, you can specify options, such as a font family and size, on the Options bar, but when you click the Commit button on the Options bar, you create a type layer. On the Layers palette, you see a layer with a T icon. For details on working with type, check out Chapter 13.

Tackling Layer Basics

Image layers are the heart and soul of the layering world. You can create multiple image layers within a single image. Even more fun is creating a composite from several different images. Add people you like; take out people you don't. Pluck people out of boring photo studios and put them in exotic locales. The creative possibilities are endless. In this section, we cover all the various ways to create image layers. We cover how to convert a background into a layer at the beginning of this chapter, in the section "Getting to Know Layers." These next few sections describe how to create an image layer by using various other methods.

Creating a new layer from scratch

If you're creating a new, blank file, you can select the Transparent option for your background contents. Your new file is created with a transparent layer and is ready to go. If you have an existing file and want to create a new, blank layer, here are the ways to do so:

- Click the Create a New Layer icon at the top of the Layers palette.
- Choose New Layer from the Layers palette pop-up menu.
- Choose Layer⇨New⇨Layer. Note that if you create a layer by using either of the menu commands, you're presented with a dialog box with options. There, you can name your layer and specify options for grouping, blending, and adjusting opacity. Provide a name for your layer and click OK. You can always adjust the other options directly on the Layers palette later.

You can also use the Copy and Paste commands without even creating a blank layer first. When you copy and paste a selection without a blank layer, Elements automatically creates a new layer from the pasted selection. A better method of copying and pasting between multiple images, however, is to use the drag-and-drop method described later in this section.

The Copy Merged command on the Edit menu creates a merged copy of all visible layers within the selection.

After you create your layer, you can put selections or other elements on that layer by doing one or more of the following:

- ✔ Grab a painting tool, such as the Brush or Pencil, and paint on the layer.

- ✔ Make a selection on another layer or on the background within the same document or from another image entirely and then choose Edit⇨Copy. Select your new, blank layer on the Layers palette and then choose Edit⇨Paste. You can also choose Select⇨All and then copy and paste to transfer an entire image to the new layer.

- ✔ Make a selection on another layer or on the background within the same document or from another image and then choose Edit⇨Cut. Select your new, blank layer and then choose Edit⇨Paste. Be aware that this action removes that selection from its original location and leaves a transparent hole, as shown in Figure 8-8.

Corbis Digital Stock

Figure 8-8: When you cut a selection from a layer, take note of the resultant hole in the original location.

Using Layer via Copy and Layer via Cut

Another way to create a layer is to use the Layer via Copy and Layer via Cut commands on the Layer menu. Make a selection on a layer or background and choose Layer⇨New⇨Layer via Copy or Layer via Cut. Elements automatically creates a new layer and puts the copied or cut selection on the layer. Remember that if you use the Layer via Cut command, your selection is deleted from its original location layer and you're left with a transparent hole. If you use the background for the source, your background color fills the space. A reminder: You can use these two commands only within the same image. You cannot use them between multiple images.

Duplicating layers

Duplicating layers can be helpful if you want to protect your original image while experimenting with a technique. If you don't like the results, you can always delete the duplicated layer. No harm, no foul.

To duplicate an existing layer, select it on the Layers palette and do one of three things:

- Drag the layer to the Create a New Layer icon at the top of the palette. Elements creates a duplicate layer with *Copy* appended to the name of the layer.

- Choose Duplicate Layer from the Layers palette pop-up menu.

- Choose Layer⇨Duplicate Layer. If you use the menu methods, a dialog box appears, asking you to name your layer and specify other options. Provide a name for your layer and click OK. You can specify the other options later, if you want.

Dragging and dropping layers

The most efficient way to copy and paste layers between multiple images is to use the drag-and-drop method. Why? Because it bypasses your clipboard, which is the temporary storage area on your computer for copied data. Storing data, especially large files, can bog down your system. By keeping your clipboard clear of data, your system operates more efficiently. If you already copied data and it's lounging on your clipboard, choose Edit⇨Clear⇨Clipboard to empty your clipboard.

Here's how to drag and drop layers from one file to another:

1. **Select your desired layer on the Layers palette.**

2. **Grab the Move tool (the four-headed arrow) from the Tools palette.**

3. **Drag and drop the layer onto your destination file.**

   The dropped layer pops in as a new layer above the active layer in the image. You don't need to have a selection border to copy the entire layer. But, if you want to copy just a portion of the layer, make your selection before you drag and drop with the Move tool. If you want the selected element to be centered on the destination file, press the Shift key as you drag and drop.

Here's a handy tip. If you have several elements (that aren't touching each other) on one layer and you want to select only one of the elements to drag and drop, use the Lasso tool to make a crude selection around the object without touching any of the other elements. Then press the Ctrl (⌘ on the Mac) key and press the up-arrow key once. The element then becomes perfectly selected. Drag and drop with the Move tool as described in Step 3 in this section.

Using the Paste into Selection command

The Paste into Selection command lets you put an image on a separate layer while also inserting that image into a selection border. For example, in Figure 8-9, we used this command to make it appear as though our surfer is in the water.

Figure 8-9: Use the Paste into Selection command to make one element appear as though it's coming out of another element.

You can do the same by following these steps:

1. **Make your desired selection on the layer in your destination image.**

   In our figure, we selected the area in the water where the surfer would be positioned.

2. **Select the image that will fill that selection.**

   The image can be within the same file or from another file. Our surfer was in another file.

3. **Choose Edit⇨Copy.**

4. **Return to the destination image layer and choose Edit⇨Paste into Selection.**

   Elements converts the selection border on the layer into a layer mask. The pasted selection is visible only inside the selection border. In our example, the surfer only shows inside the selected area. His ankles and feet are outside the border and therefore are hidden.

Moving a Layer's Content

Moving the content of a layer is a piece of cake: Grab the Move tool from the Tools palette, select your layer on the Layers palette, and drag the element on the canvas to your desired location. You can also move the layer in 1-pixel increments by using the keyboard arrow keys. Press Shift with the arrows to move in 10-pixel increments.

The Auto-Select Layer option on the Options bar enables you to switch to a layer when you click any part of that layer with the Move tool. But be careful if you have a lot of overlapping layers because this technique can sometimes be more trouble than it's worth.

The Move tool has received a couple of new options in Elements 5. Here's the lowdown:

- ✓ **Show Highlight on Rollover:** Hover your mouse anywhere over the canvas and you see an outline around the element on your layer. Click the highlighted layer to select it and then move it.

- ✓ **Link Layers:** This option connects the layers to allow ease in moving multiple layers simultaneously. Select a layer and then Shift+click to select more layers. Click the Link Layers option.

- ✓ **Arrange menu:** This menu enables you to move your selected layer in front or back of other layers.

- ✓ **Align menu:** Align your selected layers on the left, center, right, top, middle, and bottom. As with linking, select your first layer and then Shift+click to select more layers. Choose an alignment option.

- ✓ **Distribute menu:** Use this menu to evenly space your selected layers on the left, center, right, top, middle, and bottom. As with aligning, select your first layer and then Shift+click to select more layers. Choose your desired distribution option.

Transforming Layers

When working with layers, you may find the need to scale or rotate some of your images. You can do so easily by applying the Transform and Free Transform commands. The methods to transform layers and transform selections are identical.

Here's how to transform a layer:

1. **Select your desired layer.**

   You can also apply a transformation to multiple layers simultaneously by linking the layers first.

2. **Choose Image⇨Transform⇨Free Transform.**

   A bounding box surrounds the contents of your layer. Drag a corner handle to size the contents. Press Shift while dragging to constrain the proportions. To rotate the contents, move the mouse cursor just outside a corner handle until it turns into a curved arrow and then drag. To distort, skew, or apply perspective to the contents, right-click and choose the desired command from the context menu. If you would rather enter your transform values numerically, you can do so in the fields on the Options bar.

   If you want to apply just a single transformation, you can also choose the individual Distort, Skew, and Perspective commands from the Image⇨Transform menu. Or, to rotate or flip, you can choose Image⇨Rotate.

3. **When your layer is transformed to your liking, double-click inside the bounding box or click the Commit button on the Options bar.**

Try to perform all your transformations in one execution. Each time you transform pixels, you put your image through the interpolation process (see Chapter 3 for more on interpolation). Done to the extreme, this process can degrade the quality of your image. This is why it's prudent to use the Free Transform command rather than individual commands — so that all transformations can be executed in one fell swoop.

When the Move tool is active, you can transform a layer without choosing a command. Select the Show Bounding Box option on the Options bar. This option surrounds the layer, or selection, with a box with handles. Drag the handles to transform the layer or selection.

Flattening and Merging Layers

Layers are fun and fantastic, but they can quickly chew up your computer's RAM and bloat your file size. And sometimes, to be honest, having too many layers can start to make your file tedious to manage, thereby making you less productive. Whenever possible, you can merge your layers to save memory and space. *Merging* combines visible, linked, or adjacent layers into a single layer (not a background). The intersection of all transparent areas is retained.

In addition, if you need to import your file into another program, certain programs don't support files with layers. Therefore, you may need to flatten your
file before importing it. *Flattening* an image combines all visible layers into a
background. Hidden layers are discarded, and any transparent areas are filled
with white. We recommend, however, that before you flatten your image,
you make a copy of the file with all its layers intact and save it as a native
Photoshop file. That way, if you ever need to make any edits, you have the
added flexibility of having your layers.

By the way, the only file formats that support layers are native Photoshop
(.psd); Tagged Image File Format, or TIFF (.tif); and Portable Document
Format, or PDF (.pdf). If you save your file in any other format, Elements
automatically flattens your layers into a background.

Merging layers

You can merge your layers in a couple of ways. Here's how:

- **Display only those layers you want to merge.** Click the eye icon on the
  Layers palette to hide those layers you don't want to merge. Choose
  Merge Visible from the Layers palette pop-up menu or the Layer menu.

- **Arrange the layers you want to merge so that they're adjacent to each
  other on the Layers palette.** Select the topmost layer of that group and
  choose Merge Down from the Layers palette pop-up menu or the Layer
  menu. Note that Merge Down merges your active layer with the layer
  directly below it.

Flattening layers

To flatten an image, follow these steps:

1. **Make certain that all layers you want to retain are visible, because
   any hidden layers are discarded.**

2. **Choose Flatten Image from the Layers palette pop-up menu or the
   Layer menu.**

   All your layers are combined into a single background. Any transparent
   areas are filled with the background color, as shown in Figure 8-10.

   If you mistakenly flatten your image, choose Edit⇨Undo or use your
   Undo History palette. (If you're not familiar with the History palette,
   see Chapter 1 for details.)

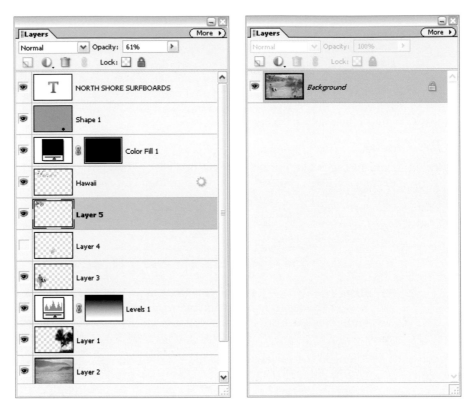

Figure 8-10: Flattening combines all your layers into a single background.

9

Simple Image Makeovers

*F*ixing images quickly without pain or hassle is probably one of the most desirable features you'll find in Elements and one that we're sure you will embrace frequently. Whether you're an experienced photographer or an amateur shutterbug, cropping away unwanted background, tweaking the lighting or color of an image, and erasing away the minor blemishes of a loved one's face are all editing tasks you'll most likely tackle. With these simple image-makeover tools in Elements, these tasks are as easy as clicking a single button or as difficult as a few swipes with a brush.

Cropping and Straightening Images

Cropping a photo is probably one of the easiest things you can do to improve the composition of your photo. Getting rid of the unnecessary background around your subject creates a better focal point. Another dead giveaway of amateurish photography is crooked horizon lines. Not a problem. Elements gives you several ways to straighten those images after the fact. So, after your next photo shoot, launch the Elements Editor and get in there and crop and straighten your images before you show them off. No one will be the wiser that the images were digitally doctored.

Cutting away with the Crop tool

The most common way to crop a photo is by using the Crop tool. Simple, quick, and easy, this tool gets the job done. Here's how to use it:

1. **Select the Crop tool from the Tools palette in either Full Edit (Standard Edit on the Mac) or Quick Fix mode.**

   You can also press the C key. For details on the different workspaces, see Chapter 1. For full details on Quick Fix mode, see the upcoming section "Editing with Quick Fix."

2. **Specify your aspect ratio options on the Options bar. Here are your choices:**

   • *No Restriction:* Allows you to freely crop the image at any size.

   • *Use Photo Ratio:* Retains the original aspect ratio of the image when you crop.

   • *Preset Sizes:* Offers a variety of common photographic sizes. When you crop, your image then becomes that specific dimension.

   When you crop an image, Elements retains the original resolution of the file. To keep your image at the same resolution, therefore, while simultaneously eliminating portions of your image, Elements must resample the file. Consequently, your image must have sufficient resolution so that the effects of the resampling aren't as noticeable. This is especially true if you're choosing a larger preset size. If all this talk about resolution and resampling is fuzzy, be sure to check out Chapter 3.

   • *Width and Height:* Enables you to specify a desired width and height to crop your image.

3. **Drag around the portion of the image you want to retain and release the mouse button.**

   As you drag, a crop marquee bounding box appears. Don't worry if your cropping marquee isn't exactly correct. You can adjust it in the next step.

   The area outside the cropping marquee (called a *shield*) appears darker than the inside in order to better frame your image, as shown in Figure 9-1. If you want to change the color and opacity of the shield, or if you don't want it at all, change your Crop preferences (choose Edit⟹Preferences⟹Display & Cursors, or choose Elements⟹Preferences⟹ Display & Cursors on the Mac).

Cropping marquee   Handle

Shield   Cancel button

Commit button

Corbis Digital Stock

Figure 9-1: The area outside the crop marquee appears darker to allow for easier framing of your image.

4. **Adjust the cropping marquee by dragging the handles of the crop marquee bounding box.**

   To move the entire marquee, position your mouse inside the marquee until you see a black arrowhead cursor and then drag.

   If you move your mouse outside the marquee, your cursor changes to a curved arrow. Drag with this cursor to rotate the marquee. This action allows you to both rotate and crop your image simultaneously — handy for straightening a crooked image. Just be aware that rotation, unless it's in 90 degree increments, also resamples your image.

5. **Double-click inside the cropping marquee.**

   You can also just press Enter (Return on the Mac) or click the green Commit button next to the marquee. Elements then discards the area outside the marquee. To cancel your crop, click the red Cancel button.

Cropping with a selection border

You can also crop an image by choosing the Image⇨Crop command in either Full Edit (Standard Edit mode on the Mac) or Quick Fix mode. First, make a selection with any of the selection tools and then choose the command. You can use this technique with any selection border shape. That is, your selection doesn't have to be rectangular. It can be round or even freeform. Your cropped image doesn't take on that shape, but Elements crops as close to the boundaries of the selection border as it can, as shown in Figure 9-2. For details about making selections, see Chapter 7.

Straightening images

There may be times when you just didn't quite get that horizon straight when you took a photo of the beach. Or, maybe you scanned a photo and it wasn't quite centered in the middle of the scanning bed. It's not a big deal. Elements gives you several ways to straighten an image.

Using the Straighten tool

This new tool enables you to specify a new straight edge and then rotates the image accordingly. Here's how to use the Straighten tool:

1. **Select the Straighten tool from the Tools palette (or press the P key) only in Full Edit mode (or Standard Edit mode on the Mac).**

2. **Specify your desired setting from the Canvas Options on the Options bar. Here are your choices:**

   • *Grow Canvas to Fit:* Rotates the image and increases the size of the canvas to fit the image area.

- *Crop to Remove Background:* Trims off background canvas outside the image area. This choice is helpful if you scan an image and white areas appear around your photo that you want removed.

- *Crop to Original Size:* Rotates your image without trimming off any background canvas.

3. **Select Rotate All Layers, if you want.**

   If you have an image with layers and you want all of them rotated, select this option.

4. **Draw a line in your image to represent the new straight edge.**

   Your image is then straightened and, if you chose either of the crop options in Step 2, also cropped.

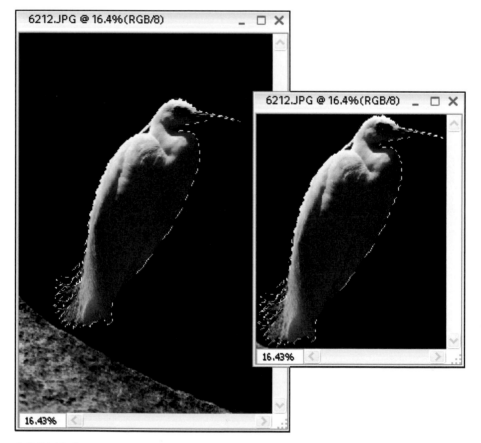

Corbis Digital Stock

Figure 9-2: Elements can crop to any selection border shape.

Using the Straighten menu commands

In addition to using the Straighten tool, you can straighten your images by using two commands on the Image menu, in either Full Edit (or Standard Edit mode on the Mac) or Quick Fix mode:

- ✔ **To automatically straighten an image without cropping, which leaves the canvas remaining around the image:** Choose Image⟹Rotate⟹ Straighten Image.

- ✔ **To automatically straighten and crop the image simultaneously:** Choose Image⟹Rotate⟹Straighten and Crop Image.

Using the Divide Scanned Photos command

The Divide Scanned Photos command is helpful if you want to save time by scanning multiple photos into one document. Cram all the photos you can on your scanning bed and get one initial scan. Just make sure that a clear separation exists between all the images. Then choose Image⟹Divide Scanned Photos in either Full Edit (or Standard Edit mode on the Mac) or Quick Fix mode. Elements divides the images and places each one in a separate file, as shown in Figure 9-3. Note that if you have images with a lot of white in them, such as snow, you should cover the scanner with a piece of dark paper to better delineate the boundaries of each image.

Corbis Digital Stock

Figure 9-3: Save time by scanning several images at a time and then applying the Divide Scanned Photos command.

Employing One-Step Auto Fixes

Elements has five automatic lighting-, contrast-, and color-correction tools that can improve the appearance of your images with just one menu command. These commands are available in either Full Edit (or Standard Edit mode on the Mac) or Quick Fix mode, and they're all on the Enhance menu. For more on Quick Fix mode, see the upcoming section "Editing with Quick Fix."

The advantage of these one-step correctors is that they're extremely easy to use. You don't need to have one iota of knowledge about color or contrast to use them. The downside to using them is that sometimes the result isn't as good as you could get via a manual color-correction method. And, sometimes these correctors may even make your image look worse than before by giving you weird color shifts. But because these correctors are quick and easy, give them a try on an image that needs some help. Usually, you don't want to use more than one of the auto fixes. If one doesn't work on your image, undo the fix and try another. If you still don't like the result, move on to one of the manual methods described in Chapter 10.

Auto Smart Fix

This all-in-one command is touted to adjust it all. It's designed to improve lighting, improve the details in shadow and highlight areas, and correct the color balance, as shown in Figure 9-4. The overexposed image on the left was improved quite nicely with the Auto Smart Fix command.

The Auto Smart Fix command is available in the Organizer, where you can apply this command to several selected images simultaneously. It's also available in the Slide Show editor.

Figure 9-4: In a hurry? Apply the Auto Smart Fix command to quickly improve an image.

If the Auto Smart Fix was just too "auto" for you, you can crank it up a notch and try Adjust Smart Fix. This command is similar to Auto Smart Fix, but gives you a slider where you, not Elements, control the amount of correction applied to the image.

Auto Levels

The Auto Levels command adjusts the overall contrast of an image. This command works best on images that have pretty good contrast (detail in the shadow, highlight, and midtone areas) to begin with and need just a minor amount of adjustment. Auto Levels works by _mapping,_ or converting, the lightest and darkest pixels in your image to black and white, thereby making highlights appear lighter and shadows appear darker, as shown in Figure 9-5.

Figure 9-5: Auto Levels adjusts the overall contrast of an image.

Although Auto Levels can improve your contrast, it may also produce an unwanted colorcast (a slight trace of color). If this happens, undo the command and try the Auto Contrast command instead. If that still doesn't improve the contrast, it's time to bring out the big guns. Try the Levels command described in Chapter 10.

Auto Contrast

The Auto Contrast command is designed to adjust the overall contrast in an image without adjusting its color. This command may not do as good a job of improving contrast as the Auto Levels command, but it does a better job of retaining the color balance of an image. Auto Contrast usually doesn't cause the funky colorcasts that can occur when you're using Auto Levels. This command works great on images with a haze, as shown in Figure 9-6.

PhotoDisc/Getty Images

Figure 9-6: The Auto Contrast command works wonders on hazy images.

Auto Color Correction

The Auto Color Correction command adjusts both the color and contrast of an image, based on the shadows, midtones, and highlights it finds in the image and a default set of values. These values adjust the amount of black and white pixels that Elements removes from the darkest and lightest areas of the image. You usually use this command to remove a colorcast or to balance the color in your image, as shown in Figure 9-7. Occasionally, this command can also be useful in correcting oversaturated or undersaturated colors.

Figure 9-7: Use Auto Color Correction to remove a colorcast.

Auto Sharpen

Photos taken with a digital camera or scanned on a flatbed scanner often suffer from a case of overly soft focus. Sharpening gives the illusion of increased focus by increasing the contrast between pixels. Auto Sharpen attempts to improve the focus, as shown in Figure 9-8, without overdoing it. What happens when you oversharpen? Your images go from soft to grainy and noisy. Always make sharpening your last fix after you have made all your other fixes and enhancements. For more precise sharpening, check out the Unsharp Mask and Adjust Sharpness features covered in Chapter 10.

Figure 9-8: Use Auto Sharpen to improve focus.

Auto Red Eye Fix

This command is self-explanatory. The Auto Red Eye Fix command automatically detects and eliminates red-eye in an image. Red-eye happens when a person or animal (where red eye can also be yellow, green, or even blue eye) looks directly into the flash. Many cameras have a red-eye prevention mode, which is a pre-flash that causes the subjects' irises to contract, making their pupils smaller when the real flash goes off. Other cameras mount the flash high or to side of the lens, which also reduces the chance of red-eye. But if you have neither of these camera options, or if it just happened, it isn't difficult to rectify demonic red-eye after the fact.

The Auto Red Eye Fix command is also available in the Organizer, where you can apply this command to several selected images simultaneously. You can also automatically apply this fix when you acquire your images. Select the Automatically Fix Red Eyes check box in the File⇨Get Photos dialog box. And, as with Auto Smart Fix, you can now access this tool in the Slide Show editor as well.

If for some reason the Auto Red Eye Fix doesn't quite do the trick, you can always reach for the Red Eye Removal tool on the Tools palette. Here's how to remove red-eye manually:

1. **Select the Red Eye Removal tool from the Tools palette.**

   Using the default settings, click the red portion of the eye in your image. This one-click tool darkens the pupil while retaining the tonality and texture of the rest of the eye, as shown in Figure 9-9.

Figure 9-9: The Auto Red Eye Fix and the Red Eye Removal tool detect and destroy dreaded red-eye.

2. **If you're unhappy with the fix, adjust one or both of these options:**

   • *Pupil Size:* Use the slider to increase or decrease the size of the pupil.

   • *Darken Pupil:* Use the slider to darken or lighten the color of the pupil.

Editing with Quick Fix

If you use the Auto Fixes we cover in the preceding section while working in Quick Fix mode, you may find all you need to repair and enhance your images and rarely visit Full Edit mode (or Standard Edit mode on the Mac). And so, in this section, we offer a closer look at Quick Fix mode.

Quick Fix mode is a pared-down version of Full Edit mode (Standard Edit mode on the Mac) that conveniently provides basic fixing tools and tosses in a few unique features, such as a before-and-after preview of your image.

Here's a step-by-step workflow that you can follow in Quick Fix mode to repair your photos:

1. **Select one or more photos in the Organizer and then choose Go to Quick Fix from the Edit menu or the Shortcuts bar. Or, if you're in Full Edit mode (Standard Edit mode on the Mac), click the Quick Fix button in the upper-right area of the application window.**

   If you happen to be in Full Edit mode (Standard Edit mode on the Mac) with an image already open, this image is transported into Quick Fix mode. Note that you can also open images by simply choosing the File⇨Open menu command.

2. **Specify your preview preference from the View pop-up menu at the bottom of the application window.**

   You choose to view just your original image (before), your fixed image (after), or both images side-by-side in either portrait or landscape orientation, as shown in Figure 9-10.

3. **Use the Zoom and Hand tools to magnify and navigate around your image. See Chapter 5 for more on these tools.**

   You can also specify the Zoom percentage by using the Zoom slider at the bottom of the application window.

4. **Crop your image by using the Crop tool on the Tools palette.**

   You can also use any of the methods described earlier, in the "Cropping and Straightening Images" section, except for the Straighten tool, which is exclusive to Full Edit mode (Standard Edit mode on the Mac).

5. **To rotate the image in 90-degree increments, click the Rotate Left or Rotate Right button at the bottom of the application window.**

6. **Use the Red Eye tool to remove the red from your subjects' eyes.**

   Note that you can also automatically fix red-eye by clicking the Auto button under Red Eye Fix on the General Fixes palette on the right side of the application window. Both these methods are described earlier in this chapter, in the section "Auto Red Eye Fix."

Figure 9-10: Quick Fix mode enables you to view before-and-after previews of your image.

7. **Apply any necessary auto fixes, such as Auto Smart Fix, Auto Levels, Auto Contrast, and Auto Color Correction.**

   All these commands are on the Enhance menu or in the General Fixes, Lighting, and Color palettes on the right side of the application window.

   Each of these fixes is described in detail earlier in this chapter. Remember that usually one of the fixes is enough. Don't stack them on top of each other. If one doesn't work, click the Reset button near the image preview and try another. If you're not happy, go to Step 8.

8. **If the auto fixes don't quite cut it, you get more control by using the sliders available for Smart Fix, Contrast, and Color, located on the palettes on the right of the application window. If auto fixes did create a result that you're happy with, skip to Step 9.**

   Here's a brief description of each available adjustment:

   • *Lighten Shadows:* When you drag the slider to the right, lightens the darker areas of your image without adjusting the highlights.

- *Darken Highlights:* When you drag the slider to the right, darkens the lighter areas of your image without adjusting the shadows.

- *Midtone Contrast:* Adjusts the contrast of the middle (gray) values and leaves the highlights and shadows as is.

- *Saturation:* Adjusts the intensity of the colors.

- *Hue:* Changes all colors in an image. Make a selection first to change the color of just one or more elements. Otherwise, use restraint with this adjustment.

- *Temperature:* Adjusts the colors warmer (red) or cooler (blue). This adjustment can be used to correct skin tones or to correct overly cool images (such as snowy winter photos) or overly warm images (such as photos shot at sunset or sunrise).

- *Tint:* Adjusts the tint after you adjust temperature to make the color more green or magenta.

If you still don't get the results you need, move on to one of the more manual adjustments, described in Chapter 10.

Note that you can also apply fixes to just selected portions of your image. Quick Fix mode offers the Selection Brush and Magic Selection Brush tools for your selection tasks. For details on using these tools, see Chapter 7.

9. **Finally, sharpen your image either automatically, by clicking the Auto button, or manually, by dragging the slider on the Sharpen palette.**

This fix should always be the last adjustment you make on your image.

Cloning with the Clone Stamp Tool

Elements enables you to clone elements without the hassle of genetically engineering DNA. In fact, the Clone Stamp tool works by just taking sampled pixels from one area and copying, or *cloning,* them onto another area. The advantage of cloning over making a selection and copying and pasting is that it's easier to realistically retain soft-edged elements, such as shadows, as shown in Figure 9-11.

The Clone Stamp doesn't stop there. You can also use this tool for fixing flaws, such as scratches, bruises, and other minor imperfections. Although the birth of the healing tools (discussed later in this chapter) has somewhat pushed the Clone Stamp tool out of the retouching arena, it can still do a good repair job in many instances.

PhotoSpin

Figure 9-11: The Clone Stamp tool enables you to realistically duplicate soft-edged elements, such as shadows.

Here's how to use the Clone Stamp tool:

1. **Choose the Clone Stamp tool from the Tools palette in Full Edit mode (Standard Edit mode on the Mac).**

   You can also press the S key.

2. **On the Options bar, choose a brush from the Brush Preset drop-down list. Use the brush as is or adjust its size with the Size slider.**

   Keep in mind that the size of the brush you specify should be appropriate for what you're trying to clone or retouch. If you're cloning a large object, use a larger brush. For repairing small flaws, use a smaller brush. Cloning with a soft-edged brush usually produces more natural results. For details on brushes, see Chapter 12.

3. **Choose your desired blend mode and opacity percentage.**

   For more on blend modes, see Chapter 11. To make your cloned image appear ghosted, use an opacity percentage of less than 100 percent.

4. **Select or deselect the Aligned option.**

With Aligned selected, the clone source moves when you move your cursor to a different location. If you want to clone multiple times from the same location, leave the Aligned option deselected.

5. **Select or deselect the Sample All Layers option.**

   This option enables you to sample pixels from all visible layers for the clone. If this option is deselected, the Clone Stamp tool clones from only the active layer. Check out Chapter 8 for details about working with layers.

6. **Alt+click (Opt+click on the Mac) the area of your image that you want to clone to define the *source* of the clone.**

7. **Click or drag along the area where you want the clone to appear, as shown in Figure 9-12.**

   As you drag, Elements displays a crosshair icon along with your Clone Stamp cursor. The crosshair is the source you're cloning from, and the Clone Stamp cursor is where the clone is being applied. As you move the mouse, the crosshair moves as well. This provides a continuous reference to the area of your image that you're cloning. Watch the crosshair, or else you may clone something you don't want.

Figure 9-12: The crosshair and Clone Stamp cursor in action.

If you're cloning an element, try to clone it without lifting your mouse. Also, when you're retouching a flaw, try not to overdo it. One or two clicks on each flaw is usually plenty. If you're heavy-handed with the Clone Stamp, you get a blotchy effect that is a telltale sign that something has been retouched.

You can also clone patterns by using the Pattern Stamp tool, which shares a flyout menu with the Clone Stamp tool. Select a pattern from the Pattern Picker drop-down palette on the Options bar. Drag with the tool to clone a pattern onto your image.

Retouching with the Healing Brush

The Healing Brush tool is similar to the Clone Stamp tool in that you clone pixels from one area onto another area. But the Healing Brush is superior in that it takes into account the tonality (highlights, midtones, and shadows) of the flawed area. The Healing Brush clones by using the *texture* from the sampled area (the source) and then using the *colors* around the brush stroke as you paint over the flawed area (the destination). The highlights, midtones, and shadow areas remain intact, making the repair more realistic and natural and not as blotchy or miscolored as with the Clone Stamp tool.

Here are the steps to heal a photo:

1. **Open an image in need of a makeover and select the Healing Brush tool from the Tools palette in Full Edit mode (Standard Edit mode on the Mac).**

   You can also heal between two images, but be sure that they have the same color mode; for example, both RGB. We chose a guy who looks like he might like to lose a few years, shown in Figure 9-13.

PhotoSpin

Figure 9-13: Wipe out ten years in two minutes with the Healing Brush tool.

2. **Specify a diameter and hardness for your brush tip from the Brush Picker drop-down palette on the Options bar.**

   You can also adjust the spacing, angle, and roundness. For details on these options, see Chapter 12. Don't be shy. Be sure to adjust the size of your brush as needed. Using the appropriate brush size for the flaw you're retouching is critical to creating a realistic effect.

3. **Choose your desired blend mode.**

   For most retouching jobs, you probably should leave the mode as Normal. Replace mode preserves textures, such as noise or film grain, around the edges of your strokes.

4. **Choose one of these Source options:**

- *Sampled:* Uses the pixels from the image. This is your choice for the majority of your repairs.

- *Pattern:* Uses pixels from a pattern chosen from the Pattern Picker drop-down palette.

5. **Select or deselect the Aligned option on the Options bar.**

For most retouching tasks, you probably should leave it on Aligned.

- *Select Aligned:* When you click or drag with the Healing Brush, Elements displays a crosshair along with the Healing Brush cursor. The crosshair represents the sampling point, also known as the source. As you move the Healing Brush tool, the crosshair also moves, providing a constant reference to the area you're sampling.

- *Deselect Aligned:* Elements applies the source pixels from your initial sampling point, no matter how many times you stop and start dragging.

6. **Select the Sample All Layers option to heal an image using all visible layers.**

If this option is deselected, you heal from only the active layer.

To ensure maximum editing flexibility later on, select the Sample All Layers option and add a new, blank layer above the image you want to heal. When you heal the image, the pixels appear on the new layer and not on the image itself. This enables you to adjust opacity and blend modes and to make other adjustment to the healed layer.

7. **Establish the sampling point by Alt+clicking (Opt+clicking). Make sure to click the area of your image that you want to clone from.**

In our example, we clicked a smooth area of the forehead.

8. **Release the Alt key (Opt key on the Mac) and click or drag over a flawed area of your image.**

Keep an eye on the crosshair because that's the area you're healing from. We brushed over the wrinkles under and around the eyes and on the forehead (refer to Figure 9-13). This guy never looked so good, and he experienced absolutely no recovery time.

Zeroing In with the Spot Healing Brush

Whereas the Healing Brush is designed to fix larger flawed areas, the Spot Healing Brush is great for smaller imperfections. The Spot Healing Brush doesn't require you to specify a sampling source. It automatically takes a sample from around the area to be retouched. It's quick and easy and often effective. But it doesn't give you control over the sampling source, so keep an eye out for less-than-desirable fixes.

Here's how to quickly fix small flaws with the Spot Healing Brush tool:

1. **Open your image and grab the Spot Healing Brush tool in Full Edit mode (Standard Edit mode on the Mac).**

   The moles on this guy's face, shown in Figure 9-14, are no match for the Spot Healing Brush.

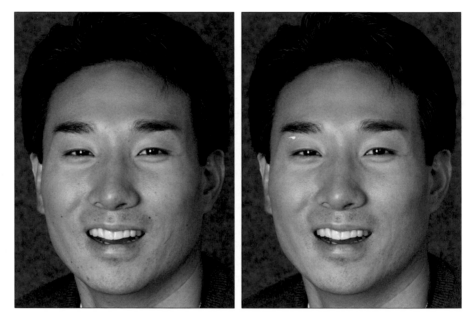

PhotoSpin

Figure 9-14: Now you see it (left), and now you don't (right).

2. **On the Options bar, click the Brush Preset Picker and select a desired diameter and hardness for your brush tip from the drop-down palette.**

   Select a brush that's a little larger than the flawed area you're fixing.

3. **Choose a blend mode from the Options bar.**

   As with the Healing Brush, the most likely mode is Normal.

4. **Choose a type from the Options bar:**

   - *Proximity Match:* Samples the pixels around the edge of the selection to fix the flawed area.

   - *Create Texture:* Uses all the pixels in the selection to create a texture to fix the flaw.

   Try Proximity Match first, and if it doesn't work, undo and try Create Texture.

5. **Choose Sample All Layers to heal an image using all visible layers.**

   If you leave this check box unselected, you heal from only the active layer.

6. **Click or drag on the area you want to fix.**

   We clicked the moles with the Spot Healing Brush. For the wrinkles around the eyes, we broke out the Healing Brush. We needed more control of the sampling source to achieve realistic results.

Lightening and Darkening with Dodge and Burn Tools

The techniques of dodging and burning originated in the darkroom, where photographers fixed negatives that had overly dark or light areas by adding or subtracting exposure, using holes and paddles as an enlarger made prints. The Dodge and Burn tools in Elements are even better than their analog ancestors in that they're more flexible and much more precise. In Elements, you can specify the size and softness of your tool by simply selecting from one of the many brush tips. You can also limit the correction to various tonal ranges in your image — shadows, midtones, or highlights. Finally, you can adjust the amount of correction that's applied by specifying an exposure percentage.

Use these tools only on small areas, such as the girl's face shown in Figure 9-15, and in moderation. Also, keep in mind that you can't add detail that isn't there to begin with. If you try to lighten extremely dark shadows that contain little detail, you get gray areas. If you try to darken overly light highlights, you just end up with white blobs.

Figure 9-15: Use the Dodge and Burn tools to lighten and darken small areas.

Follow these steps to dodge or burn an image:

1. **Choose either the Dodge or Burn tool (or press O) from the Tools palette in Full Edit mode (Standard Edit mode on the Mac).**

2. **Select a brush from the Brush Preset Picker drop-down palette and also adjust the brush size, if necessary.**

   Larger, softer brushes spread the dodging or burning effect over a larger area, making blending with the surrounding area easier.

3. **From the Range pop-up list, select Shadows, Midtones, or Highlights.**

   Select Shadows to darken or lighten the darker areas of your image. Select Midtones to adjust the tones of average darkness. Select Highlights to make the light areas lighter or darker.

   In Figure 9-15, the original image had mostly dark areas, so we dodged the shadows.

4. **Choose the amount of correction you want to apply with each stroke by adjusting the Exposure setting on the Options bar.**

   Start with a lower percentage to better control the amount of darkening or lightening. Exposure is similar to the opacity setting you use with the regular Brush tool. We used a setting of 10 percent.

5. **Paint over the areas you want to lighten or darken.**

6. **If you overdo it, press Ctrl+Z (⌘+Z on the Mac) to undo the stroke.**

Smudging Away Rough Spots

The Smudge tool, one of the focus tools, pushes your pixels around using the color that's under the cursor when you start to drag. Think of it as dragging a brush through wet paint. You can use this tool to create a variety of effects. When it's used to the extreme, you can create a warped effect. When it's used more subtly, you can soften the edges of objects in a more natural fashion than you can with the Blur tool. Or, you can create images that take on a painterly effect, as shown in Figure 9-16. Keep an eye on your image as you paint, however, because you can start to eliminate detail and wreak havoc if you're not careful with the Smudge tool.

To use the Smudge tool, follow these steps:

1. **Choose the Smudge tool from the Tools palette in Full Edit mode (Standard Edit mode on the Mac).**

   You can also press the R key (press Shift+R to cycle through the available focus tools).

2. **Select a brush from the Brushes presets drop-down palette.**

   Use a small brush for smudging tiny areas, such as edges. Larger brushes produce more extreme effects.

3. **Select a blending mode from the Mode pop-up list.**

4. **Choose the strength of the smudging effect with the Strength slider or text box.**

   The lower the value, the lighter the effect.

5. **If your image has multiple layers, select Sample All Layers, and Elements uses pixels from all the visible layers to produce the effect.**

   The smudge still appears only on the active layer, but the look is a bit different, depending on the colors of the underlying layers.

6. **Use the Finger Painting option to begin the smudge by using the foreground color.**

   Rather than use the color under your cursor, this option smears your foreground color at the start of each stroke. If you want the best of both worlds, you can quickly switch into Finger Painting mode by pressing the Alt key (Opt key on the Mac) as you drag. Release Alt to go back to Normal mode.

PhotoSpin

Figure 9-16: The Smudge tool can make your images appear to be painted.

7. **Paint over the areas you want to smudge.**

   Pay attention to your strokes because this tool can radically change your image. If you don't like the results, press Ctrl+Z (⌘+Z on the Mac) to undo and then lower the Strength percentage even more.

Softening with the Blur Tool

The Blur tool can be used for both repair and more artistic endeavors. You can use the Blur tool to soften a small flaw or part of a rough edge. You can add a little blur to an element to make it appear as though it were moving when photographed. You can also blur portions of your image to emphasize the focal point, as shown in Figure 9-17, where we blurred everything except the girl's face. The Blur tool works by decreasing the contrast among adjacent pixels in the blurred area.

The mechanics of using the Blur tool and its options are similar to those of the Smudge tool, described earlier in this chapter. You obviously just don't find the Finger Painting option with the Blur tool. When you use the Blur tool, be sure to use a small brush for smaller areas of blur.

PhotoSpin

Figure 9-17: The Blur tool can soften just the edges of a larger portion of an image element.

Focusing with the Sharpen Tool

If the Blur tool is yin, the Sharpen tool is yang. The Sharpen tool increases the contrast among adjacent pixels to give the illusion that things are sharper. This tool needs to be used with restraint, however. Sharpen can quickly give way to overly grainy and noisy images if you're not cautious.

Use a light hand and keep the areas you sharpen small. Sometimes, the eyes in a soft portrait can benefit from a little sharpening, as shown in Figure 9-18. You can also slightly sharpen an area to emphasize it against a less-than-sharp background.

PhotoSpin

Figure 9-18: Reserve the Sharpen tool for small areas, such as eyes.

To use the Sharpen tool, grab the tool from the Tools palette and follow the steps provided for the Smudge tool. In addition, here are some tips for using the Sharpen tool:

- Use a lower value, around 25 percent or less.
- Remember that you want to gradually sharpen your element to avoid the nasty, noisy grain that can occur from oversharpening.
- Because sharpening increases contrast, if you use other contrast adjustments, such as Levels, you boost the contrast of the sharpened area even more.

If you need to sharpen your overall image, try choosing either the Enhance⇨ Unsharp Mask or Enhance⇨Adjust Sharpness feature instead. They offer more options and better control.

Sponging Color On and Off

The Sponge tool soaks up color or squeezes it out. In more technical terms, this tool reduces or increases the intensity, or *saturation,* of color in both color and grayscale images. Yes, the Sponge tool also works in Grayscale mode by darkening or lightening the brightness value of those pixels.

As with the Blur and Sharpen tools, you can use the Sponge tool to reduce or increase the saturation in selected areas in order to draw attention to or away from those areas.

Follow these steps to sponge color on or off your image:

1. **Choose the Sponge tool from the Tools palette in Full Edit mode (Standard Edit mode on the Mac).**

   Press the O key or press Shift+O to cycle through the Sponge, Dodge, and Burn tools.

2. **Select a brush from the Brushes presets drop-down palette.**

   Use large, soft brushes to saturate or desaturate a larger area.

3. **Choose either Desaturate or Saturate from the Mode pop-up list to decrease or increase color intensity, respectively.**

4. **Choose a flow rate with the Flow slider or text box.**

   The *flow rate* is the speed with which the saturation or desaturation effect builds as you paint.

5. **Paint carefully over the areas you want to saturate or desaturate with color.**

   In the example shown in Figure 9-19, we saturated one of the kids to make her more of a focal point and desaturated the others.

PhotoSpin

Figure 9-19: The Sponge tool increases or decreases the intensity of the color in your image.

Replacing One Color with Another

The Color Replacement tool allows you to replace the original color of an image with the foreground color. You can use this tool in a multitude of ways:

PhotoSpin

Figure 9-20: The Color Replacement tool replaces the color in your image with the foreground color.

✔ Colorize a grayscale image to create the look of a hand-painted photo.

✔ Completely change the color of an element, or elements, in your image, as shown in Figure 9-20.

✔ Eliminate red-eye if other, more automated methods don't work to your satisfaction.

What we particularly like about the Color Replacement tool is that it preserves all the tones in the image. The color that's applied isn't like the opaque paint that's applied when you paint with the Brush tool. When you're replacing color, the midtones, shadows, and highlights are retained. The Color Replacement tool works by first sampling the original colors in the image and then replacing those colors with the foreground color. By specifying different sampling methods, limits, and tolerance settings, you can control the range of colors that Elements replaces.

Follow these steps to replace existing color with your foreground color:

1. **Select the Color Replacement tool from the Tools palette in Full Edit mode (Standard Edit mode on the Mac).**

   This tool shares a flyout menu with the Brush and Pencil tools.

   Alternatively, press the B key (or Shift+B).

2. **Specify your desired brush tip diameter and hardness from the Brush Preset Picker drop-down palette.**

3. **Choose your desired blend mode. Here's a brief rundown of each one:**

   • *Color:* The default, this mode works well for most jobs. This mode works great in eliminating red-eye.

   • *Hue:* Similar to color, this mode is less intense and provides a subtler effect.

   • *Saturation:* This mode is the one to use to convert your color image to grayscale. Set your foreground color to Black on the Tools palette.

- *Luminosity:* This mode, the opposite of Color, doesn't provide much of an effect.

4. **Choose your sampling method (represented by the icons):**

   - *Continuous:* Samples and replaces color continuously as you drag your mouse.

   - *Once:* Replaces colors only in areas that contain the color you first sampled when you initially clicked.

   - *Background Swatch:* Replaces colors only in areas containing your current Background color.

5. **Select your limits mode:**

   - *Contiguous:* Replaces the color of adjacent pixels containing the sampled color.

   - *Discontiguous:* Replaces the color of the pixels containing the sampled color, whether or not they're adjacent.

6. **Set your tolerance percentage.**

   Tolerance refers to a range of color. The higher the value, the broader range of color that is sampled, and vice versa.

7. **Select anti-aliasing.**

   Anti-aliasing slightly softens the edges of the sampled areas.

8. **Click or drag on your image.**

   The foreground color replaces the original colors of the sampled areas. In our example (refer to Figure 9-20), we used a black foreground color.

Correcting Contrast, Color, and Clarity

*I*f you've tried the quick and easy automatic fixes on your images and they didn't quite do the job, you've come to the right place. The great thing about Elements is that it offers multiple ways and multiple levels of repairing and enhancing your images. If an auto fix doesn't cut it, move on to a manual fix. If you're still not happy, you can consider shooting in Camera Raw format, as long as your camera can do so. Elements has wonderful Camera Raw support, enabling you to process your images to your exact specifications. Chances are that if you can't find the tools to correct and repair your images in Elements, they're probably beyond salvaging.

REMEMBER

With information in Chapter 9 and this chapter at your fingertips, try to employ some kind of logical workflow when you tackle the correction and repair of your images:

1. **Crop, straighten, and resize your images, if necessary.**

2. **After you have the images in their proper physical state, correct the lighting and establish good tonal range for your shadows, highlights, and midtones in order to display the greatest detail possible.**

   Often, just correcting the lighting solves minor color problems. If not, move on to adjusting the color balance.

3. **Eliminate any color casts and adjust the saturation, if necessary.**

4. **Grab the retouching tools, such as the healing tools and filters, to retouch any flaws.**

5. **Sharpen your image if you feel that it could use a boost in clarity and sharpness.**

   By following these steps and allocating a few minutes of your time, you should be able to get all your images in shape to print, post, and share with family and friends.

Adjusting Lighting

Elements has several simple, manual tools you can use to fix lighting if the Auto tools, described in Chapter 9, didn't work or were just too, well, automatic for you. You'll find that the manual tools offer more control over adjusting overall contrast as well as bringing out details in shadow, midtones, and highlight areas of your images.

Fixing lighting with Shadows/Highlights

The Shadows/Highlights command offers a quick and easy method of correcting over- and underexposed areas. This feature works especially well with images shot in bright, overhead light or in light coming from the back (backlit). These images usually suffer from having the subject partially or completely surrounded in shadows, such as the original image (left) in Figure 10-1.

To use the Shadows/Highlights adjustment, follow these steps:

1. **In Full Edit mode (Standard Edit mode on the Mac), choose Enhance⇨ Adjust Lighting⇨Shadows/Highlights. Make sure that the Preview check box is selected.**

   In either Quick Fix or Full Edit mode (Standard Edit mode on the Mac), when the dialog box appears, the correction is automatically applied in your preview.

2. **If the automatic adjustment doesn't quite do the job, move the sliders (or enter a value) to adjust the amount of correction for your shadows (dark areas), highlights (light areas), and midtones (middle-toned areas).**

Before

Adjusted with the
Shadows/Highlights command

Figure 10-1: Correct the lighting in your images with the Shadows/Highlights adjustment.

Remember that you want to try to reveal more detail in the dark and light areas of your image. If, after you do so, your image still looks like it needs more correction, add or delete contrast in your midtone areas.

3. Click OK to apply the adjustment and close the dialog box.

If you want to start over, press Alt (Option on the Mac) and click the Reset button (previously the Cancel button).

Using Brightness/Contrast

Despite its aptly descriptive moniker, the Brightness/Contrast command doesn't do a great job of brightening (making an image darker or lighter) or adding or deleting contrast. Initially, users tend to be drawn to this command because of its appropriate name and ease of use. But, after users realize its limitations, they move on to better tools with more controls, such as Shadows/Highlights and Levels.

The problem with the Brightness/Contrast command is that it applies the adjustment equally to all areas of your image. For example, you may have a photo that has some highlights that need darkening but all the midtones and shadows are perfect. The Brightness slider isn't smart enough to recognize that, so when you start to darken the highlights in your image, the midtones and shadows also become darker. To compensate for the unwanted darkening, you try to adjust the Contrast, which doesn't fix the problem.

The moral is, if you want to use the Brightness/Contrast command, select only the areas that need the correction, as shown in Figure 10-2. (For more on selections, see Chapter 7.) Then choose Enhance⇨Adjust Lighting⇨Brightness/Contrast.

Figure 10-2: The Brightness/Contrast adjustment is best reserved for correcting selected areas (left) rather than the entire image (right).

Pinpointing proper contrast with Levels

If you want real horsepower when it comes to correcting the brightness and contrast (and even the color) in your image, look no further than the Levels command. Granted, the dialog box is a tad more complex than what you find with the other lighting and color adjustment commands, but when you understand how it works, it can be downright user-friendly.

You can get a taste of what Levels can do by using Auto Levels, detailed in Chapter 9. The Levels command, its manual cousin, offers much more control. And, unlike the primitive Brightness/Contrast control, Levels enables you to darken or lighten 256 different tones. Keep in mind that Levels can be used on your entire image, a single layer, or a selected area. You can also apply the Levels command by using an adjustment layer, as described in Chapter 8.

If you're serious about image editing, the Levels command is one tool you want to seriously figure out how to use. Here's how it works:

1. **In Full Edit mode (Standard Edit mode on the Mac), choose Enhance⇨ Adjust Lighting⇨Levels.**

The Levels dialog box appears, displaying a *histogram*. This graph displays how the pixels of the image are distributed at each of the 256 available brightness levels. Shadows are shown on the left side of the histogram, midtones are in the middle, and highlights are on the right. Note that, in addition to viewing the histogram of the composite RGB channel (the entire image), you can view the histogram of just the Red, Green, or Blue channel by selecting one of them from the Channel drop-down menu.

Although you generally make changes to the entire document by using the RGB channel, you can apply changes to any one of an image's component color channels by selecting the specific channel in the Channel pop-up menu. You can also make adjustments to just selected areas, which can be helpful when one area of your image needs adjusting and others don't.

2. **In Full Edit mode (Standard Edit mode on the Mac), choose Window⇨ Info to open the Info palette.**

3. **Set the black and white points manually by using the eyedroppers in the dialog box. Select the White Eyedropper tool and move the cursor over the image.**

4. **Look at the Info palette and try to find the lightest white in the image. Select that point by clicking it.**

5. **Repeat Steps 3 and 4 using the Black Eyedropper tool and trying to find the darkest black in the image.**

When you set the pure black and pure white points, the remaining pixels are redistributed between those two points.

You can also reset the white and black points by moving the position of the white and black triangles on the input sliders (just under the histogram). Or, you can enter values in the Input Levels boxes. The three boxes represent the black, gray, and white triangles, respectively. Use the numbers 0 to 255 in the white and black boxes.

6. **Use the Gray Eyedropper tool to remove any color casts. Select a neutral gray portion of your image, one in which the Info palette shows equal values of red, green, and blue.**

If your image is grayscale, you can't use the Gray Eyedropper tool.

If you're not sure where there's a neutral gray, you can also remove a color cast by choosing a color channel from the Channel pop-up menu and doing one of the following:

- Choose the Red channel and drag the midtone slider to the right to add cyan or to the left to add red.

- Choose the Green channel and drag the midtone slider to the right to add magenta or to the left to add green.

- Choose the Blue channel and drag the midtone slider to the right to add yellow or to the left to add blue.

7. **If your image requires it, adjust the output sliders at the bottom of the Levels dialog box.**

   Moving the black triangle to the right reduces the contrast in the shadows and lightens the image. Moving the white triangle to the left reduces the contrast in the highlights and darkens the image.

8. **Adjust the midtones (or gamma values) with the gray triangle input slider.**

   The default value for gamma is 1.0. Drag the triangle to the left to lighten midtones, and drag to the right to darken them. You can also enter a value.

9. **Click OK to apply your settings and close the dialog box.**

   Your image should be greatly improved, as shown in Figure 10-3.

Figure 10-3: Improve the contrast of an image with the intelligent Levels command.

When you click the Auto button, Elements applies the same adjustments as the Auto Levels command, explained in Chapter 9. Note the changes, and subsequent pixel redistribution, made to the histogram after you click it.

Adjusting Color

Getting the color you want sometimes seems about as attainable as winning the state lottery. Sometimes, an unexpected color cast (a shift in color) can be avoided at the shooting stage, for example, by using (or not using, in some cases) a flash or lens filter. After the fact, you can usually do a pretty good job of correcting the color with one of the many Elements adjustments. Occasionally, you may want to change the color of your image to create a certain special effect. Conversely, you also may want to strip out the color from your image altogether to create a vintage feel. Remember that all these color adjustments can be applied to your entire image, a single layer, or just a selection. Whatever your color needs, they'll no doubt be met in Elements.

TIP

If you shoot your photos in the Camera Raw file format, you can open and fix your files in the Camera Raw dialog box. Remember that Camera Raw files haven't been processed by your camera. You're in total control of the color and the exposure. For more on Camera Raw, see Chapter 4.

Removing color casts automatically

If you ever took a photo in an office or classroom and got a funky green tinge in your image, it was probably the result of the overhead fluorescent lighting. To eliminate this green color cast, you can apply the Color Cast command. This feature is designed to adjust the image's overall color and remove the cast.

Follow these short steps to correct your image:

1. **Choose Enhance⇨Adjust Color⇨Remove Color Cast in either Quick Fix or Full Edit mode (Standard Edit mode on the Mac).**

   The Remove Color Cast dialog box appears. Move the dialog box to better view your image.

2. **Click an area in your photo that should be white, black, or neutral gray, as shown in Figure 10-4. In our example, we clicked the sky in the image on the left.**

   The colors in the image are adjusted according to the color you choose. Which color should you choose? The answer depends on the subject matter of your image. Feel free to experiment. Your adjustment is merely a preview at this point and isn't applied until you click OK. If you goof up, click the Reset button, and your image reverts to its unadjusted state.

3. **If you're satisfied with the adjustment, click OK to accept it and close the dialog box.**

Figure 10-4: Get rid of nasty color shifts with the Remove Color Cast command.

If the Remove Color Cast command doesn't cut it, try applying a photo filter (described in the later section "Adjusting color temperature with photo filters"). For example, if your photo has too much green, try applying a magenta filter.

Adjusting with Hue/Saturation

The Hue/Saturation command enables you to adjust the colors in your image based on their hue, saturation, and lightness. *Hue* is the color in your image. *Saturation* is the intensity, or richness, of that color. And, *lightness* controls the brightness value.

Follow these steps to adjust color by using the Hue/Saturation command:

1. **In either Quick Fix or Full Edit mode (Standard Edit mode on the Mac), choose Enhance⇨Adjust Color⇨Adjust Hue/Saturation.**

   The Hue/Saturation dialog box appears. Be sure to select the Preview check box so that you can view your adjustments.

2. **Select all the colors (Master) from the Edit pop-up menu, or choose one color to adjust.**

3. **Drag the slider for one or more of the following attributes to adjust the colors as described:**

   • *Hue:* Shifts all the colors clockwise (drag right) or counterclockwise (drag left) around the color wheel.

   • *Saturation:* Increases (drag right) or decreases (drag left) the richness of the colors. Note that dragging all the way to the left gives you the appearance of a grayscale image.

   • *Lightness:* Increases the brightness values by adding white (drag right) or decreases the brightness values by adding black (drag left).

   The top color bar at the bottom of the dialog box represents the colors in their order on the color wheel before you make any changes. The lower color bar displays the colors after you make your adjustments.

   When you select an individual color to adjust, sliders appear between the color bars so that you can define the range of color to be adjusted. You can select, add, or subtract colors from the range by choosing one of the Eyedropper tools and clicking in the image.

   The Hue/Saturation dialog box also lets you colorize images, a useful option for creating sepia-colored images.

4. **(Optional) Check the Colorize option to change the colors in your image to a new, single color. Drag the Hue slider to change the color to your desired hue.**

The pure white and black pixels remain unchanged, and the intermediate gray pixels are colorized.

Use the Hue/Saturation command, with the Colorize option, to create tinted photos, such as the one shown in Figure 10-5. You can also make selections in a grayscale image and apply a different tint to each selection. This can be especially fun with portraits. Tinted images can create vintage or moody feels and can transform even mediocre photos into something more special.

PhotoDisc/Getty Images

Figure 10-5: Adjust the color, intensity, or brightness of your image with the Hue/Saturation command.

Eliminating color with Remove Color

Despite all the talk in this chapter about color, we realize that there may be times when you don't want *any* color. With the Element Remove Color command, you can easily eliminate all the color from an image, layer, or selection. In Figure 10-6, we made a selection on the right side of the image and applied the Remove Color command. To use this one-step command, simply choose Enhance⇨ Adjust Color⇨Remove Color.

Figure 10-6: Wash away all color with the Remove Color command.

Sometimes, stripping away color with this command can leave your image *flat,* or low in contrast. If this is the case, adjust the contrast using one of Element's many lighting fixes such as Auto Levels, Auto Contrast, or Levels.

Elements 5.0 introduces the new feature Convert to Black and White, shown in Figure 10-7. As with the Remove Color command, you can convert to black and white a selection, a layer, or an entire image. But, rather than just arbitrarily strip color as the Remove Color command does, the Convert to Black and White command enables you to select a conversion method by first choosing an image style. To further tweak the results, you can move the Intensity slider to adjust the More or Less thumbnails. Finally, add or subtract colors or contrast by clicking those thumbnails until your grayscale image looks the way you want. Note that you aren't really adding color; you're simply altering the amount of data in the color channels. For more information on channels, see Chapter 2.

Switching colors with Replace Color

The Replace Color command enables you to replace designated colors in your image with other colors. You first select the colors you want to replace by creating a *mask,* which is a selection made by designating white (selected), black (unselected), and gray (partially selected) areas. See Chapter 7 for more details on masks. You can then adjust the hue and or saturation of those selected colors.

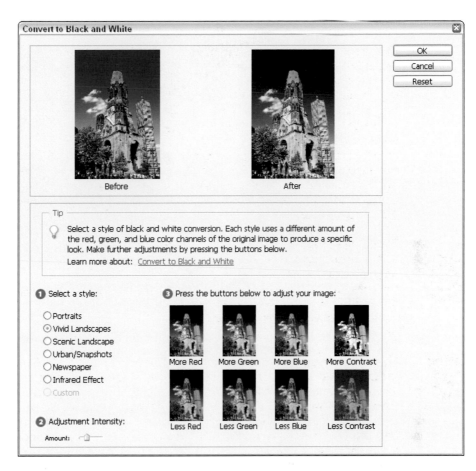

Figure 10-7: Change color photos to grayscale ones with the Convert to Black and White command.

Follow these steps to get on your way to replacing color:

1. **In Quick Fix or Full Edit mode (Standard Edit mode on the Mac), choose Enhance⇨Adjust Color⇨Replace Color.**

   The Replace Color dialog box appears. Make sure to select the Preview check box.

2. **Choose either Selection or Image:**

   • *Selection:* Shows the mask in the Preview window. The unselected areas are black, partially selected areas are gray, and selected areas are white.

   • *Image:* Shows the actual image in the Preview window.

3. **Click the colors you want to select in either the image or the Preview window.**

4. **Press the Shift key and click, or use the plus (+) Eyedropper tool, to add more colors.**

5. **Press the Alt key (Option key on the Mac) or use the minus (–) Eyedropper tool to delete colors.**

6. **To add colors similar to the ones you select, use the Fuzziness slider to fine-tune your selection, adding or deleting from the selection based on the Fuzziness value.**

7. **Move the Hue and or Saturation sliders to change the color or color richness, respectively. Move the Lightness slider to lighten or darken the image.**

   Be careful to use a light hand (no pun intended) with the Lightness slider. You can reduce the tonal range too much and end up with a mess.

8. **View the result in the Image window. If you're satisfied, click OK to apply the settings and close the dialog box.**

   Figure 10-8 shows how we substituted the color of our tulips to change them from orange to yellow.

Corbis Digital Stock

Figure 10-8: The Replace Color command enables you to replace one color with another.

Correcting with Color Curves

Elements borrowed a much-used feature from Photoshop named Curves. However, it added the word *Color* and took away some of its sophistication. Nevertheless, the Color Curves adjustment attempts to improve the tonal range in color images by making adjustments to highlights, shadows, and midtones in each color channel (for more on channels, see Chapter 2). Try using this command on images where the foreground elements appear overly dark due to backlighting. Conversely, the adjustment is also designed to correct images that appear overexposed and washed out.

Here's how to use this new adjustment on a selection, a layer, or an entire image:

1. **In Quick Fix or Full Edit mode (Standard Edit mode on the Mac), choose Enhance⇨Adjust Color⇨Adjust Color Curves.**

   The Adjust Color Curves dialog box appears. Make sure to select the Preview check box. Move the dialog box to the side so that you can view the Image window while making adjustments.

2. **Various curve adjustments appear in the Samples area. Click the thumbnails to make your desired adjustments while viewing your image.**

3. **If you need greater precision, click Advanced Options to display additional highlight, brightness, contrast, and shadow adjustment sliders, as shown in Figure 10-9. Adjust the sliders as desired.**

   The graph on the left represents the distribution of tones in your image. When you first access the Color Curves dialog box, the tonal range of your image is represented by a straight line. As you drag the sliders, the straight line is altered and the tonal range is adjusted accordingly.

4. **Click OK when you have adjusted the image satisfactorily. To start over, click the Reset button. Check out Figure 10-10 for before-and-after images.**

Adjusting skin tones

Occasionally, you may find that the loved ones in your photos have taken on a rather sickly shade of green, red, or some other non-flesh-colored tone. To rectify that problem, Elements has a command specifically designed to adjust the overall color in the image and get skin tones back to a natural shade.

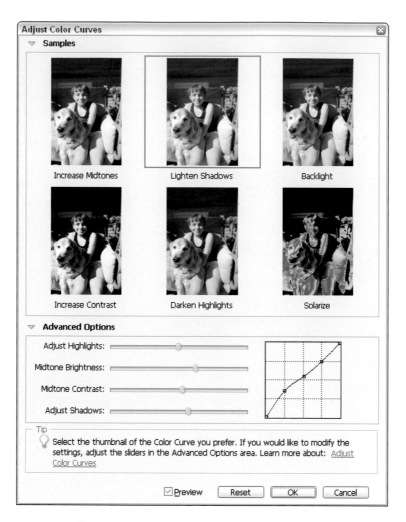

Figure 10-9: The new Color Curves adjustment provides both basic and advanced adjustment controls.

Here's how to use this feature:

1. **Open your image in Quick Fix or Full Edit mode (Standard Edit mode on the Mac), select the Preview check box, and do one or both of the following:**

Original   After the Color Curves Adjustment

Figure 10-10: Color Curves improves tonal range in color images.

- *Select the layer that needs to be adjusted.* If you don't have any layers, your entire image is adjusted.

- *Select your desired areas of skin that need to be adjusted.* Only the selected areas is adjusted. This is a good way to go if you're happy with the color of your other elements and you just want to tweak the skin tones. For more on selection techniques, see Chapter 7.

2. **Choose Enhance⇨Adjust Color⇨Adjust Color for Skin Tone.**

   The Adjust Color for Skin Tone dialog box appears, as shown in Figure 10-11.

3. **In the Image window, click the portion of skin that needs to be corrected.**

   The command adjusts the color of the skin tone as well as the color in the overall image, layer, or selection, depending on what you selected in Step 1.

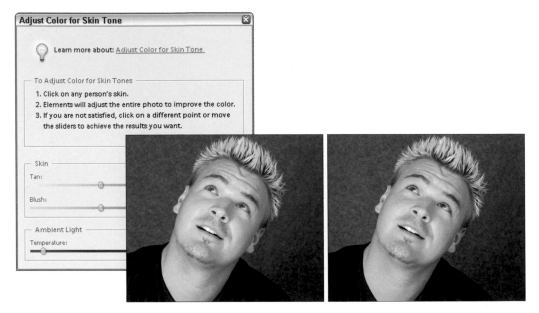

PhotoSpin

Figure 10-11: Give your friends and family a complexion makeover with the new Adjust Color for Skin Tone command.

4. **If you're not satisfied with the results, click another area or fiddle with the Skin and Ambient Light sliders:**

   • *Tan:* Adds or removes the amount of brown in the skin.

   • *Blush:* Adds or removes the amount of red in the skin.

   • *Temperature:* Adjusts the overall color of the skin, making it warmer (right toward red) or cooler (left toward blue).

5. **When you're happy with the correction, click OK to apply the adjustment and close the dialog box.**

   To start anew, click the Reset button. And, of course, to bail out completely, click Cancel.

Defringing layers

A telltale sign of haphazardly composited images is selections with fringe. We don't mean the cute kind hanging from your leather jacket or upholstery; we mean the unattractive kind that consists of those background pixels that surround the edges of your selections, as shown in Figure 10-12. Inevitably, when you move or paste a selection, some of the background pixels are bound to go along for the ride. These pixels are referred to as a *fringe* or *halo*. Luckily, the new Defringe command replaces the color of the fringe pixels with the colors of neighboring pixels that don't contain the background color. In our example, we plucked the boat out of a white studio background and placed it on an image of water. Some of the background pixels were included in our selection and appear as a white fringe. When we apply the Defringe command, those white fringe pixels are changed to colors of nearby pixels, such as blue or red, as shown in Figure 10-12.

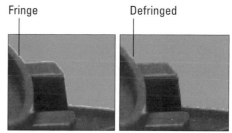

Fringe   Defringed

PhotoSpin

Figure 10-12: Remove the colored halo around your selections with the Defringe command.

Here are the steps to defringe your selection:

1. **In Quick Fix or Full Edit mode (Standard Edit mode on the Mac), copy and paste a selection onto a new or existing layer, or drag and drop a selection onto a new document.**

   For more on selections, see Chapter 7.

2. **Choose Enhance⇨Adjust Color⇨Defringe Layer.**

   The Defringe dialog box appears.

3. **Enter a value for the number of pixels that need to be converted.**

   Try entering 1 or 2 first to see whether that does the trick. If not, you may need to enter a slightly higher value.

4. **Click OK to accept the value and close the dialog box.**

Correcting with Color Variations

Although we give you in this chapter several ways to eliminate color casts in an image, now we throw in one more. The Variations command is a digital color-correction feature that has been around for years and is largely unchanged. That's probably because it's one of those great features that's easy to use and easy to understand, and it works. The command works by enabling you to make corrections by visually comparing thumbnails of color variations of your image. You may use this command when you're not quite sure what's wrong with the color or what kind of color cast your image has.

Here's how to use the Color Variations command:

1. **Choose Enhance⇨Adjust Color⇨Color Variations in Quick Fix or Full Edit mode (Standard Edit mode on the Mac).**

   The Color Variations dialog box appears, displaying a preview of your original image (before) and the corrected image (after), as shown in Figure 10-13.

2. **Select your desired tonal range or color richness (if you're unsure which range to select, start with the Midtones):**

   • *Shadows, Midtones, Highlights:* Adjusts the dark, middle, or light areas in the image, respectively.

   • *Saturation:* Adjusts the color intensity or richness, making colors more intense (saturated) or less intense (desaturated). If your image is faded from time, be sure to increase the saturation after you correct any color cast issues.

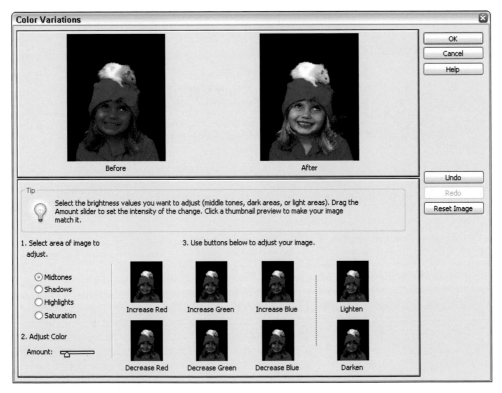

PhotoSpin

Figure 10-13: Color Variations enables you to visually correct your images by comparing thumbnails.

Usually, just correcting the midtones is enough to get your image's color in order, but if it's not, you can always adjust the shadows and highlights as well.

3. **Specify how much adjustment you want with the Adjust Color slider.**

   Drag left to decrease the amount of adjustment, and drag right to increase the amount.

4. **If you selected Midtones, Shadows, or Highlights in Step 2, adjust the color by clicking the various Increase or Decrease (color) buttons. Click more than once if your initial application wasn't sufficient to correct the problem.**

   Be sure to keep an eye on the After thumbnail, which reflects your corrections as you make them.

5. **Click the Darken or Lighten buttons to make the colors a little darker or lighter.**

6. **If you selected Saturation in Step 2, click the Less Saturation or More Saturation buttons.**

7. **If you make a mistake — or several mistakes, for that matter — click the Undo button.**

   The Color Variations dialog box supports multiple levels of undo. If you botch something, you can always click the Reset Image button to start again. Keep in mind that you cannot undo the Reset Image command after you click it. Click Cancel to bail out entirely.

8. **To apply your color adjustments and close the dialog box, click OK.**

The Color Variations command is a great tool to correct those old, faded, green- (or some other unwanted color) tinted circa yesteryear photos. Color Variations allows you to easily correct the color and saturation of these precious, but damaged, images. Remember to either decrease the offending color or add the color that's the opposite of the cast in the image. If it's too red, add green and vice versa.

Adjusting color temperature with photo filters

Light has its own color temperature. A photo shot in a higher-color temperature of light makes an image blue. Conversely, an image shot in a lower-color temperature makes a photo yellow. In the old days, photographers used to place colored glass filters in front of their camera lenses to adjust the color temperature of the light. They did this to either warm up or cool down photos, or to just add a hint of color for subtle special effects. Elements gives you the digital version of these filters with the Photo Filter command.

To apply the Photo Filter adjustment, follow these steps:

1. **Choose Filter➪Adjustments➪Photo Filter in Full Edit mode (Standard Edit mode on the Mac).**

   The Photo Filter dialog box appears.

   Note that you can also apply the photo filter to an individual layer by creating a photo-filter adjustment layer. For details, see Chapter 8.

2. **In the dialog box, select Filter to choose a preset filter from the drop-down list, or select Color to select your own filter color from the Color Picker.**

   Here's a brief description of each of the preset filters:

   - *Warming Filter (85), (81), and (LBA):* Adjusts the white balance in an image to make the colors warmer, or more yellow. Filter (81) is like (85) and (LBA), but is best used for minor adjustments. In our example in Figure 10-14, we used the Warming Filter (85) to warm up an overly cool winter shot.

   - *Cooling Filter (80), (82), and (LBB):* Also adjusts the white balance that's shown, but instead makes the colors cooler, or bluer. Filter (82) is like (80) and (LBB), but is designed for slight adjustments.

   - *Red, Orange, Yellow, and so on:* The various color filters adjust the hue, or color, of a photo. Choose a color filter to try to eliminate a color cast or to apply a special effect.

Figure 10-14: Apply a Photo Filter to adjust the color temperature of an image.

3. **Adjust the Density option to specify the amount of color applied to your image.**

4. **Check Preserve Luminosity to prevent the photo filter from darkening your image.**

5. **Click OK to apply your filter and close the dialog box.**

Mapping your colors

Elements provides some commands referred to as *color mappers,* which change the colors in your image by mapping them to other values. The color mappers are found on the Filter➪Adjustments submenu. Figure 10-15 shows an example of each command, which is also briefly described in the following subsections.

Equalize　　　Gradient Map　　　Invert

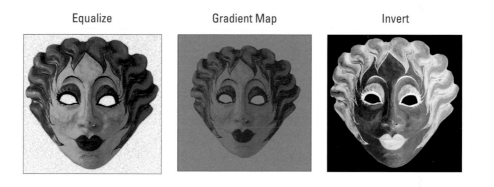

Threshold　　　Posterize

Figure 10-15: Change the colors in your image by remapping them to other values.

Equalize

This mapper first locates the lightest and darkest pixels in the image and assigns them values of white and black. It then redistributes all the remaining pixels among the grayscale values. The exact effect depends on your individual image.

Gradient Map

This command maps the tonal range of an image to the colors of your chosen gradient. For example, colors such as orange, green, and purple are mapped to the shadows, highlight, and midtone areas.

Invert

This command reverses all the colors in your image, creating a kind of negative. Black reverses to white, and colors convert to their complementary hues (blue goes to yellow, red goes to green, and so on).

Threshold

Threshold makes your image black and white, with all pixels that are brighter than a value you specify represented as white, and all pixels that are darker than that value as black. You can change the threshold level to achieve different high-contrast effects.

The Threshold command can come in handy when you need to clean up scans of line art, such as hand-drawn sketches, people's signatures, pages from a book, or even sheet music. Often, when you scan things on paper, the slight color from the paper appears as a dull gray background in the scan. By applying the Threshold command, you can adjust the tones in your image to black and white and drop out the gray. Simply move the slider to get your desired balance of white and black areas.

Posterize

This command reduces the number of colors in your image. Choose a value between 2 and 255 colors. Lower values create an illustrative, poster look, and higher values produce a more photo-realistic image.

Adjusting Clarity

After your image has the right contrast and color and you fix any flaws, as described in Chapter 9, you're ready to finally work on the overall clarity of that image. Although you may have fixed the nitpicky little blemishes with the healing tools, if your image suffers from an overall problem like dust, scratches, or *artifacts* (blocky pixels or halos), you may need to employ the help of a filter. After you totally clean up your image, your last chore is to give it a good sharpening. Why wait until the bitter end to do so? That's because sometimes, while you're improving the contrast and color and getting rid of flaws, you can reduce the clarity and sharpness of an image. So, you want to be sure that your image is as soft as it's going to get before you tackle your sharpening tasks. On the other hand, also be aware that sharpening itself increases contrast, so depending on how much of your image you're sharpening, you may need to go back and fine-tune it by using the lighting adjustments described previously in this chapter.

Finally, with all this talk about sharpening, we know that you may find it strange when we say that you may also need to occasionally blur your image. Blurring can be done to eliminate unpleasant patterns that occur during scanning, soften distracting backgrounds to give a better focal point, or even to create the illusion of motion.

Removing noise, artifacts, dust, and scratches

Surprisingly, the tools you want to use to eliminate junk from your images are found on the Filter⇨Noise filter submenu in Standard Edit mode. With the exception of the Add Noise filter, the others help to hide noise, dust, scratches, and artifacts. Here's the list of junk removers:

- **Despeckle:** Decreases the contrast, without affecting the edges, to make the dust in your image less pronounced. You may notice a slight blurring of your image (that's what's hiding the junk), but hopefully the edges are still sharp.

- **Dust & Scratches:** As its name says, hides dust and scratches by blurring those areas of your image that contain the nastiness (it looks for harsh transitions in tone). Specify your desired Radius value, which is the size of the area to be blurred. Also specify the Threshold value, which determines how much contrast between pixels must be present before they are blurred.

  Use this filter with restraint because it can obliterate detail and make your image go from bad to worse.

- **Median:** Reduces contrast around dust spots. The process the filter goes through is rather technical, so suffice it to say that the light spots darken, the dark spots lighten, and the rest of the image isn't changed. Specify your desired radius, which is the size of the area to be adjusted.

- **Reduce Noise:** Designed to remove luminance noise and artifacts from your images. We used this filter to correct the original image (on the left) in Figure 10-16. *Luminance noise* is grayscale noise that makes images look overly grainy. Specify these options to reduce the noise in your image:

- *Strength:* Specify the amount of noise reduction.

- *Preserve Details:* A higher percentage preserves edges and details but reduces the amount of noise that's removed.

- *Reduce Color Noise:* Remove random colored pixels.

- *Remove JPEG Artifact:* Remove the blocks and halos that can occur from low-quality JPEG compression.

Figure 10-16: Use the Reduce Noise filter to remove noise and artifacts.

Blurring when you need to

It may sound odd that anyone would intentionally want to blur an image. But, if your photo is overly grainy or suffers from a nasty moiré pattern (described in the following list), you may need to blur the image to correct the problem. And, occasionally, you may even want to blur the background of an image to deemphasize distractions or to make the foreground elements appear sharper and provide a better focal point.

All the blurring tools are found on the Filter➪Blur menu in Full Edit mode (Standard Edit mode on the Mac), with the exception of the Blur tool, which is explained in Chapter 9:

✔ **Average:** This one-step filter calculates the average value of the image or selection and fills the area with that average value. You can use it for smoothing overly noisy areas in your image.

✓ **Blur:** Another one-step filter, this one applies a fixed amount of blurring to the whole image.

✓ **Blur More:** This one-step blur filter gives the same effect as Blur, but more intensely.

✓ **Motion Blur:** This filter mimics the blur given off by moving objects. Specify the angle of motion and the distance of the blur. Make sure to select the Preview check box to see the effect as you enter your values.

✓ **Radial Blur:** Need to simulate a moving Ferris wheel or some other round object? This filter produces a circular blur effect. Specify the amount of blur you want. Choose the Spin method to blur along concentric circular lines, as shown in the thumbnail. Or, choose Zoom to blur along radial lines and mimic the effect of zooming in to your image. Specify your desired Quality level. Because the Radial Blur filter is notoriously slow, Elements gives you the option of Draft (fast but grainy), Good, or Best (slower but smoother). The difference between Good and Best is evident only on larger, higher-resolution images. Finally, indicate where you want the center of your blur by moving the blur diagram thumbnail.

✓ **Smart Blur:** This filter provides several options to enable you to specify how the blur is applied. Specify a value for the radius and threshold, both defined later in this chapter, in the "Sharpening for better focus" section. Start with a lower value for both and adjust from there. Choose a quality setting from the pop-up menu. Choose a mode setting. Normal blurs the entire image or selection. Edge Only blurs only the edges of your elements and uses black and white in the blurred pixels. Overlay Edge also blurs just the edges, but it applies only white to the blurred pixels.

✓ **Gaussian Blur:** The last Blur filter we discuss is probably the one you'll use most often. It offers a Radius setting to let you adjust the amount of blurring you desire.

Use the Gaussian Blur filter to camouflage moiré patterns on scanned images. A *moiré pattern* is caused when you scan halftone images. A *halftone* is created when a continuous tone image, such as a photo, is digitized and converted into a screen pattern of repeating lines (usually between 85 and 150 lines per inch) and then printed. When you then scan that halftone, a second pattern results and is overlaid on the original pattern. These two different patterns bump heads and create a nasty moiré pattern. The Gaussian Blur filter doesn't eliminate the moiré — it simply merges the dots and reduces the appearance of the pattern, as shown in Figure 10-17. Play with the Radius slider until you get an acceptable tradeoff between less moiré and less focus. If you happen to have a descreen filter built into your scanning software, you can use that as well during the scanning of the halftone image.

Figure 10-17: Use the Gaussian Blur filter to reduce moiré patterns caused by scanning halftones.

Sharpening for better focus

Of course, if your images don't need any contrast, color, and flaw fixing, feel free to jump right into sharpening. Sometimes, images captured by a scanner or a digital camera are a little soft, and it's not due to any tonal adjustments. Occasionally, you may even want to sharpen a selected area in your image just so that it stands out more.

First, let us say that you can't really improve the focus of an image after it's captured. But, you can do a pretty good job of faking it. All sharpening tools work by increasing the contrast between adjacent pixels. This increased contrast causes the edges to appear more distinct, thereby giving the illusion that the focus is improved, as shown in Figure 10-18.

Figure 10-18: Sharpening mimics an increase in focus by increasing contrast between adjacent pixels.

Elements eliminated the less-than-useful one-step Sharpen filters in favor of a new, smarter sharpening command. Thankfully, Elements also retained a long-time favorite command, Unsharp Mask. Remember that you can also use the Sharpen tool for small areas, as described in Chapter 9. Here's a description of the two sharpening commands:

✔ **Unsharp Mask:** If you're looking for this filter on the Filter menu in Version 5.0, don't bother. It moved to the Enhance menu with the new sharpening command. Unsharp Mask, which gets its odd name from a darkroom technique, is the sharpening tool of choice. It gives you several options that enable you to control the amount of sharpening and the width of the areas to be sharpened. Use them to pinpoint your desired sharpening:

  • *Amount:* Specify your desired amount (from 1 to 500 percent) of edge sharpening. The higher the value, the more contrast between pixels around the edges. Start with a value of 100 percent (or less), which usually gives good contrast without appearing overly grainy.

  • *Radius:* Specify the width (from .1 to 250 pixels) of the edges that the filter will sharpen. The higher the value, the wider the edge. The value you use is largely based on the resolution of your image. Low-resolution images require a smaller radius value. High-resolution images require a higher value.

    Be warned that specifying a value that's too high overemphasizes the edges of your image and makes it appear too "contrasty" or even "goopy" around the edges.

    A good guideline in selecting a starting radius value is to divide your image's resolution by 150. For example, if you have a 300 ppi image, set the radius at 2 and then use your eye to adjust from there.

  • *Threshold:* Specify the difference in brightness (from 0 to 255) that must be present between adjacent pixels before the edge is sharpened. A lower value sharpens edges with very little contrast difference. Higher values sharpen only when adjacent pixels are very different in contrast. We recommend leaving Threshold set at 0 unless your image is very grainy. Increasing the value too high can cause unnatural transitions between sharpened and unsharpened areas.

Occasionally, the values you enter for Amount and Radius may sharpen the image effectively but in turn create excess *grain,* or noise, in your image. You can sometimes reduce this noise by increasing the Threshold value.

Adjust Sharpness: When you're looking for precision in your image sharpening, Unsharp Mask is one option. The new Adjust Sharpness command, shown in Figure 10-19, is the other. This feature enables you to control the amount of sharpening applied to shadow and highlight areas. It also allows you to choose from various sharpening algorithms.

Here are the various options you can specify:

- *Amount and Radius:* See the two descriptions under the preceding Unsharp Mask bullet.

- *Remove:* Choose your sharpening algorithm. Gaussian Blur is the algorithm used for the Unsharp Mask command. Lens Blur detects detail in the image and attempts to respect the details while reducing the nasty halos that can occur with sharpening. Motion Blur tries to sharpen the blurring that occurs with moving the camera (or if your subject doesn't sit still).

- *Angle:* Specify the direction of motion for the Motion Blur algorithm, described in the preceding Remove bullet.

- *More Refined:* Runs the algorithm more slowly for better accuracy.

Figure 10-19: The new Adjust Sharpness command.

Part IV
Exploring Your Inner Artist

The 5th Wave   By Rich Tennant

"I'm going to assume that most of you — but not all of you — understand that this session on 'masking' has to do with Photoshop Elements."

In this part . . .

*I*n addition to correcting photos to improve their appearance, you can delve into the world of the Photoshop Elements artist, where you can use tools to draw and paint on existing photos or create new, blank documents and create your own drawings. The tools available to you rival an artist's analog tools, and Photoshop Elements capabilities are limited only by your imagination. In this part, you find out how to apply different artistic effects by using many tools and customizing them for your own use, and you get some helpful tips to create some dazzling images.

In addition to describing the artistic effects you can apply to your photos, this section tells you how to handle working with text. When it comes time for creating a poster, an advertisement, or some Web icons, the text features in Elements offer you many options for creating headline type, body copy, and special type effects.

Playing with Filters, Effects, Styles, and More

*A*fter giving your images a makeover — edges cropped, color corrected, flaws repaired, focus sharpened — you may want to get them all gussied up for a night out on the town. You can do just that with filters, effects, layer styles, and blend modes. These tools enable you to add that touch of emphasis, drama, whimsy, or just plain goofy fun. We're the first to admit that often the simplest art (and that includes photographs) is the best. That gorgeous landscape shot or the portrait that perfectly captures the expression on a child's happy face is something you may want to leave unembellished. But, for the times when a little artistic experimentation is in order, turn to this chapter as your guide.

Having Fun with Filters

Filters have been around since the early days of digital imaging, when Photoshop was just a little bitty program. *Filters,* also called *plug-ins* because they can be installed or removed independently, change the look of your image in a variety of ways, as shown in Figure 11-1. They can correct less-than-perfect images by making them appear sharper or by covering up flaws, as described in Chapter 10. Or, they can enhance your images by making them appear as though they were painted, tiled, photocopied, or lit by spotlights. Just make sure to create a backup of your original image if you plan on saving your filtered one. This section gives you the basics on how to apply a filter and gives you a few filtering tips.

Original	Unsharp Mask filter	Water Paper filter

Figure 11-1: Use filters to correct image imperfections or to completely transform them.

Applying filters

You can apply a filter in three ways:

- **In either Full Edit (Standard Edit on the Mac) or Quick Fix mode:** From the Filter menu, choose your desired filter category, and then select a specific filter.

- **In Full Edit mode only (Standard Edit on the Mac):** Choose Window⇨ Artwork and Effects to open the palette. Click the Apply Effects, Filters and Layer Styles, the middle button at the top of the palette. Select Filters from the drop-down list in the upper-left corner of the palette. Select your filter category from the drop-down list in the upper-right corner of the palette. Double-click the thumbnail of your desired filter or drag the filter onto your image window.

- **In either Full Edit (Standard Edit on the Mac) or Quick Fix mode:** Choose Filter⇨Filter Gallery to apply one or more filters in a flexible editing environment. The Filter Gallery is described later in this chapter.

You cannot apply filters to images that are in Bitmap or Index Color mode. And, some filters don't work on images in Grayscale mode. For a refresher on color modes, see Chapter 3.

Corrective or destructive filters

Although there are no hard and fast rules, most digital-imaging folks classify filters into two basic categories, *corrective* and *destructive:*

- **Corrective filters** usually fix some kind of image problem. They adjust color, improve focus, remove dust or artifacts, and so on. Don't get us wrong — pixels are still modified. It's just that the basic appearance of the image remains the same, albeit hopefully improved. Two of the most popular corrective filters, Sharpen and Blur, are covered in Chapter 10.

- **Destructive filters** are used to create some kind of special effect. Pixels are also modified, but the image may look quite a bit different from its original. These kinds of filters create effects such as textures, brush strokes, mosaics, lights, and clouds. They can also distort an image with waves, spheres, and ripples.

One-step or multistep filters

All corrective and destructive filters are either one-step filters or multistep filters. One-step filters have no options and no dialog boxes; select the filter and watch the magic happen. Multistep filters act almost like mini-applications. Choose the filter and you're presented with a dialog box with options to specify. The options vary widely depending on the filter, but most come equipped with at least one option to control the intensity of the filter. A multi-step filter appears on the menu with an ellipsis following its name, indicating that a dialog box follows the execution of the command.

Giving a filter an encore

If you like the filter you applied so much that you want to reapply it, to either the same image or a different one, all you have to do is either press Ctrl+F (⌘+F on the Mac) or choose the name of the filter from the Filter menu. Either way, your last filter, with the same settings, is reapplied to your image. You may want to reapply a filter to make the effect more pronounced. Or, maybe you want to apply the same filter with the same settings to a series of different images. If you want to reapply the filter but need to tweak the settings, press Ctrl+Alt+F (⌘+Option+F on the Mac), which brings up the last applied filter's dialog box.

Fading a filter

Sometimes, you don't want the full effects of a filter applied to your image. Sometimes, fading a filter a bit softens the effect and makes it look less "computerish." Here's what you can do:

1. **Choose Layer⟹Duplicate Layer. Click OK when the dialog box appears.**

2. **Apply your desired filter to the duplicate layer.**

3. **Use the blend modes and opacity settings located on the Layers palette to merge the filtered layer with the original unfiltered image.**

4. **(Optional) Using the Eraser tool, selectively erase portions of your filtered image to enable the unfiltered image to show through.**

   For example, if you applied a Gaussian Blur filter to soften a harshly lit portrait, try erasing the blurred portion that covers the subject's eyes to let the unblurred eyes of the layer below show through, as shown in Figure 11-2. The sharply focused eyes provide a natural focal point.

PhotoSpin

Figure 11-2: Fading a filter allows you to mix the filtered and unfiltered images.

Selectively applying a filter

Up to this point in the book, we have referred to applying filters to your *images*. But we use this word rather loosely. You don't necessarily have to apply filters to your entire image. You can apply filters to individual layers, or even to selections. You can often get better effects when you apply a filter just to a portion of an image or layer. For example, you can blur a distracting background so that the person in your image gets due attention. Or, as shown in Figure 11-3, you can apply an Ocean Ripple or Wave filter to the ocean, leaving your surfer unfiltered to avoid that overly "Photoshopped" effect.

Corbis Digital Stock

Figure 11-3: Selectively applying a filter can prevent an image from looking overly manipulated.

Exercising a little restraint in applying filters usually produces a more attractive image.

Working in the Filter Gallery

When you apply a filter, don't be surprised if you're presented with a gargantuan dialog box. This *editing window,* as it's officially called, is the Filter Gallery. You can also access it by choosing Filter➪Filter Gallery. In the flexible Filter Gallery, you can apply multiple filters as well as edit them *ad nauseum.*

Even when you're using the Filter Gallery, make a backup copy of your image, or at least create a duplicate layer, before you apply filters. Filters change the pixels of an image permanently, and when you exit the Filter Gallery, the filters that are applied can't be removed.

Follow these steps to work in the Filter Gallery:

1. **Choose Filter➪Filter Gallery in either Full Edit (Standard Edit on the Mac) or Quick Fix mode.**

   The Filter Gallery editing window appears, as shown in Figure 11-4.

2. **In the center of the editing window, click your desired filter category folder.**

   The folder expands and shows the filters in that category. A thumbnail displays each filter's effect.

3. **Select your desired filter.**

   You get a large, dynamic preview of your image on the left side of the dialog box. To preview a different filter, just select it. Use the magnification controls to zoom in and out of the preview. To hide the Filter menu and get a larger preview box, click the arrow to the left of the OK button.

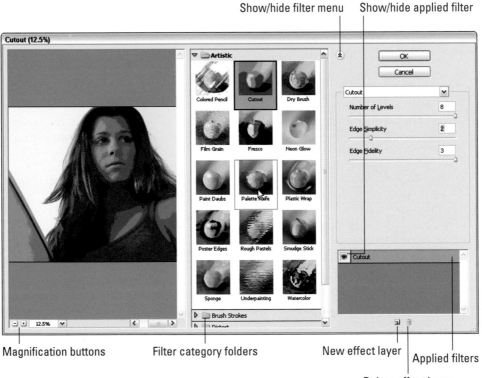

PhotoSpin

Figure 11-4: Apply and edit multiple filters in the Filter Gallery.

4. **Specify any settings associated with the filter.**

   The preview is updated accordingly.

5. **When you're happy with the results, click OK to apply the filter and close the editing window.**

6. **If you want to apply another filter, click the New Effect Layer button at the bottom of the editing window.**

   This step duplicates the existing filter.

7. **Choose your desired new filter, which then replaces the duplicate in the Applied Filters area of the dialog box.**

   Each of the filters you apply is displayed in the lower-right area of the Filter Gallery dialog box. To delete a filter, select it and click the Delete Effect Layer button. To edit a filter's settings, select it from the list and make any changes. Keep in mind that when you edit a filter's settings, the edit may affect the look of any subsequent filters you have applied. Finally, you can rearrange the order of the applied filters. Doing so changes the overall effect, however.

8. **When you're completely done, click OK to apply the filters and close the editing window.**

Distorting with the Liquify Filter

The Liquify filter is really much more than a filter. It's a distortion that allows you to manipulate an image as though it were warm taffy. You can interactively twist, pull, twirl, pinch, and bloat parts of your image. You can apply this distortion filter on the entire image, on a layer, or on a selection. This *überfilter* comes equipped with a "mega" dialog box with its own set of tools (on the left) and options (on the right), as shown in Figure 11-5.

Follow these steps to turn your image into a melted Dalí-esque wannabe:

1. **Choose Filter⇨Distort⇨Liquify in either Full Edit (Standard Edit on the Mac) or Quick Fix mode.**

   Your image appears in the preview area.

2. **Choose your distortion weapon of choice.**

   You also have a number of tools to help zoom and navigate around your image window.

   Here's a description of each tool to help you decide. See Figure 11-6 to get a visual look at the effect of each distortion tool (the letter in parentheses is the keyboard shortcut):

PhotoSpin

Figure 11-5: The Liquify filter enables you to interactively distort your image.

- *Warp (W):* This tool pushes pixels forward as you drag, creating a stretched effect. Use short strokes or long pushes.

- *Turbulence (T):* Drag to randomly jumble your pixels. Use this tool to re-create maelstroms of air, fire, and water with clouds, flames, and waves. Adjust how smooth the effect is by dragging the Turbulent Jitter slider in the Tool Options area. The higher the value, the smoother the effect.

- *Twirl Clockwise (R) and Twirl Counterclockwise (L):* These options rotate pixels either clockwise or counterclockwise. Place the cursor in one spot, hold down the mouse button, and watch the pixels under your brush rotate, or drag the cursor to create a moving twirl effect.

- *Pucker (P):* Press and hold or drag to pinch your pixels toward the center of the area covered by the brush. To reverse the pucker direction *(bloat),* press the Alt key (Option key on the Mac) as you hold or drag.

- *Bloat (B):* Press and hold or drag to push pixels toward the edge of the brush area. To reverse the bloat direction *(pucker),* press the Alt key (Opt key on the Mac) as you hold or drag.

- *Shift Pixels (S):* This tool moves pixels to the left when you drag the tool straight up. Drag down to move pixels to the right. Drag clockwise to increase the size of the object being distorted. Drag counterclockwise to decrease the size. To reverse any of the directions, press Alt (Option on the Mac) as you hold or drag.

- *Reflection (M):* This tool drags a reversed image of your pixels at a 90-degree angle to the motion of the brush. Hold down the Alt key to force the reflection in the direction opposite the motion of the brush. This tool works well for making reflections on water.

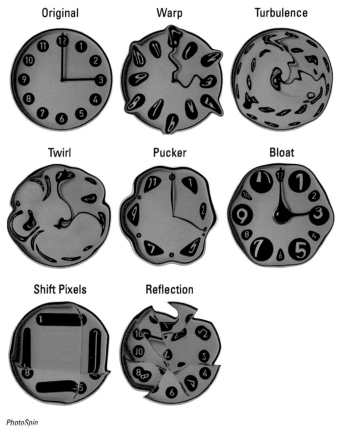

PhotoSpin

Figure 11-6: The Liquify filter can transform a clock into something far from ordinary.

- *Hand (H):* This tool works like the Hand tool on the Elements Tools palette. Drag with the Hand tool to move the image around the preview window.

- *Zoom (Z):* This tool, which works like the Zoom tool on the Elements Tools palette, zooms you in and out (hold down the Alt key) so that you can better see your distortions. You can also zoom by selecting a magnification percentage from the pop-up list in the lower-left corner of the dialog box.

3. **Specify your options in the Tool Options area:**

   - *Brush Size:* Drag the pop-up slider or enter a value from 1 to 600 pixels to specify the width of your brush.

   - *Brush Pressure:* Drag the pop-up slider or enter a value from 1 to 100 to change the pressure. The higher the pressure, the faster the distortion effect is applied.

   - *Turbulent Jitter:* Drag the pop-up slider or enter a value from 1 to 100 to adjust the smoothness when you're using the Turbulence tool.

   - *Stylus Pressure:* If you're lucky enough to have a graphics tablet and stylus, click this option to select the pressure of your stylus.

4. **Did you get a little carried away? Select the Reconstruct tool (R) and hold down or drag the mouse on the distorted portions of the image that you want to reverse or reconstruct.**

   Note that the reconstruction occurs faster at the center of the brush's diameter. To partially reconstruct your image, set a low brush pressure and watch closely as your mouse drags across the distorted areas.

5. **Click OK to apply the distortions and close the dialog box.**

   However, if you mucked things up and want to start again, click the Revert button to get your original, unaltered image back. This action also resets the tools to their previous settings.

Correcting Camera Distortion

Elements 5 has acquired a new member in the Filter family: Correct Camera Distortion. If you've ever tried to capture a looming skyscraper or cathedral in the lens of your camera, you know that it often involves tilting your camera and putting your neck in some unnatural position. And then, after all that, what you end up with is a distorted view of what was an impressive building in "real life," as shown with the "before" image on the left in Figure 11-7. That's not a problem — now. The Correct Camera Distortion filter fixes the distorted perspective created by both vertical and horizontal tilting of the camera. As a bonus, this filter also corrects other kinds of distortions caused by lens snafus.

Figure 11-7: The Correct Camera Distortion filter fixes distortions caused by camera tilt and lens flaws.

Here's how to fix all:

1. **Choose Filter⇨Correct Camera Distortion in either Full Edit (Standard Edit on the Mac) or Quick Fix mode.**

2. **In the Correct Camera Distortion dialog box, be sure to select the Preview option.**

3. **Specify your correction options:**

   • *Remove Distortion:* Corrects *lens barrel,* which causes your images to appear spherised or bloated. This can occur when you're using wide angle lenses. It also corrects *pincushion* distortion, which creates images that appear to be pinched in at the center, a flaw that's found in using telephoto or zoom lenses. Slide the slider while keeping an eye on the preview. Use the handy grid as your guide for proper alignment.

   • *Amount:* Adjusts the amount of lightening or darkening around the edges of your photo that you can get sometimes from incorrect lens shading. Change the width of the adjustment by specifying a midpoint value. A lower *midpoint* value affects more of the image. Then move the Amount slider while viewing the preview.

- *Vertical Perspective:* Corrects the distorted perspective created by tilting the camera up or down. Again, use the grid to assist in your correction. We used the Vertical Perspective to correct the building shown in Figure 11-7.

- *Horizontal Perspective:* Corrects halos and blurs caused by moving the camera (or if your subject can't sit still). For better results, set the angle of movement under the Angle option.

- *Angle:* Enables you to rotate the image to compensate for tilting the camera. You may also need to tweak the angle slightly after correcting the vertical or horizontal perspective.

- *Scale:* When you correct the perspective on your image, you may be left with blank areas on your canvas. You can scale your image up or down to crop into the image and eliminate these "holes." Note that scaling up results in interpolating your image up to its original pixel dimensions. Therefore, if you do this, be sure and start with an image that has a high enough pixel dimension, or resolution, to avoid severe degradation. For more on resolution and interpolation, see Chapter 3.

- *Show Grid:* Shows and hides the grid as needed.

- *Zoom:* Zooms in and out for your desired view.

Dressing Up with Photo and Text Effects

In addition to the multitude of filters at your disposal, Elements also provides lots of different effects that you can apply to enhance your photos. Note that some effects automatically create a duplicate of the selected layer, whereas other effects can work only on flattened images. (See Chapter 8 for details on layers.) Finally, unlike with filters, you cannot preview how the effect will look on your image or type, nor do you have any options to specify.

Here are the short steps to follow to apply an effect:

1. **Select your desired image layer on the Layers palette. Or, if you're applying the effect to just a selection, make the selection before applying the effect.**

2. **Choose Window⇨Artwork and Effects.**

3. **Select the Apply Effects, Filters and Layer Styles button at the top of the palette.**

4. **Select Photo Effects from the drop-down list in the upper-left area of the palette.**

5. Select your desired category of effects from the drop-down list in the upper-right area of the palette:

- *Show All:* Shows all the effects described in this list.

- *Frames:* Includes effects that enhance the edges of the layer or selection, as shown in Figure 11-8.

- *Image Effects:* Includes a wide variety of effects to make your image appear as though it is snowing, made of lizard skin or neon tubes, or painted with oil pastels.

6. On the Effects palette, double-click your desired effect or drag the effect onto the image.

Note that you can view your styles and effects by thumbnails or by list. To change the view, click More in the upper-right corner of the palette.

PhotoSpin

Figure 11-8: Enhance your images by adding effects to your image and type layers.

Previously lumped with the effects for images, Elements 5 moved the type effects to its own subpalette. Although the steps for applying text effects are similar to those for applying photo effects, here are the steps, for good measure:

1. **Create your desired type.**

   For details on working with type, see Chapter 13.

2. **Choose Window⇨Artwork and Effects.**

3. **Click the Add Text to Your Document button at the top of the palette.**

4. **Select your type layer on the Layers palette and then double-click your desired text effect.**

   You can also drag the effect onto the type. Refer to Figure 11-8 to see some artwork with both image and text effects.

Adding Shadows, Glows, and More

Going hand in hand with filters and effects are layer styles. Also designed to enhance your image and type layers, layer styles range from simple shadows and bevels to the more complex styles, such as buttons and patterns. The wonderful thing about layer styles is that they're completely nondestructive. Unlike filters, layer styles don't change your pixel data. You can edit them or even delete them if you're unhappy with the results.

Here are some important facts about layer styles:

- **Layer styles can be applied only to layers.** Therefore, if all you have in your image is a background, be sure to convert it to a layer first.

- **Layer styles are *dynamically linked* to the contents of a layer.** If you move or edit the contents of the layers, the results are updated.

- **When you apply a layer style to a layer, a starburst symbol appears next to the layer's name on the Layers palette.** Double-click the starburst to bring up the Styles Settings dialog box and perform any editing that's necessary to get the look you want.

Applying layer styles

Layer styles are stored in a few different libraries. You can add shadows, glows, beveled and embossed edges, and more complex styles, such as neon, plastic, chrome, and various other image effects. A sampling of styles is shown in Figure 11-9.

Drop Shadow   Inner Shadow   Bevel

Outer Glow   Inner Glow

PhotoSpin

Figure 11-9: Add dimension by applying shadows, glows, and bevels to your object or type.

Here are the steps to apply a style and a description of each of the style libraries.

1. **Select your desired image or type layer on the Layers palette.**

2. **Choose Window➪Artwork and Effects.**

3. **Select Layer Styles from the drop-down list in the upper-left area of the palette.**

4. **Select your desired library of styles from the drop-down list in the upper-right area of the palette:**

   - *Bevels:* Bevels add a three-dimensional edge on the outside or inside edges of the contents of a layer, giving the element some dimension. Emboss styles make elements appear as though they're raising off or are punched into the page. You can change the appearance of these styles depending on the type of bevel chosen. Adjust parameters such as the lighting angle, distance (how close the shadow is to the layer contents), size, bevel direction, and opacity.

   - *Drop and Inner Shadows:* Add a soft drop or inner shadow to a layer. Choose from the garden-variety shadow or one that includes noise, neon, or outlines. You can adjust the lighting angle, distance, size, and opacity as desired.

   - *Outer and Inner Glows:* Add a soft halo that appears on the outside or inside edges of your layer contents. Adjust the appearance of the glow by changing the lighting angle, size, and opacity of the glow.

   - *Visibility:* Click Show, Hide, or Ghosted to either display, hide, or partially show the layer contents. The Layer Style remains fully displayed.

   - *Complex and others:* The remaining layer styles are a cornucopia of different effects ranging from simple glass buttons to the more exotic effects, such as Groovy and Rose Impressions. You can customize all these layer styles to a certain extent by adjusting the various settings, which are similar to those for other styles in this list.

5. **On the Layer Styles palette, double-click your desired effect or drag the effect onto the image.**

   The style, with its default settings, is applied to the layer. Note that layer styles are cumulative. You can apply multiple styles — specifically, one style from each library — to a single layer.

   To edit the style's settings, either double-click the sunburst on the Layers palette or choose Layer➪Layer Style➪Style Settings.

Working with layer styles

Here are a few last tips for working with layer styles:

- **Delete a layer style or styles:** Choose Layer➪Layer Style➪Clear Layer Style or drag the florin on the Layers palette to the trash can icon.

- **Copy and paste layer styles onto other layers:** Select the layer containing the layer style and choose Layer➪Layer Style➪Copy Layer Style. Select the layer or layers on which you want to apply the effect and choose Layer➪Layer Style➪Paste Layer Style. If it's easier, you can also just drag and drop an effect from one layer to another while holding down the Alt key (Option key on the Mac).

✔ **Hide or show layer styles:** Choose Layer➪Layer Style➪Hide All Effects or Show All Effects.

✔ **Scale a layer style:** Choose Layer➪Layer Style➪Scale Effects. Select Preview and enter a value between 1 and 1,000 percent. This action allows you to scale the style without scaling the element.

Mixing It Up with Blend Modes

Elements sports a whopping 23 blend modes. *Blend modes* affect how colors interact between layers and also how colors interact when you apply paint to a layer. Not only do blend modes create interesting effects, but you can also easily apply, edit, or remove blend modes without touching your image pixels.

The various blend modes are located on a pop-up menu at the top of your Layers palette in Full Edit mode (Standard Edit mode on the Mac). The best way to get a feel for the effect of blend modes is not to memorize the descriptions we give you in this section. Instead, grab an image with some layers and apply each of the blend modes to one or more of the layers to see what happens. The exact result varies depending on the colors in your image layers. Combine these blend modes with varying opacity settings and who knows what amazing images can materialize?

General blend modes

The Normal blend mode needs no introduction. It's the one you probably use the most. Dissolve is the next one on the list and, ironically, is probably the one you use the least. Both blend modes are illustrated in Figure 11-10.

✔ **Normal:** The default mode lets each pixel display unadjusted.

✔ **Dissolve:** This mode can be seen only on a layer with an opacity setting of less than 100 percent. It allows some pixels from lower layers, which are randomized, to show through the target (selected) layer.

Normal   Dissolve

Corbis Digital Stock

Figure 11-10: The Dissolve blend mode allows pixels from one layer to peek randomly through another.

Darken blend modes

These blend modes produce effects that darken your image in various ways, as shown in Figure 11-11:

- **Darken:** Turns lighter pixels transparent if the pixels on the target layer are lighter than those below. If the pixels are darker, they're unchanged.

- **Multiply:** Burns the target layer onto the layers underneath, thereby darkening all colors where they mix. When you're painting with the Brush or Pencil tool, each stroke creates a darker color, as though you're drawing with markers.

- **Color Burn:** Darkens the layers underneath the target layer and burns them with color, creating a contrast effect, like applying a dark dye to your image.

- **Linear Burn:** Darkens the layers underneath the target layer by decreasing the brightness. This effect is similar to Multiply, but often makes parts of your image black.

Darken	Multiply	Color Burn	Linear Burn

Corbis Digital Stock

Figure 11-11: These blend modes darken your image layers.

Lighten blend modes

The lighten blend modes are the opposite of the darken blend modes. All these blend modes create lightening effects on your image, as shown in Figure 11-12:

- **Lighten:** Turns darker pixels transparent if the pixels on the target layer are darker than those below. If the pixels are lighter, they're unchanged. This effect is the opposite of Darken.

- **Screen:** Lightens the target layer where it mixes with the layers underneath. This effect is the opposite of Multiply.

- ✔ **Color Dodge:** Lightens the pixels in the layers underneath the target layer and infuses them with colors from the top layer. This effect is similar to applying a bleach to your image.

- ✔ **Linear Dodge:** Lightens the layers underneath the target layer by increasing the brightness. This effect is similar to Screen but often makes parts of your image white.

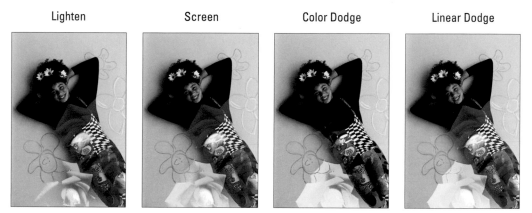

| Lighten | Screen | Color Dodge | Linear Dodge |

Corbis Digital Stock

Figure 11-12: These blend modes lighten your image layers.

Lighting blend modes

This group of blend modes plays with the lighting in your layers, as shown in Figure 11-13:

- ✔ **Overlay:** Overlay multiplies the dark pixels in the target layer and screens the light pixels in the underlying layers. It also enhances the contrast and saturation of colors.

- ✔ **Soft Light:** This mode darkens the dark (greater than 50 percent gray) pixels and lightens the light (less than 50 percent gray) pixels. The effect is like shining a soft spotlight on the image.

- ✔ **Hard Light:** This mode multiplies the dark (greater than 50 percent gray) pixels and screens the light (less than 50 percent gray) pixels. The effect is similar to shining a bright, hard spotlight on the image.

- ✔ **Vivid Light:** If the pixels on the top layer are darker than 50 percent gray, this mode darkens the colors by increasing the contrast. If the pixels on the top layer are lighter than 50 percent gray, the mode lightens the colors by decreasing the contrast.

- ✔ **Linear Light:** If the pixels on the top layer are darker than 50 percent gray, the mode darkens the colors by decreasing the brightness. If the pixels on the top layer are lighter than 50 percent gray, the mode lightens the colors by increasing the brightness.

✔ **Pin Light:** If the pixels on the top layer are darker than 50 percent gray, the mode replaces pixels darker than those on the top layer and doesn't change lighter pixels. If the pixels on the top layer are lighter than 50 percent gray, the mode replaces the pixels lighter than those on the top layer, and doesn't change pixels that are darker. The mode is usually reserved for special effects.

✔ **Hard Mix:** This mode is similar to Vivid Light, but reduces the colors to a total of eight — cyan, magenta, yellow, black, red, green, blue, and white. This mode creates a posterized effect.

Overlay	Soft Light	Hard Light	Vivid Light

Linear Light	Pin Light	Hard Mix

Corbis Digital Stock

Figure 11-13: Some blend modes adjust the lighting between your image layers.

Inverter blend modes

The Inverter blend modes invert your colors and tend to produce some radical effects, as shown in Figure 11-14:

Difference   Exclusion

Corbis Digital Stock

Figure 11-14: Difference and Exclusion blend modes invert colors.

- **Difference:** Produces a negative effect according to the brightness values on the top layers. If the pixels on the top layer are black, no change occurs in the underlying layers. If the pixels on the top layer are white, the mode inverts the colors of the underlying layers.

- **Exclusion:** Like Difference, but with less contrast and saturation. If the pixels on the top layer are black, no change occurs in the underlying layers. If the pixels on the top layer are white, this mode inverts the colors of the underlying layers. Medium colors blend to create gray.

HSL blend modes

These blend modes use the HSL (Hue, Saturation, Lightness) color model to mix colors, as shown in Figure 11-15:

- **Hue:** Blends the luminance (brightness) and saturation (intensity of the color) of the underlying layers with the hue (color) of the top layer.

- **Saturation:** Blends the luminance and hue of the underlying layers with the saturation of the top layer.

- **Color:** Blends the luminance of the underlying layers with the saturation and hue of the top layer. This mode enables you to paint color while preserving the shadows, highlights, and details of the underlying layers.

The Color mode is a great tool for colorizing images. If you've ever admired those hand-tinted black-and-white photos used in greeting cards and posters, you can create the same effect fairly easily. First, make sure that your black-and-white image is in RGB mode so that it can accept color. Create a new layer on the Layer palette and set it to the Color blend mode. Grab the Brush tool (with a soft-edged tip), choose your desired color, and paint over your image. Adjust your opacity to less than 100 percent to create a softer effect.

> ✔ **Luminosity:** The opposite of Color, this mode blends the hue and saturation of the underlying layers with the luminance of the top layer. This mode also preserves the shadows, highlights, and details from the top layer and mixes them with the colors of the underlying layers.

Hue	Saturation	Color	Luminosity

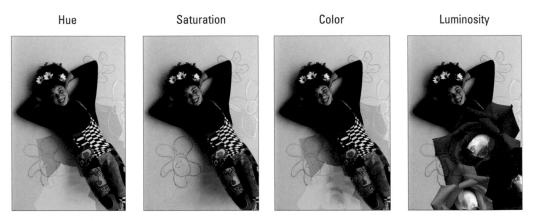

Corbis Digital Stock

Figure 11-15: Some blend modes mix colors based on the actual hue, richness, and brightness of color.

Using Photomerge Panorama

This awesome tool enables you to combine multiple images into a single panoramic image, as shown in Figure 11-16. From skylines to mountain ranges, you can take several overlapping shots and stitch them together into one.

To be successful at merging photos into a panorama, you need to start with good source files. First of all, make sure that when you shoot your photos, you overlap your individual images by 15 to 40 percent, but no more than 50 percent. Then, avoid using distortion lenses (such as fish-eye) and your camera's zoom setting. Also try to keep the same exposure settings for even lighting. Lastly, try to stay in the same position and keep your camera at the same level for each photo. Using a tripod and rotating the head can help you get shots at the same camera level.

Follow these steps to create a Photomerge Panorama image:

1. **Choose File⟳New⟳Photomerge Panorama in Full Edit mode (Standard Edit mode on the Mac).**

   Note that you can also select this command in the Organizer.

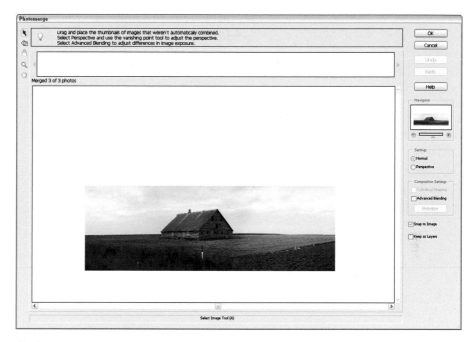

PhotoSpin

Figure 11-16: Combine multiple images into a single panorama with Photomerge.

2. **In the first Photomerge dialog box, select your source files. Click the Browse button and navigate to where your files are located.**

3. **After you have selected all applicable images, click OK.**

   Elements opens and automatically assembles the source files to create the composite panorama in the work area of the dialog box. If it looks good, skip to Step 6.

   Elements alerts you if it cannot automatically composite your source files. You then have to assemble the images manually.

4. **To manually assemble your panorama, drag the image thumbnails from the lightbox area onto the work area with the Select Image tool (the arrow), or simply double-click the lightbox thumbnail to add it to the composition.**

5. **Arrange and position your images:**

   • Position the images by using the Select Image tool.

   • Use the Rotate Image tool to make rotations.

   • Use the Zoom and Move View tools to help view and navigate around your panorama.

You can also use the Navigator view box to zoom in and out of your composition by dragging the slider.

- Select the Snap to Image option to enable overlapping images to automatically snap into place.

6. **To adjust the Vanishing Point, first select the Perspective option in the Settings area. Click your desired image with the Set Vanishing Point tool.**

   Elements changes the perspective of the composition. By default, Elements selects the center image as the vanishing point. If necessary, you can move the other images.

   Note that when you select the Perspective setting, Elements links non-Vanishing Point images to the Vanishing Point image. To break the link, click the Normal Setting button or separate the images in the work area.

7. **Adjust the blending of the composition.**

   Select the Perspective setting first and then choose Cylindrical Mapping to reduce the bowed distortion you can get when you add perspective to your composition.

   If you have some color inconsistencies from having photos with different exposures, select Advanced Blending to blend the different colors and tones.

   Click Preview to view your settings. Click Exit Preview to return to Edit mode.

8. **Select the Keep As Layers option to save each image in the composite as an individual layer.**

9. **Click OK to create the panorama.**

   The file opens as a new Photoshop Elements (.psd) file with a layer named Photomerge (if you didn't retain your layers in Step 8).

Drawing and Painting

*E*lements is such a deluxe, full-service image editing program that it doesn't just stop at giving you tools to select, repair, organize, and share your images. It figures that you may need to add a swash of color, either freeform with a brush or pencil or in the form of a geometric or organic shape. Don't worry: This drawing and painting business isn't just for those with innate artistic talent. In fact, Elements gives you plenty of preset brushes and shapes that you can use. If you can pick a tool and drag your mouse, you can draw and paint.

Choosing Color

Before you start drawing or painting, you may want to change your color to something other than the default black. If you've read the earlier chapters in this book, we're sure that you checked out the Elements Tools palette and noticed the two overlapping color swatches at the bottom of the palette. These two swatches represent two categories of color: *foreground* and *background.* Here's a quick look at how they work with different tools:

✔ When you add type, paint with the Brush tool, or create a shape, you're using the foreground color.

✔ On the background layer of an image, when you erase with the Eraser tool, or when you increase the size of your canvas, you're accessing the background color.

✔ When you drag with the Gradient tool, as long as your gradient is set to the default, you're laying down a blend of color from the foreground to the background.

Elements gives you three ways to choose your foreground and background colors: the Color Picker, the Color Swatches, and the Eyedropper tool, which samples color in an image. In the following sections, we explore each one.

Working with the Color Picker

By default, Elements uses a black foreground color and a white background color. If you're experimenting with color and want to go back to the default color, press the D key. If you want to switch between foreground and background colors, press the X key. If you want any other color of the rainbow, click your desired swatch to change either the foreground or background color. This action transports you to the Color Picker, shown in Figure 12-1.

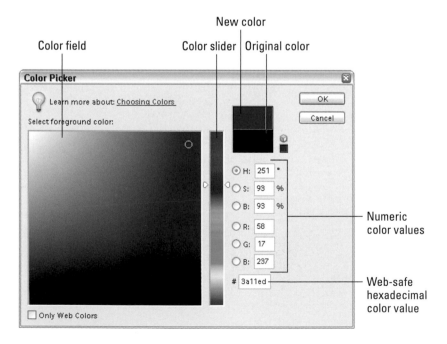

Figure 12-1: The Color Picker.

Here are the steps to choose your color via the Color Picker:

1. **Click either the Foreground or Background color swatch on the Tools palette.**

   The Color Picker appears.

2. **Drag the color slider or click the color bar to get close to the general color you desire.**

3. **Choose the exact color you want by clicking in the large square, called a *color field,* on the left.**

   The circle cursor targets your selected color. The two swatches in the upper-right corner of the dialog box represent your newly selected color and the original foreground or background color.

   The numeric values on the right side of the dialog box also change according to the color you selected. If you happen to know the values of your desired color, you may also enter them in the text boxes. Remember that RGB values are based on brightness levels, from 0 (black) to 255 (white). You can also enter HSB (Hue, Saturation, Brightness) values or the hexadecimal formula for Web-safe colors.

   When you're happy with your color, click OK.

Dipping into the Color Swatches palette

Another way Elements enables you to choose a foreground or background color is by selecting a color on the Color Swatches palette. The Color Swatches palette is a digital version of the artist's paint palette. In addition to preset colors, you can mix and store your own colors for use now and later. You can have several palettes for certain types of projects or images. For example, you may want a palette of skin tones for retouching portraits. Choose Window➪Color Swatches to bring up the palette, shown in Figure 12-2.

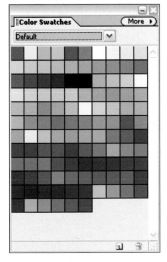

Figure 12-2: The Color Swatches palette.

To grab a color from the Color Swatches palette, just click the color swatch you want. By the way, it doesn't matter which tool you have. As soon as you move the tool over the palette, it temporarily converts to an eyedropper that samples the color and makes it your new foreground or background color.

Although the Color Swatches palette is a breeze to use, here are a few tips to help you along:

- ✓ **Change the background color**. Either first select the background swatch on the Tools palette or Ctrl+click (⌘+click on the Mac) a swatch.

- ✓ **Use preset colors.** To load a particular preset swatch library, select it from the Color Swatches palette drop-down list. Elements offers libraries specific to Web graphics, photo filters, and Windows systems.

- ✓ **Add a color to the Color Swatches palette.** To add a color to the Swatches palette, choose New Swatch from the More pop-up menu. Name your swatch and click OK.

- ✓ **Save swatches.** Choose Save Swatches from the More pop-up menu in the upper-right corner of the palette. We recommend saving the swatch library in the default Color Swatches folder in the Presets folder. If by chance this folder doesn't come up by default, just navigate to the Color Swatches folder by following this path: `Adobe Elements 5.0\Presets\ Color Swatches`.

- ✓ **Load swatches.** If you want to load a custom library created by you or by someone else, choose More⇨Load Swatches. In the dialog box, select your desired library from the Color Swatches folder. The new library is appended (added) to your current library.

  You can also work with swatches by using the Preset Manager. For more on the Preset Manager, see Chapter 2.

- ✓ **Delete swatches.** To delete a swatch, drag it to the trash can at the bottom of the palette or Alt+click (Option+click on the Mac) the swatch.

- ✓ **Change the palette's appearance.** Click the More button in the upper-right corner to choose from Small or Large Thumbnail (swatch squares) or Small or Large List (swatch squares with a name).

- ✓ **Replace your current swatch library with a different library.** Choose Replace Swatches from the More pop-up menu. Choose a library from the Color Swatches folder.

Sampling with the Eyedropper tool

Another way that Elements enables you to choose color is via the Eyedropper tool. The Eyedropper tool comes in handy when you want to sample an existing color in an image and use it for another element. For example, you may want your text to be the same color as the green background in the images shown in Figure 12-3. We grab the Eyedropper tool (or press I) and click a shade of green in the background. The tool samples the color and makes it our new foreground color. We then create the type with our new foreground color.

Figure 12-3: The Eyedropper tool enables you to sample color from your image to use with other elements, such as type.

Here are few things to remember when you're using the Eyedropper tool:

- ✓ **Sample a new foreground or background color.** Obviously, you can select either the foreground or background swatch on the Tools palette before you sample a color. But if the foreground color swatch is active, pressing the Alt key (Option key on the Mac) samples a new background color, and vice versa.

- ✓ **Choose a color from any open image.** If you have multiple images open, you can even sample a color from an image that you're not working on!

- ✓ **Choose your sample size on the Options bar.** You can select the color of just the single pixel you click (Point Sample), or Elements can average the colors of the pixels in a 3-x-3- or 5-x-5-pixel area.

✔ **Make colors Web safe.** If you right-click your image to bring up the context menu, you have a hidden option: Copy Color As HTML. This option provides the Web-safe hexadecimal color formula for that sampled color and copies it to the Clipboard. You can then paste that formula into an HTML file or grab the Type tool and choose Edit⇨Paste to view the formula in your image.

✔ **Toggle between the Eyedropper and other tools.** Elements, multitasker that it is, enables you to temporarily access the Eyedropper tool when you're using the Brush, Pencil, Color Replacement, Gradient, Paint Bucket, Cookie Cutter, or Shape tools. Simply press the Alt key (Option key on the Mac) to access the Eyedropper. Release the Alt key (Option key on the Mac) and you're back to your original tool.

Getting Artsy with the Pencil and Brush Tools

If you've read the first part of this chapter and have been thoroughly doused with every way to choose a color, you probably want to find out how to paint and draw with that color. The Pencil and Brush tools give you the power to put your creative abilities to work, and the following sections show you how.

When you use these two tools, you benefit immensely from the use of a pressure-sensitive digital drawing tablet. The awkwardness of trying to draw or paint with a mouse disappears and leaves you with tools that behave much closer to their analog ancestors.

Drawing with the Pencil tool

Drawing with the Pencil tool creates hard edges. You can't get the soft, feathery edges that you can with the Brush tool. In fact, the edges of a pencil stroke cannot even be *anti-aliased*. (For more on anti-aliasing, see the following section.) Keep in mind that if you draw anything other than vertical or horizontal lines, your lines will have some jaggies when they're viewed up close. But hey, don't diss the Pencil just yet. Those hard-edged strokes can be perfect for Web graphics. What's more, the Pencil tool can erase itself, and it's great for digital sketches, as shown in Figure 12-4.

Follow these steps to become familiar with the Pencil tool:

1. **Select the Pencil tool from the Tools palette.**

Illustration credit: Chris Blair

Figure 12-4: The Pencil tool can be used for digital drawings.

You can also press the N key. By default, the Pencil tool's brush tip is the 1-pixel brush. Yes, even though the Pencil tip is hard-edged, we still refer to it as a brush.

2. **On the Options bar, choose your desired pencil options, beginning with a brush preset. Click the arrow and select your desired brush from the Brush Preset Picker drop-down palette.**

   To load another preset library, click the Brushes menu at the top of the palette.

   Remember that you aren't limited to the standard old brush strokes. Check out the Assorted and Special Effects brushes. You'll be surprised at some of the interesting brushes lurking on these palettes. Use them to create stand-alone images or to enhance your photographic creations.

   Access the pop-up menu on the drop-down palette to save, rename, or delete individual brushes and also save, load, and reset brush libraries. For more on these operations, see the following section.

3. **Choose your brush size.**

   A preset brush's pixel diameters are shown as text below a thumbnail image of the brush shape. If you want to change the size of that brush tip, drag the Size slider or enter a value.

4. **Select a blending mode.**

   Blend modes alter the way the color you're applying interacts with the color on your canvas. You can find more about blend modes in Chapter 11.

5. **If you want the background to show through your strokes, adjust the opacity by dragging the slider or entering an Opacity percentage less than 100 percent.**

   The lower the percentage, the more the background images show through.

   Your strokes must be on a separate layer above your images for you to be able to adjust the opacity and blend modes after you draw them. For more on layers, see Chapter 8.

6. **Select Auto Erase if you want to enable that option.**

   This option removes portions of your pencil strokes. For example, if your foreground color is black and your background color is white and you apply some black strokes, with Auto Erase enabled, you apply white if you drag back over the black strokes. If you drag over the white background, you apply black.

7. **Click and drag with the mouse to create your freeform lines.**

   To draw straight lines, click at a starting point, release the mouse button, and then Shift+click at a second point.

Painting with the Brush tool

The Brush tool creates soft-edged strokes. How soft those strokes are depends on which brush you use. By default, even the hardest brush has a slightly soft edge because it's anti-aliased. Remember that anti-aliasing creates a single row of partially filled pixels along the edges to produce the illusion of a smooth edge. You can also get even softer brushes, which employ feathering. For details on feathering, see Chapter 7.

The Brush tool shares most of the options found in the Pencil tool, except that the Auto Erase feature isn't available. Here's the lowdown on the unique Brush options:

- **Airbrush:** Click the Airbrush button on the Options bar to apply the Airbrush mode. In this mode, the longer you hold down the mouse button, the more paint pumps out of the Brush and the wider the airbrush effect spreads.

- **Tablet Options:** If you're using a pressure-sensitive digital drawing tablet, check the settings you want the tablet to control, including size, scatter, opacity, roundness, and hue jitter. The harder you press with the stylus, the greater the effect of these options.

- **More Options:** Click the brush icon to the right of the More Options label to access the additional options described in the following list. These options, referred to as brush *dynamics,* change while you apply your stroke. See Figure 12-5 for an example of each one.

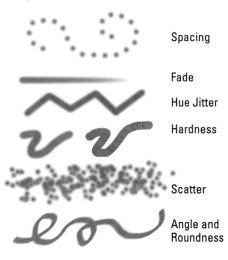

Figure 12-5: Change brush options to create a custom brush.

  - *Spacing:* The higher the number, the more space between marks.

  - *Fade:* The lower the value, the quicker the stroke fades. Zero, however, creates no fade.

  - *Hue Jitter:* Vary the stroke between the foreground and background colors. The higher the value, the more frequent the variation.

  - *Hardness:* The higher the value, the harder the brush.

  - *Scatter:* The higher the value, the higher the number of brush marks and the farther apart they are.

- *Angle:* If you have created an oval brush by adjusting the round-ness (see the next bullet), this option controls the angle of that oval brush stroke. It's so much easier to drag the points and the arrow on the diagram than to "guesstimate" values in the text boxes.

- *Roundness:* A setting of 100 percent is totally circular. The lower the percentage, the more oval your brush becomes.

- *Keep These Settings for All Brushes:* You can lock in these brush dynamics by selecting this check box. This ensures that every brush you choose adopts these settings.

Like the Pencil tool, additional features for the Brush tool appear on the pop-up list on the Brush Preset Picker drop-down palette. Here's a quick description of each:

✓ **Save Brush:** Allows you to save a custom brush as a preset. See the fol-lowing section for details.

✓ **Rename Brush:** Don't like your brush's moniker? Change it with this option.

✓ **Delete Brush:** Don't like your entire brush? Eliminate it with this option.

✓ **Reset Brushes:** Reverts your current brush library to the default.

✓ **Save Brushes:** Saves custom brushes in a separate library.

✓ **Load Brushes:** Loads a preset or custom brush library.

✓ **The display options:** Not a single command but rather a set of commands that enable you to change the way your brush tips are displayed. The default view is Stroke Thumbnail, which displays the appearance of the stroke. These commands include Text Only, Small and Large Thumbnail, and Small and Large List.

You can also manage brush tip libraries by using the Preset Manager. See Chapter 2 for information on using the Preset Manager.

Creating your own brush

After playing with all the various options, if you really like the Franken-brush you have created, feel free to save it as a preset that you can access again in the future. Choose Save Brush from the pop-up menu on the Brush Preset Picker palette. Name the Brush and click OK. Your new custom brush shows up at the bottom of the Brush Preset Picker drop-down palette.

There's one additional way to create a brush. Elements allows you to create a brush from all or part of your image. The image can be a photograph or something you have painted or drawn.

Here's how to create a brush from your image:

1. **Select part of your image with any of the selection tools. If you want to use the entire image or entire layer, deselect everything.**

   For more on selections, see Chapter 7.

2. **Choose Edit⇨Define Brush or Edit⇨Define Brush from Selection.**

   You see one command or the other, depending on what you do in Step 1.

3. **Name the brush and click OK.**

   The new brush shows up at the bottom of your Brush Preset Picker drop-down palette. Note that your brush is only a grayscale version of your image. When you use the brush, it automatically applies the color you have selected as your foreground color, as shown in Figure 12-6.

Digital Vision

Figure 12-6: Create a custom brush from a portion of your image.

Using the Impressionist Brush

In this section, we introduce the Impressionist Brush. This tool is designed to paint over your photos in a way that makes it look like a fine art painting. You can set various options that change the style of the brush strokes.

Here's how to use this artistic brush:

1. **Select the Impressionist Brush from the Tools palette.**

It looks like a brush with a curlicue next to it.

2. Set your brush options.

The Brushes, Size, Mode, and Opacity options are identical to those found with the Brush tool, described in "Painting with the Brush tool," earlier in this chapter. You can also find some unique options on the More Options palette:

- *Style:* This drop-down list contains various brush stroke styles, such as dab and tight curl.

- *Area:* Controls the size of your brush stroke. The larger the value, the larger the area covered.

- *Tolerance:* Controls how similar color pixels have to be before they're changed by the brush stroke.

3. Drag on your image and paint with your brush strokes, as shown in Figure 12-7.

The best way to get a feel for what this tool does is to open your favorite image, grab the tool, and take it for a test drive.

Figure 12-7: The Impressionist Brush turns your photo into a painting.

Filling and Outlining Selections

There may be times when you want to create an element on your canvas that can't quite be created with a brush or pencil stroke. Maybe it's a perfect circle or five-point star. Elements offers a couple of other ways to create these objects. If you have a selection, you can fill or stroke that selection to create that element rather than draw or paint it on. The Fill command adds a color or a pattern to the entire selection, whereas the Stroke command applies the color to only the edge of the selection border.

Fill 'er up

You won't find a Fill tool on the Tools palette. Elements decided to avoid the overpopulated palette and placed the Fill and Stroke commands on the Edit menu. Here are the simple steps to fill a selection:

1. **Grab the selection tool of your choice and create your selection on a new layer.**

   Although you don't have to create a new layer to make a selection to fill, we recommend it. That way, if you don't like the filled selection, you can delete the layer, and your image or background below it remains safe. See Chapter 7 for more on selections and Chapter 8 for details on working with layers.

2. **Select either the foreground or background color and then choose a fill color.**

   See "Choosing Color," earlier in this chapter, if you need a refresher.

3. **Choose Edit➪Fill Selection.**

   The Fill Layer dialog box, shown in Figure 12-8, appears.

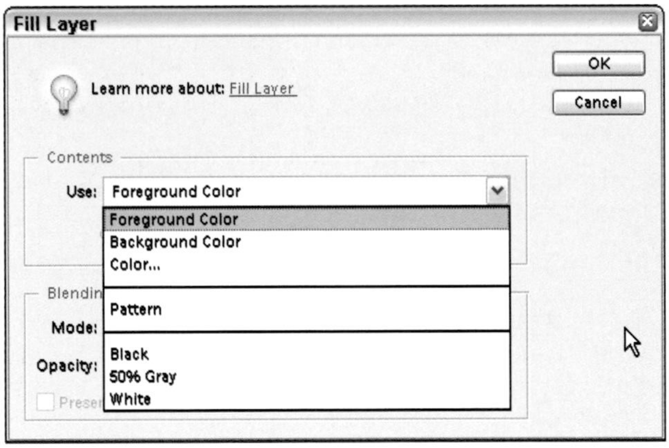

Fill Layer

Learn more about: Fill Layer

OK
Cancel

Contents

Use: Foreground Color

Foreground Color
Background Color
Color...

Pattern

Black
50% Gray
White

Blendin
Mode:
Opacity:
Prese

Figure 12-8: Fill your selection or layer with color or a pattern.

If you want to bypass the Fill dialog box (and the rest of these steps), you can use these handy keyboard shortcuts instead:

- *To fill the selection with the foreground color:* Press Alt+Backspace (Option+Delete on the Mac).

- *To fill it with the background color:* Press Ctrl+Backspace (⌘+Delete on the Mac).

4. **Choose your desired fill from the Use pop-up menu.**

You can select whether to fill with the foreground or background color. You also can choose Color, Black, 50% Gray, White, or Pattern. If you select Color, you're transported to the Color Picker. If you choose Pattern, you must then choose a pattern from the Custom Pattern drop-down palette. For more on patterns, see the upcoming section.

If you don't have an active selection border in your image, the command says Fill Layer and your entire layer is filled with your color or pattern.

5. **In the blending area, you can choose whether to preserve transparency, which enables you to fill the whole selection or only portions of the selection that contain pixels (the nontransparent areas).**

Although you can also choose a blend mode (how the fill color interacts with colors below it) and opacity percentage, we urge you not to adjust your blend mode and opacity in the Fill Layer dialog box. Make those adjustments on your layer later, by using the Layer palette commands, where you have more flexibility for editing.

6. **Click OK.**

The color or pattern fills the selection.

Outlining with the Stroke command

Stroking a selection enables you to create colored outlines, or borders, of selections or layers. You can put this border inside or outside the selection order or centered on it. Here are the steps to stroke a selection:

1. **Choose a foreground color and make a selection.**

2. **Choose Edit➪Stroke (Outline) Selection.**

   The Stroke dialog box opens.

3. **Select your desired settings.**

   Many settings are the same as those found in the Fill dialog box, as explained in the preceding section. Here's a brief rundown of those options that are unique to strokes:

   • *Width:* Enter a width of 1 to 250 pixels for the stroke.

   • *Location:* Specify how Elements should apply the stroke: outside the selection, inside the selection, or centered on the selection.

4. **Click OK to apply the stroke.**

   We gave a 30-pixel centered stroke to our selection, shown in Figure 12-9.

Figure 12-9: Stroke a selection to create a colored border.

Splashing On Color with the Paint Bucket Tool

The Paint Bucket tool has been a longtime occupant of the Tools palette. This tool, whose icon looks just like a bucket, behaves like a combination of the Fill command and the Magic Wand tool. This means that it makes a selection based on similarly colored pixels and then immediately fills that selection with color or a pattern. Just like the Magic Wand tool, this tool is the most successful when you have a limited number of colors, as shown in Figure 12-10.

To use the Paint Bucket tool, simply click inside the selection you want to fill. Before you click, however, specify your options:

Corbis Digital Stock

Figure 12-10: The Paint Bucket tool makes a selection and fills it at the same time.

- ✐ **Fill:** Choose between a fill of the foreground color or a pattern.

- ✐ **Pattern:** If you choose pattern, select a preset pattern from the drop-down palette. For more details on patterns, see the upcoming section.

- ✐ **Mode:** Select a blending mode to change how your fill color interacts with the color below it.

- ✐ **Opacity:** Adjust the opacity to make your fill more or less transparent.

- ✐ **Tolerance:** Choose a tolerance level that specifies how similar in color a pixel must be before it's selected and then filled. The lower the value, the more similar the color must be. For more on tolerance, see the section on the Magic Wand in Chapter 7.

- ✐ **Anti-alias:** Choose this option to smooth the edges between the filled and unfilled areas.

- ✐ **Contiguous:** If selected, this option selects and fills only pixels that are touching within your selection. If the option is unselected, pixels are selected and filled wherever they lie within your image.

- ✐ **All Layers:** This option selects and fills pixels in all layers that are within your tolerance level.

Working with Multicolored Gradients

If one color isn't enough for you, you'll be pleased to know that Elements enables you to fill a selection or layer with a gradient. A *gradient* is a blend of two or more colors that gradually dissolve from one to another. Elements provides a whole slew of various preset gradients. But creating your own custom gradient is also fun and easy.

Applying a preset gradient

Similar to colors, patterns, and brushes, gradients have a whole slew of presets that you can apply to your selection and layers. You can also load other libraries of gradients from the Gradient palette pop-up menu.

Here's how to apply a preset gradient:

1. **Make the selection you want to fill with a gradient.**

   We recommend making the selection on a new layer so that you can edit the gradient later without harming the underlying image.

   If you don't make a selection, the gradient is applied to the entire layer or background.

2. **Select the Gradient tool from the Tools palette or press the G key.**

3. **On the Options bar, click the downward-pointing arrow on the Gradient Picker drop-down palette and choose a preset gradient.**

   Remember that you can choose other preset libraries from the palette pop-up menu. Libraries such as Color Harmonies and Metals contain interesting presets.

4. **Choose your desired gradient type by clicking one of the icons.**

   See Figure 12-11 for an example of each type.

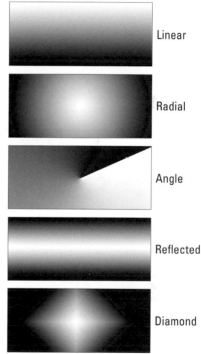

Linear

Radial

Angle

Reflected

Diamond

Figure 12-11: Choose from one of five gradient types.

5. **Choose from the following additional options on the Options bar:**

   - *Mode:* Choose a blending mode to change how the color of the gradient interacts with the colors below it.

   - *Opacity:* Choose how opaque or transparent the gradient is.

   - *Reverse:* Reverse the order in which the colors are applied.

   - *Dither:* Add *noise,* or random information, to produce a smoother gradient that prints with less *banding* (weird stripes caused by printing limitations).

   - *Transparency:* Deselect this option and Elements ignores any transparent areas in the gradient and makes them opaque instead.

6. **Position your gradient cursor at your desired starting point within your selection or layer.**

7. **Drag in any direction to your desired end point for the gradient.**

   TIP

   Longer drags result in a subtler transition between colors, whereas shorter drags result in a more abrupt transition. Hold down the Shift key to restrain the direction of the gradient to a 45-degree angle.

8. **Release the mouse button to apply the gradient.**

   We applied an Orange Yellow radial gradient from the Color Harmonies 2-preset library to a selection of a sun in Figure 12-12. We selected the Reverse option and dragged from the center of the sun to the tip of the top ray.

Figure 12-12: We filled our sun selection with a radial Orange Yellow gradient.

Customizing gradients

If you can't find the exact gradient you need, you can easily create your own. The Gradient Editor lets you create your own, custom gradient, using as many colors as you want. After you create a custom gradient, you can save it as a preset to reuse in the future.

Follow these steps to create a custom gradient:

1. **Select the Gradient tool from the Tools palette.**

2. **Click the Edit button on the Options bar.**

   The Gradient Editor dialog box opens, as shown in Figure 12-13.

3. **Pick an existing preset to use as the basis for your new gradient.**

4. **Choose your gradient type, either Solid or Noise, from the pop-up menu.**

   A Noise gradient contains random colors. Interestingly, each time you create a Noise gradient, the result is different.

   Note that as soon as you start to edit the existing gradient, the name of the gradient changes to Custom.

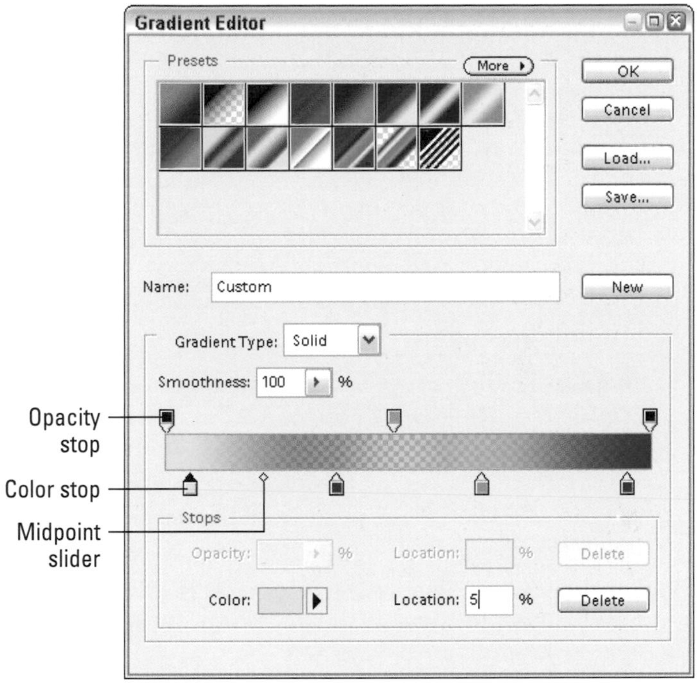

Figure 12-13: Use the Gradient Editor to edit and customize gradients.

5. **Choose your options for either a Solid or Noise gradient, depending on what you chose in Step 4.**

   - *If you chose Solid:* Adjust the Smoothness percentage to determine how smoothly one color blends into another.

   - *If you chose Noise:* You can choose which Color Model to use to set the color range. You can also adjust the Roughness, which affects how smoothly or abruptly the color transitions from one to another. Click Restrict Colors to avoid oversaturated colors. The Add Transparency option adds transparency to random colors. Click the Randomize button to randomly generate a new gradient. You can then skip down to Step 15 to finish the gradient-making process.

6. **If you're creating a solid gradient, begin choosing the first color of your gradient by first clicking the left color stop under the gradient bar (refer to Figure 12-13).**

   The triangle on top of the stop turns black to indicate that you're working with the starting point of the gradient.

7. **Choose the starting color by double-clicking the left color stop and selecting a color from the Color Picker.**

   In the Stops area, you can also click the Color Swatch or choose Foreground, Background, or User Color from the Color pop-up menu. If you select color with the Foreground or Background option when you change either of those colors, the color in the gradient changes automatically for gradients you make. However, when you open the Gradient Editor again, you can revert to your original foreground or background color by selecting the User Color option.

8. **Select the ending color by clicking the right color stop. Repeat Step 7 to define the color.**

9. **Change the percentage of the amount of one color versus the other by moving the starting or ending point's color stop to the left or right. Drag the midpoint slider (a diamond icon) to adjust where the colors mix equally, 50-50.**

   You can also change the position of the midpoint by typing a value in the Location box.

10. **To add another color, click below the gradient bar at the position you want to add the color. Define a color in the same way you did in Step 7.**

11. **Repeat Step 10 to add colors.**

12. **To add transparency to your gradient, select an opacity stop (refer to Figure 12-13), and adjust the Opacity slider to specify the amount of transparency you desire.**

    By default, a gradient has colors that are 100 percent opaque. You can fade a gradient to transparency so that the portion of the image under the gradient shows through.

    You can also add additional opacity stops in the same way you add color stops.

13. **Adjust your color and opacity stops and their midpoint sliders to vary the percentages of each color.**

14. **You can also redefine any of the colors. To delete a color stop, drag it up or down off the gradient bar.**

15. **When you're done, name your gradient and click the New button.**

    Your gradient is added to the Presets menu.

After all that work, you may want to consider saving your gradients for later use. To save a gradient, click the Save button in the Gradient Editor dialog box. Save the current presets, with your new gradient, under the current library's name or a new name altogether. You can then later load that preset library. You can also manage your gradient presets with the Preset Manager, explained in Chapter 2.

Working with Patterns

If you've ever seen someone wearing leopard-print pants with an argyle sweater and a plaid blazer, you're familiar with patterns. Not always pretty when used without restraint, patterns can be used to occasionally fill selections or layers. You can also stamp your image by using the Pattern Stamp tool. You can even retouch by using a pattern with the Healing Brush tool. Elements offers lots of preset patterns to keep you happy. And, if you're not, you can, of course, create your own.

Applying a preset pattern

Although you can apply patterns by using many different tools, this chapter sticks with applying patterns as fills. To fill a layer or selection with a preset pattern, follow these steps:

1. **Choose the layer or selection you want to fill with a pattern.**

   Again, we recommend making your selection on a new layer above your image for more flexible editing later on.

2. **Choose Edit⇨Fill Selection or Fill Layer and choose Pattern from the Use drop-down menu.**

3. **Click the downward-pointing arrow and select a pattern from the Custom Pattern drop-down palette, as shown in Figure 12-14.**

   If you don't see a pattern to your liking, choose another preset library by clicking the palette pop-up menu and choosing another preset library at the bottom of the submenu.

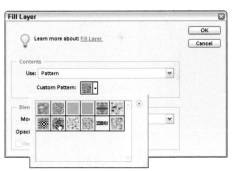

Figure 12-14: Fill your selection with one of the many Elements preset patterns.

4. **Choose any other fill options you want to apply, such as Mode, Opacity, or Preserve Transparency.**

   For details on these options, see the section "Filling and Outlining Selections," earlier in this chapter.

5. **Click OK to fill the layer or selection with the chosen pattern.**

Creating a new pattern

You may someday want to create your own pattern. Patterns can be easily created from any existing photo or painting you create in Elements. You can even scan your signature or logo, define it as a pattern, and use it with the Pattern Stamp tool to sign all your work.

To create your own pattern, follow these steps:

1. **Open the photographic, painted, or scanned image that contains the area you want to use as a pattern.**

2. **Use the Rectangular Marquee tool to select the area you want to convert into a pattern. Make sure that your Feather option is set to 0.**

   If you don't make a selection, Elements uses your entire layer as a basis for the pattern.

3. **Choose Edit⇨Define Pattern from Selection or Edit⇨Define Pattern.**

4. **Enter a name for your pattern in the Pattern Name dialog box.**

   Your new pattern now appears in every Pattern palette, wherever it may lurk in Elements.

In addition to filling your selection with a pattern, you can stamp on a pattern with the Pattern Stamp tool. For details, see Chapter 9.

Creating Shapes of All Sorts

In this section, we leave the land of pixels and head into uncharted territory — Vectorville. Before we discuss the ins and outs of creating shapes, here's a little overview that explains the difference between pixels and vectors:

- ✓ **Pixel images describe a shape in terms of a grid of pixels.** When you increase the size of a pixel-based image, it loses quality and begins to look blocky, mushy, and otherwise nasty. For more details on resizing pixel-based images and the ramifications of doing so, see Chapter 3.

- ✓ **Vectors describe a shape mathematically.** The shapes comprise paths made up of lines, curves, and anchor points. Because vector shapes are math-based, you can resize them without any loss of quality whatsoever.

Figure 12-15: Elements images can be vector-based (top) or pixel-based (bottom).

In Figure 12-15, you can see both types of images.

When you create a shape in Elements, you're creating a vector-based element. Shapes reside on a special kind of layer called, not surprisingly, a shape layer. Use shapes to create simple logos, Web buttons, and other small spot illustrations.

Drawing a shape

Elements offers an assortment of shape tools for you to choose from. Follow these steps to draw a shape in your document:

1. **Choose your desired shape tool from the Tools palette.**

   You can also press the * key and choose the shape tool from the Options bar. All the following tools have associated geometry options, which are described in an upcoming section. Here are the tools that are available:

   - *Rectangle and Ellipse:* As with their Marquee counterparts, you can hold down the Shift key while dragging to produce a square or circle; hold down the Alt key (Option key on the Mac) to draw the shape from the center outward.

   - *Rounded Rectangle:* This tool works like the regular Rectangle but with the addition of a radius value used to round off the corners of the rectangle.

   - *Polygon:* This tool creates a polygon with a specified number of sides, from 3 to 100.

   - *Line:* Draw a line with a width from 1 to 1000 pixels. You can also add arrowheads at either end.

   - *Custom:* Custom is the most varied shape tool. You have numerous preset custom shapes to choose from. As with any shape, hold down Shift to constrain proportions or Alt to draw from the center out.

2. **Select your desired color from the Color drop-down palette on the Options bar.**

   Click the More Colors button to access the Color Picker for additional color choices.

3. **Select a style from the Style drop-down palette.**

   To jazz up the shape with bevels and other fancy edges, choose a style from the palette. For more on styles, see Chapter 11.

4. **Click the downward-pointing arrow just to the right of the Shape tools to specify your geometry options.**

   For detailed explanations on the various geometry options, see the upcoming sections.

If you chose the Custom Shape tool in Step 1, click the downward-pointing arrow to access the drop-down shapes palette and choose your desired shape. You can access more preset shape libraries via the pop-up menu at the top of the palette.

5. **Drag in the document to draw the shape you defined.**

The shape appears in the Image window on its own shape layer. Check out the Layers palette to see this phenomenon. Figure 12-16 shows our shape, a Japanese hairstyle, which we add to in the next section.

Figure 12-16: Custom shapes run the gamut from the ordinary to the exotic, such as this hairstyle.

Drawing multiple shapes

After you create a shape layer, you can draw additional shapes to that layer. You can add, subtract, overlap, and intersect shapes in exactly the same way you do with selections (see Chapter 7). Just follow these steps:

1. **Select your desired state button on the Options bar. You can choose from the following options:**

   - *New Shape Layer:* Creates your initial shape layer

   - *Add to Shape Area:* Combines and joins two or more shapes

   - *Subtract from Shape Area:* Subtracts one shape from another shape

   - *Intersect Shape Areas:* Creates a shape only from the areas that overlap

   - *Exclude Overlapping Shape Areas:* Creates a shape only from the areas that don't overlap

2. **Choose your desired Shape tool and draw the next shape.**

We completed the shape by adding the face, shown in Figure 12-17.

Figure 12-17: Add to your shape layer by pressing the Shift key.

Specifying geometry options

Geometry options help define how your shapes look. Click the downward-pointing arrow on the Options bar to access the geometry options described in the sections that follow.

Rectangle and Rounded Rectangle geometry options

Here are the Geometry options for the rectangle and rounded rectangle shapes:

- **Unconstrained:** Enables you to have free reign to draw a rectangle at any size or shape.
- **Square:** Constrains the shape to a perfect square.
- **Fixed Size:** Lets you draw rectangles in fixed sizes, as specified by your width and height values.
- **Proportional:** Allows you to define a proportion for the rectangle. For example, specifying 2W and 1H makes a rectangle twice as wide as it is high.
- **From Center:** Enables you to draw from the center out.
- **Snap to Pixels:** Aligns the shape to the pixels on your screen.
- **Radius:** For Rounded Rectangles, applies the radius of a circle used to round off the corners.

Ellipse geometry options

The ellipse shape has the same options that are available for rectangles except for the Snap to Pixels option. The only differences are that, rather than be able to create a perfect square, you can create a perfect circle with the Circle option.

Polygon geometry options

The geometry options for the Polygon shape are as follows:

- **Radius:** Enter the radius of a circle used to round off the corners of a polygon when you have the Smooth Corners option selected.
- **Smooth Corners:** Round off the corners.
- **Star:** Create an inward-pointing polygon called a star.
- **Indent Sides By:** Determine the amount the sides indent inward.
- **Smooth Indents:** Round off the inner corners of indented sides.
- **Sides:** Specify the number of sides for your polygon or the number of points for your star.

Line geometry options

The line's geometry settings include whether to put arrowheads at the start or end of the line. You can also adjust the width, length, and concavity settings to change the arrowhead shapes.

Custom shape geometry options

The custom shape options are similar to those you find for the other shapes, but with a couple of unique options:

- **Defined Proportions:** Draws a shape based on the original proportions you used when you created it.
- **Defined Size:** Draws a shape based on its original size when you created it.

Editing shapes

You can edit shapes you create by using a variety of tools and techniques. Here's a list of the things you can do to modify your shapes:

- **Select:** Choose the Shape Selection tool to move one or more shapes in their layers. This tool shares a flyout menu with the Shapes tools.
- **Move:** Choose the Move tool (press V) to move the entire contents of the shape layer.
- **Delete:** Select a shape and press Delete to remove it.
- **Transform shapes:** Choose the Shape Selection tool and select your shape. Choose Image⇨Transform Shape and choose your desired transformation.
- **Change the color:** Double-click the thumbnail of the shape layer on the Layers palette. This action transports you to the Color Picker, where you can choose a new color.
- **Clone a shape:** Press Alt (Option on the Mac) and move the shape with the Move tool.

To convert your vector-based shape into a pixel-based shape, click the Simplify button on the Options bar or choose Layer⇨Simplify Layer. Note that you cannot edit a shape after you simplify it, except to modify the pixels.

13

Working with Type

In This Chapter

▶ Understanding type basics

▶ Creating point type and paragraph type

▶ Setting type options

▶ Editing type

▶ Simplifying (rasterizing) type

▶ Masking with type

▶ Stylizing and warping type

*A*lthough we spout on in this book about how a picture says a thousand words, we would be terribly negligent if we didn't at least give a nod to the power of the written word as well. You may find that you never need to go near the type tools. That's fine. We won't be offended if you skip right past this chapter.

Then again, you may have an occasional need to add a caption or a headline or maybe even a short paragraph to an image. Although it's by no means a word-processing or even page-layout program, Elements does give you ample tools for creating, editing, stylizing, and even distorting type.

Understanding Type Basics

Elements has four type tools. Two of them are for entering horizontally oriented type, and two are for entering vertically oriented type. Don't worry about the vertical type tools. Although you can use them, they're really designed for the Asian market, to enter Chinese and Japanese characters. The horizontal and vertical type tools are identical in their attributes, so we just cover the two horizontal type tools from here on, and, for the sake of simplicity, we just call them the Type and Type Mask tools:

- ✔ **Type tool:** Use this tool to enter type. This type is created on its own type layer except when used in Bitmap mode or Indexed Color mode, neither of which supports layers.

  We refer to layers a lot in this chapter, so if your layer knowledge is rusty, check out Chapter 8.

- ✔ **Type Mask tool:** This tool doesn't create actual type; instead, it creates a selection border in the shape of the type you want to enter. The selection border is added to the active layer. You can do anything with a type selection that you can do with any other selection.

  We also talk more about selections in this chapter; even for more detail on selections, see Chapter 7.

You can enter text in Elements in two different modes: point type and paragraph type. Both the Type and Type Mask tools can enter either one. Here's a brief description of each one; for the step-by-step process of creating the text, see the following sections.

- ✔ **Point type:** Use this mode if all you want to enter is a few words or so. To create point type, select the Type tool, click in your image, and, well, type. The text appears as you type and continues to grow. In fact, it even continues past the boundary of your image! Remember that point type *never* wraps around to a new line. To wrap to the next line, you must press Enter (Return on the Mac).

- ✔ **Paragraph type:** Use this mode to enter longer chunks of text on an image. To create paragraph type, click and drag your type tool to create a text bounding box and then type. All the text is entered in this resizable bounding box. If a line of text is too long, Elements automatically wraps it around to the next line.

Elements is capable of displaying and printing type in two different formats. Each format has its pros and cons, and which format you use depends on your needs. Here's the lowdown on each one:

- ✔ **Vector type:** All text in Elements is initially created as vector type. *Vector* type provides scalable outlines that you can resize without producing jaggy edges in the diagonal strokes. Vector type remains fully editable and always prints with optimum quality, appearing crisp and clean. Vector type is the default type format in Elements.

✔ **Raster type:** When Elements converts vector type into pixels, the text is *rasterized.* Elements refers to this rasterization process as simplifying. When text is *simplified,* it's no longer editable but is converted into a raster image. You usually simplify your vector type when you want to apply filters to the type to produce a special effect or when you want to merge the type with the image. You can't resize simplified type without losing some quality or risking jagged edges. For more details, see the section "Simplifying Type," later in this chapter.

Creating Point Type

The majority of your type entry will most likely be in point type mode. Point type is useful for short chunks of text, like headlines, labels, logos, and headings for Web pages.

Point type is so called because it's preceded by a single anchor point. Remember that point type lines don't wrap automatically, as shown in Figure 13-1.

Figure 13-1: Point type doesn't wrap automatically, but instead can run off your image into a type Neverland.

Follow these steps to create point type:

1. **Open an image or create a new, blank Elements file.**

2. **Select the Type tool from the Tools palette.**

   You can also press the T key.

3. **On the image, click where you want to insert your text.**

   Your cursor is called an *I-beam.* When you click, you make an insertion point.

A small, horizontal line about one-third of the way up the I-beam shows the *baseline* (the line on which the text sits) for horizontal type.

4. **Specify your type options from the Options bar.**

   All the options are described in detail in the section "Specifying Type Options," later in this chapter.

5. **Type your text. Press Enter (Return on the Mac) to begin a new line.**

   When you press Enter (Return on the Mac), you insert a hard return that doesn't move.

6. **When you finish entering the text, click the Commit button (the check-mark icon) on the Options bar.**

   You can also commit the type by pressing Enter on the numeric keypad or by clicking any other tool on the Tools palette. A new type layer with your text is created. Type layers appear on your Layers palette and are indicated by the T icon.

Creating Paragraph Type

If you have larger chunks of text, it's more practical to enter the text as paragraph type. Entering paragraph type is similar to entering text in a word-processing or page-layout program, except that it's contained inside a bounding box. As you type and come to the end of the bounding box, Elements automatically wraps the text to the next line.

To enter paragraph type, follow these steps:

1. **Open an image or create a new, blank Elements file.**

2. **Select the Type tool from the Tools palette or press the T key.**

3. **On the image, insert and size the bounding box by using one of two methods:**

   • Drag to create a bounding box close to your desired size. After you release the mouse button, you can drag any of the handles at the corners and sides of the box to resize the box.

   • Hold down the Alt key (Option key on the Mac) and click the image. The Paragraph Text Size dialog box appears. Enter the exact dimensions of your desired bounding box. When you click OK, your specified box appears, complete with handles for resizing later, if necessary.

4. **Specify your type options from the Options bar.**

Options are described in detail in the following section.

5. **Enter your text. To start a new paragraph, press Enter (Return on the Mac).**

   Each line wraps around to fit inside the bounding box, as you can see in Figure 13-2.

   If you type more text than can squeeze into the text box, an overflow icon appears. Just resize the text box by dragging any of the bounding box handles.

6. **Click the Commit button (the check-mark icon) on the Options bar or press Enter on the numeric keypad.**

   Elements creates a new type layer.

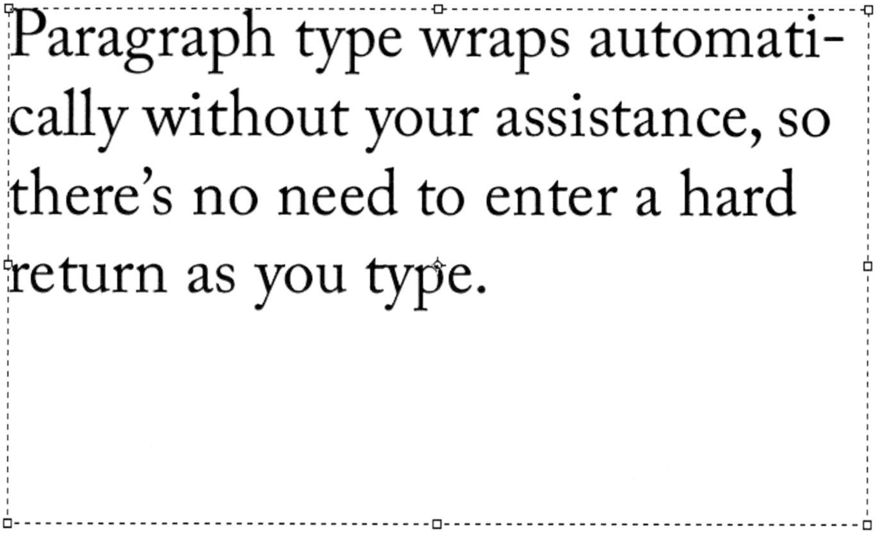

Paragraph type wraps automatically without your assistance, so there's no need to enter a hard return as you type.

Figure 13-2: Paragraph type automatically wraps to fit within your bounding box.

Specifying Type Options

You can find several character and paragraph type settings on the Options bar, shown in Figure 13-3. Although you can't use some of the more specialized options, such as small caps and superscript, you do have access to the most commonly used options, and they should be more than sufficient if all you want to do is pair a small amount of type with your images.

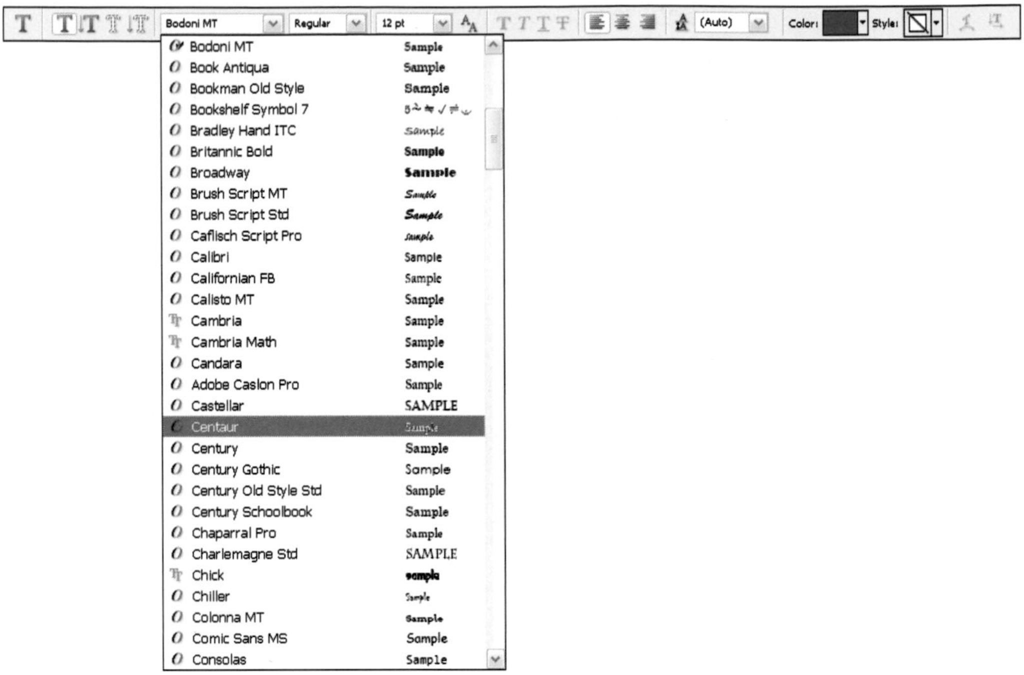

Figure 13-3: Specify your type options, such as font family and size, before you type.

Here's an explanation of each available option on the Options bar, from left to right:

- **Type tools:** You can choose your type tool flavor from the Options bar as well as from the Tools palette.

- **Font family:** Select the font you want from the drop-down list. Elements provides a WYSIWYG (What You See Is What You Get) font menu. After each font name, the word *Sample* is rendered in the actual font — no more selecting a font without knowing what it really looks like. You also find one of these abbreviations before each font name to let you know what type of font it is:

  - *a* for Adobe Type 1 (PostScript) fonts

  - *TT* for TrueType fonts

  - *O* for OpenType fonts

Fonts with no abbreviation are bitmapped fonts.

✔ **Font style:** Some font families have additional styles, such as light or condensed. Only the styles available for a particular font appear in the list. This is also now a WYSIWYG menu.

✔ **Font size:** Select your type size from the drop-down list or just type a size in the text box. Note that type size is most commonly measured in points (72 points equals about 1 inch at a resolution of 72 ppi). You can switch to millimeters or pixels by choosing Edit⇨Preferences⇨Units and Rulers (Elements⇨Preferences⇨Units and Rulers on the Mac).

✔ **Anti-aliasing:** Select Anti-aliasing to slightly smooth out the edges of your text. Anti-aliasing softens that edge by 1 pixel, as shown in Figure 13-4. For the most part, you want to keep this option turned on. The one occasion in which you may want it turned off is when you're creating small type to be displayed on-screen, such as on Web pages. The soft edges can sometimes be tough to read easily.

Anti-aliased   Not anti-aliased

Figure 13-4: Anti-aliasing softens the edges of your type.

- **Faux Bold:** Use this option to create a fake bold style when a real bold style (which you would choose under Font Style) doesn't exist. Be warned that although the sky won't fall, applying faux styles can distort the proportions of a font. You should use fonts with real styles, and if they don't exist — oh, well.

- **Faux Italic:** This option creates a phony italic style and carries the same warning as the Faux Bold option.

- **Underline:** This setting obviously underlines your type, like <u>this</u>.

- **Strikethrough:** Choose this option to apply a ~~strikethrough~~ style to your text.

- **Text alignment:** These three options align your horizontal text on the left or right or in the center. If you happen to have vertical text, these options rotate 90 degrees clockwise and change into Top, Center Vertical, and Bottom settings.

- **Leading:** Leading (pronounced "ledding") is the amount of space between the baselines of lines of type. A *baseline* is the imaginary line on which a line of type sits. You can choose Auto Leading or specify the amount of leading to apply. When you choose Auto Leading, Elements uses a value of 120 percent of your type point size. Therefore, 10-point type gets 12 points of leading. Elements adds that extra 20 percent so that the bottoms of the lowest letters don't crash into the tops of the tallest letters on the line below them.

- **Text Color:** Click the color swatch to select a color for your type from the Color Picker. You can also choose a color from the Swatches palette.

- **Style:** Click this option to access a drop-down palette of preset styles that you can apply to your type. For more on this option and the Create Warped Text option (described next), see "Stylizing and Warping Type," later in this chapter.

- **Create Warped Text:** This fun option lets you distort type in more than a dozen ways.

- **Change the Text Orientation:** Select your type layer and then click this option to switch between vertical and horizontal type orientations.

- **Cancel:** Click this button (or press Esc) to cancel and keep the type from being entered. You use this option, and the Commit option, only after you have clicked the type tool on your canvas.

- **Commit:** Click this button to apply the type to your canvas.

Editing Text

If you have read the first part of this chapter and slogged with us through all the available options for type in Elements, just remember that you can apply these settings either before or after you enter your text. To correct typos, add and delete type, or change any of the type options, simply follow these steps:

1. **Select the Type tool from the Tools palette.**

2. **Select your desired type layer on the Layers palette or click within the text to automatically select the type layer.**

3. **Do one of the following:**

   - *To change the font family, size, color, or other type option:* If you want to change all the text, simply select that type layer on the Layers palette. To select only portions of the text, highlight the text by dragging across it with the I-beam of the Type tool.

   - *To delete text:* Highlight the text by dragging across it with the I-beam of the Type tool. Then press the Backspace key.

   - *To add text:* Make an insertion point by clicking your I-beam within the line of text. Then type your new text.

4. **When you're done editing your text, click the Commit button.**

You may also occasionally need to transform your text. To do so, make sure that the type layer is selected on the Layers palette. Then choose Image⇨ Transform⇨Free Transform. Grab a handle on the bounding box and drag to rotate or scale. Press Ctrl and drag a handle to distort. When you're done, double-click inside the bounding box to commit the transformation. For more details on transformations, see Chapter 9.

Simplifying Type

As we explain in the section "Understanding Type Basics," at the beginning of this chapter, Elements can display and print type in two different formats: vector and raster. Remember that as long as you keep type in a vector format in a type layer, you can edit and resize that type all day long.

Occasionally, however, you may find the need to *simplify* your type — to convert your type into pixels. After they're simplified, you can apply filters, paint on the type, and apply gradients and patterns. If you're working with layers and you flatten your image (merge your layers into a single background image), your type layer is also simplified and merged with the other pixels in your image. By the way, if you try to apply a filter to a type layer, Elements barks at you that the type layer must be simplified before proceeding and gives you the opportunity to click OK (if you want to simplify) or Cancel.

To simplify your type, select the type layer on the Layers palette and choose Layer⇨Simplify Layer. Your type layer is then converted (the T icon disappears) into a regular layer on which your type is now displayed as pixels against a transparent background, as shown in Figure 13-5.

Simplified pixel type

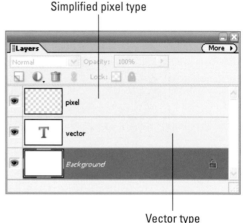

To avoid re-creating your type from scratch, be sure to make all necessary edits before simplifying. This includes sizing your text. After you simplify your type, you cannot resize your text without risking the dreaded jaggies. The other downside to remember about simplified type is that

Vector type

Figure 13-5: Simplifying your type layer converts vector type into pixels.

although it looks identical to vector type on-screen, it never prints as crisply and cleanly as vector type. Even at higher-resolution settings, a slight jagged edge always appears on simplified type. So, if you're experimenting with painting or filters on your type, just make a duplicate of your type layer before simplifying it and then hide that layer.

Masking with Type

Using the Type Mask tool epitomizes the combination of type and image. Unlike its conventional cousin, the Type Mask tool doesn't create a new layer. Instead, it creates a selection on the active layer. This is the tool of choice for filling text with an image or cutting text out of an image so that the background shows through, as shown in Figure 13-6.

A selection is a selection, no matter how it was created. So, even though they look like letters, they act like selections. You can move, modify, and save them.

The Ancient Art of
MASKS

Corbis Digital Stock

Figure 13-6: The Type Mask tool enables you to cut type out of solid color or image layers.

Here are the steps to create a type mask:

1. **Open the image of your choice.**

   We selected a stone texture.

2. **Convert your background into a layer by double-clicking the word** *Background* **on the Layers palette. Click OK.**

   This step enables you to jazz up the type with styles later on.

3. **Choose the Horizontal Type Mask tool from the Tools palette and then click the image where you want your text.**

4. **Specify your type options, such as font family, style, and size, on the Options bar.**

5. **Type your desired text. When you're done, click the Commit button on the Options bar.**

   A selection border in the shape of your type appears on your image.

6. **Choose Select⇨Inverse, which deselects your letter selections and selects everything else.**

7. **Press the Backspace (Delete on the Mac) key to delete everything outside your selection border.**

   Your type is now filled with your image.

8. **Choose Select⇨Deselect.**

9. **Experiment with applying layer styles to your type.**

   If the Layer Styles palette isn't visible, choose Window⇨Styles and Effects. Select the Apply Effects, Filters, and Layer Styles button selected in the palette. Select Layer Styles from the drop-down list on the palette. Choose the style you want. We used a drop shadow and an inner bevel in Figure 13-7. You can find more details about layer styles in Chapter 11.

Corbis Digital Stock

Figure 13-7: Fill type with imagery by using the Type Mask tool.

If you want to admire your type against a solid background, as we did, create a new layer and then choose Edit⇨Fill Layer and choose your desired color from the Use drop-down menu.

Stylizing and Warping Type

If you tried your hand at creating a type mask in the preceding section, you know that Elements is capable of much more than just throwing a few black letters at the bottom of your image. With a few clicks here and there, you can warp, distort, enhance, and stylize your type. If you're not careful, your creative typography can outshine your image.

Adjusting type opacity

If you checked out Chapter 8 before reading this chapter, you know that layers are a digital version of the old analog transparency sheets. You can change the opacity of elements on layers to enable the underlying layer to show through in varying degrees. This is also possible on a type layer. Peek at Figure 13-8 to see how varying the percentage of opacity of our type layer makes more of the underlying layer of water show through.

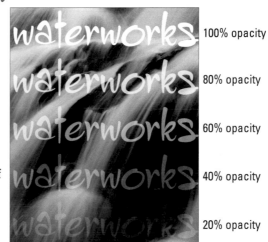

Corbis Digital Stock

Figure 13-8: You can vary the opacity of type layers to allow the underlying layer to peek through.

To change the opacity of a type layer, simply select the layer on the Layers palette, click the arrow to the right of the Opacity setting, and drag the slider. The lower the percentage, the less opaque the type (and the more the underlying layer shows through).

Applying filters to your type

One of the most interesting things you can do with type in Elements that you can't do in a word-processing or page-layout program is apply special effects, such as filters. You can make type look like it's on fire, underwater, or on the move, as shown in Figure 13-9, where we applied a motion blur. The only caveat, as we mention earlier, is that type has to be simplified first before a filter can be applied. Be sure to do all your text editing before you get to the filtering stage. Applying the filter is as easy as just selecting the simplified type layer on the Layers palette and choosing a filter from the Filter menu. For more on filters, see Chapter 11.

Corbis Digital Stock

Figure 13-9: Applying a motion blur to type can make it appear as fast as the car.

Painting your type with color and gradients

Changing the color of text is as easy as highlighting it and selecting a color from the Color Picker. But what if you want to do something a little more unconventional, like apply brush strokes of paint randomly across the type, like we did in the first image shown in Figure 13-10? It's really easier than it looks. Again, as with applying filters to text, the only criterion is that the type has to be simplified first. After that's done, choose a color, grab the Brush tool with settings of your choice, and paint. In our example, we used the Granite Flow brush, found in the Special Effect Brushes presets. We used a diameter of 39, 15, and 6 pixels and just swiped our type a few times.

Figure 13-10: Bring your type to life with color (left) or a gradient (right).

If you want the color or gradient to be confined to only the type area, you can select the text by either Ctrl+clicking (⌘+clicking on the Mac) the layer containing the text or locking the transparency of the layer on the Layers palette.

You can also apply a gradient to your type. Here are the steps to follow after simplifying your type:

1. **Select the Gradient tool from the Tools palette.**

2. **On the Options bar, click the downward-pointing arrow next to the Gradient Picker to access the Gradient Picker drop-down palette.**

3. **Choose your desired gradient.**

   If you want to create a custom gradient, find out how in Chapter 12.

4. **Position your gradient cursor on the text where you want your gradient to start and drag to where you want your gradient to end.**

   Don't like the results? Drag again until you get the look you want. Remember that you can drag at any angle and to any length, even outside your type. In the second image shown in Figure 13-10, we used the copper gradient and just dragged from the top of the letters to the bottom.

Warping your type

If horizontal or vertical text is just way too regimented for you, try out some of the distortions you can apply to your type with the Warp feature. The best part about the distortions you apply to the type is that the text remains fully editable. This feature is fun and easy to use. Click the Create Warped Text button at the far right end of the Options bar. (It's the T with a curved line under it.) This action opens the Warp Text dialog box, where you find a vast array of distortions on the Style pop-up menu with descriptive names like Bulge, Inflate, and Squeeze.

After selecting a warp style, you can adjust the orientation, amount of bend, and degree of distortion by dragging the sliders. The Bend setting affects the amount of warp, and the Horizontal and Vertical Distortions apply perspective to that warp. Luckily, you can also view the results as you adjust. We could give you technical explanations of these adjustments, but the best way to see what they do is to just play with them. See Figure 13-11 to get a quick look at a few of the warp styles. The names speak for themselves.

Figure 13-11: Text remains fully editable even after applying distortions with the Warp command.

Part V
Printing, Creating, and Sharing

The 5th Wave — By Rich Tennant

"Are you using that 'clone' tool again?!"

In this part . . .

Regardless of whether you read much of what is contained in the first four parts of this book, this last part finishes up with photo output and deployment. As is the case with so many other editing features, you have an abundance of opportunities for outputting your files. Beginning with the most familiar method, which is simply printing to your desktop color printer, we talk about how to get the best results on your printed images. We start with printing to your personal desktop printer and then cover issues related to submitting photos to commercial photo labs and service centers.

In addition to printing, you have a number of different options for sharing images, and they're all covered in the final chapters, where you find out about slide shows and videodiscs and about Web hosting, e-mailing, and sharing via online services. The opportunities are enormous, and you'll want to look over all that Photoshop Elements has to offer related to photo output and file sharing.

Aloha!
Wish you were here

14

Getting It on Paper

*P*erhaps the greatest challenge to individuals using programs like Photoshop Elements, and even the professionals who use its granddaddy, Adobe Photoshop, is getting what you see on your monitor to render a reasonable facsimile on a printed page. You can find all sorts of books on color printing — how to get color right, how to calibrate your equipment, and how to create and use color profiles — all for the purpose of getting a good match between your computer monitor and your printer. It's downright discouraging to spend a lot of time tweaking an image so that all the brilliant blue colors jump out of your computer monitor only to find that all those blues turn to murky purples when the photo is printed.

If you already read Chapters 2 and 3, you're ahead of the game because you know a little bit about color management, color profiles, and printer resolutions. After you check out those chapters, your next step is to get to know your printer or your print service center and understand how to correctly print your pictures.

In this chapter, we talk about options — many options — for setting print attributes for printing to your own color printer, and we toss in some tips on how to get better results when you're using print service centers. If you need to, reread this chapter a few times just to be certain that you understand the process for printing good-quality images. A little time spent here will, we hope, save you some headaches down the road.

Getting Pictures Ready for Printing

The first step toward getting your photos to your desktop printer or to a printing service is to prepare each image for optimum output. You have several considerations when you're preparing files, including the ones in this list:

- **Set resolution and size.** Before you print a file, use the Image Size dialog box (Image⇨Resize⇨Image Size) to set your image size and the optimum resolution for your printer. Files that have too much resolution can print images that are inferior to files optimized for a printer. See your printer's documentation for recommendations for resolution. As a general rule, 300 ppi (pixels per inch) works best for most printers printing on high-quality papers. If you print on plain paper, you may find that lower resolutions work just as well.

- **Make all brightness and color corrections before printing.** It stands to reason that you want to make sure that your pictures appear their best before sending them off to your printer. If you have your monitor properly calibrated, as we discuss in Chapter 3, you should see a fair representation of what your pictures will look like before you print them.

- **Decide how color will be managed before you print.** You can color-manage output to your printer in three ways, as we discuss in the next section. Know your printer's profiles and how to use them before you start to print your files.

Working with Color Printer Profiles

In Chapter 2, we talk about creating color profiles for your monitor and selecting a color workspace. The final leg in a color-managed workflow is to convert color from your color workspace profile to your printer's color profile. Basically, this conversion means that the colors you see on your monitor in your current workspace are accurately converted to the color that can be reproduced by your printer. To print accurate color, you need to have a color profile used by your printer at print time.

Understanding how Elements uses color profiles

You can manage color in Photoshop Elements in three ways when it comes time to print your files:

- **Let the printer driver determine color.** This method permits your printer to decide which profile is used when your photo is printed to your desktop color printer. Your printer makes this decision according to the paper you select as the source paper used to print your photos. If you choose Epson Premium Glossy Photo Paper, for example, your printer chooses the profile that goes along with that particular paper. If you choose another paper, your printer chooses a different color profile. This method is all automatic, and color profile selection is made when you print your file.

- **Choose a specific profile.** In the Elements Print dialog box, a list of color profiles appears on the Printer Profile drop-down menu. Many printers install individual color profiles at the time the software for your printer is installed. You can choose to select a profile at print time.

- **Print files with converted color.** Also on the Printer Profile drop-down menu is the Same As Source choice. You use this option if your file has been converted to a printer profile.

Each of these three options requires you to make some kind of choice about how color is managed. You make choices (as we discuss later in this chapter, when we walk you through the steps for printing) about whether to color-manage your output. These selections are all unique to the Print dialog box for your individual printer.

Converting color to a printer profile

The third option in the previous section mentions printing a file with converted color. If you choose one of the first two options for converting color (either you select a profile or you let the printer select one), the image on your monitor doesn't change. The conversion happens at print time.

You can physically convert the color in your image to a given printer profile and doing so actually shows you how the color is converted *before* you print your file. In a way, you're proofing color before wasting paper and ink. If you want to print files with accurate color, we recommend using this method.

Converting from your color workspace (remember that the workspaces are either sRGB or Adobe RGB) is handled differently in Windows and on the Mac. In the following sections, we first point out how to use a third-party tool in Windows to convert color and then later talk about using an AppleScript on the Mac that Mac users get free with their OS X installation.

Using third-party tools for converting color (Windows)

In Windows you can download a free utility from Dry Creek Photo (www.drycreekphoto.com) that converts color from a workspace to a color profile. Suppose that you want to print some pictures at a discount store like Costco and you want to be certain to use the correct profile for the photo equipment that prints your pictures. You want to convert color from your color workspace (in this case, sRGB will work best for you) to the profile used for a photo printer and paper you want to order.

Follow these steps to prepare a file for a photo service, such as Costco, or when printing to your own desktop printer that installs profiles for the papers you use:

1. **Make all the necessary edits you need to make in Elements and save your files in TIFF format.**

   You must use TIFF format to use the converter we mention in Step 6.

2. **Download color profiles from your provider's Web site.**

   Almost all service centers post color profiles for their printing equipment. You can visit the Costco Web site at www.costco.com, click the Services link on the home page, and click Photo Center on the next page. You're prompted to set up an account, and then you see a page where profiles are listed. Costco makes the profiles available for stores in their geographic regions, and usually you find profiles for printing on the store's equipment and profiles best suited for different papers. *Note:* If several profiles are available for downloading, be certain to use the right profile for the paper you want your pictures to be printed on.

   If you use a photo lab that wants you to convert color and embed profiles, you can visit independent lab Web sites and download profiles as well.

   If you want to convert color to your own printer, use a color profile installed for your printer.

3. **Copy the profiles to your system color folder:** C:\WINDOWS\system32\spool\drivers\color.

   This folder is where all your color profiles are stored.

   If you're converting color for your own printer, this folder contains all the color profiles installed by your printer when you installed the printer driver.

4. **Download a converter by going to** http://drycreekphoto.com/tools/profile_converter **and clicking the ProfileConverterSetup.zip link.**

   You need a utility to convert your files that use the Adobe RGB (1998) or sRGB color space to the color space used by machines at your service center. Fortunately, the Dry Creek Photo converter is a great free tool.

The Dry Creek Photo Web site is one of the best sources of information available for color management and color profiling. In addition to offering custom color-profiling services, Dry Creek Photo hosts a number of different color profiles for many different commercial printers.

5. **After downloading the file to your hard drive, double-click the Setup file and follow the brief steps in the install wizard.**

6. **Choose Start⇨Programs⇨Dry Creek Photo⇨Profile Converter⇨ICC Profile Converter.**

   The simple program interface opens, as you see in Figure 14-1.

Figure 14-1: Select the options for converting the color profile and select the Embed Profile in Image check box before clicking the Convert button.

7. **Click the Source Image ellipsis (. . .) and select the source file.**

   The source file is the file saved in TIFF format that you want to print.

8. **Click the Source Color Profile ellipsis and select the source color profile.**

   This color profile is currently embedded in your source file.

9. **Click the Destination Image ellipsis and select the folder where you want to save your file.**

10. **Click the Destination Color Profile ellipsis and select the color profile used by the equipment where you place your order.**

    You saved your color profiles to the Windows color folder, so be certain to look in this folder for the target printer color profiles.

11. **If you want to process multiple files, select the Process Multiple Files check box.**

12. **Be certain to select the Embed Profile in Image check box and then click the Convert button.**

    After you click Convert, the profile converter handles the profile conversion and saves your files to the target folder.

Converting profiles using operating system tools (Macintosh)

If you're a Mac user, you don't have to look far when you want to convert color spaces in your photos to output profiles. Mac OS X has a number of AppleScripts that few people know about. You can convert profiles for individual images or batch-process the conversion just like Windows users who work with the Dry Creek Photo utility.

On the Mac, follow these steps when you want to prepare files for a service such as the Costco photo centers or when you're printing to your desktop printer:

1. **Make all the necessary edits in Elements and save your files in the format needed by your service center.**

   In many cases, JPEG files are used by service centers. If you intend to print your pictures to your own desktop printer, use TIFF for the format. Also, be certain to use sRGB or Adobe RGB (1998) as your working space and save your files with the working space embedded in the images. (See Chapter 2 to find out how to save your photos while embedding a working space profile.)

2. **Open the AppleScripts ColorSync folder.**

   AppleScripts are miniature programs installed with your operating system and custom scripts you can create with the Apple Script Editor, also installed with your operating system installation. On Mac OS X, a number of short scripts are installed for you to convert color spaces in files saved as JPEG or TIFF. To find the scripts used for converting color profiles, open `Macintosh HD/Library/ColorSync/Scripts`.

3. **Locate the script to convert the color in your photo or photos.**

   Open the `ColorSync` folder and identify the scripts used for converting and embedding color output profiles. Locate the Embed chosen profile script in the Scripts folder inside the ColorSync folder as shown in Figure 14-2.

   The Embed Chosen Profile script prompts you in a dialog box to select the profile you want to use for your color output source.

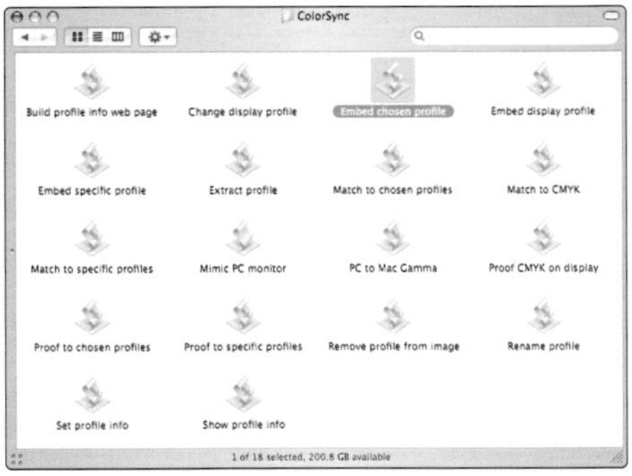

Figure 14-2: Locate the Embed Chosen Profile icon in the Scripts folder.

4. **Drag a file or multiple files to the Embed a Chosen Profile script icon:**

A dialog box opens where you're prompted to identify only your output profile. Assuming that you saved all your images by embedding either the sRGB or Adobe RGB (1998) color profile (in Step 1), drag the files to the Embed Chosen Profile Script icon; the dialog box shown in Figure 14-3 opens. To select a specific output profile, click OK.

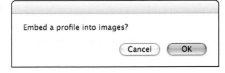

Figure 14-3: You're prompted to confirm your profile conversion first.

The Choose a File dialog box opens, as shown in Figure 14-4. The AppleScript automatically opens the folder where your color profiles are stored.

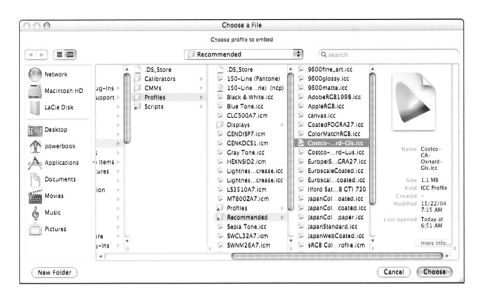

Figure 14-4: Select the output color profile.

5. **From the drop-down list, select the profile you want to use and click the Choose button.**

That's it. Your file is converted to your chosen output profile.

Printing to Epson Inkjet Printers

Print settings vary according to manufacturers, and we can't hope to cover all printers in this chapter. We choose to discuss Epson printers as an introduction to printing to desktop color printers in this chapter, but we also show some print options for HP and Canon low-end inkjets later in the chapter.

If you own a different brand of printer or use a service that uses other printers, what's important to know in reviewing this section is the process involved in printing your files. Regardless of what type of printer you own, be aware of when a color profile is used and how color is either managed or not managed. You may have different check box selections and menu commands, but the process is identical for any printer printing your photos.

Over the past few years, at least half of many service provider troubleshooting tech calls coming from clients involved problems with accurate color output from Epson and some other ink jet printers. We're not talking about subtle changes between monitor and printer, but, rather, huge monstrous color changes on output prints. As it turns out, almost all the strange output results originated from just one minor error when setting up a file to print — when and how to manage color in the Print dialog box.

We've come up with settings that will work well for you to get accurate results without stress or frustration. Just remember to use the settings exactly as described, and you can achieve superior results with either desktop or professional printers.

When you install your printer driver, the installation utility also installs a number of color profiles. You can choose the profiles in the Photoshop Elements Print dialog box and control all the printing by using the profile provided by your printer manufacturer.

You can also print from the Organizer by selecting one or more image thumbnails in the Organizer window and then choosing File⇨Print. We use printing from Standard Edit mode for the examples shown here because you may often want to perform some final corrections before printing.

You have a choice for how these profiles are used. You can

- ✓ Choose an automatic method where the manufacturer created a no-nonsense process of automatic profile selection using your printer driver.
- ✓ Choose to select the printer profile in the Print dialog box. The color profile is automatically selected when you choose the paper source.

Both methods are described in the following sections.

Automatic profile selection for Epson printers

The automatic profile selection method exists, and we want to explain to you what goes on with it so that you're aware, but we don't recommend that you use it for your printing chores. Among other things, you really can't tell by looking in the Print Preview dialog box what profile you're using to print your file. In addition, you don't have a way to convert your working space color to the device profile for accurate color viewing on your monitor. But you should understand what goes on when the selection is made so that you're aware of some potential consequences.

The color engines in Photoshop Elements — ICM (Image Color Management in Windows), Colorsync (on the Mac), and the Epson print driver — work in a similar manner, although they all show subtle differences when they're used to convert a file.

For your first setup instructions, we use the Epson Color Engine and work with an unconverted file, letting the printer driver automatically select the color profile. Our unconverted file is a photo still in its native color space, such as sRGB or Adobe RGB (1998). Assuming that your file is open in Elements and you already sized your file for the target dimensions and resolution for output, follow the steps in the next section to print from the native color space (sRGB or Adobe RGB [1998]).

Sizing files for output

When we talk about sizing files, we're referring to the physical width and height dimensions and the resolution. If you print your pictures at 8 inches by 10 inches, be certain that you visit the Image Size dialog box by choosing Image⇨Resize⇨Image Size and verify that the width and height dimensions are established for your desired paper size. Also critically important is the image resolution, which you can also adjust in the Image Size dialog box. Use your printer manufacturer recommendations for resolution according to the paper type you use. If you can't find a recommendation in the user manual, use 300 ppi (pixels per inch) as a standard for printing to quality coated-paper stocks, such as Epson premium glossy photo paper.

Above all, don't size your image resolution larger than the default size of your photo. For example, if you have a 5 x 7 inch photo at 300 ppi, don't try to size the photo up to 8 x 10 inches at 300 ppi. Doing so can produce unexpected results. If you need an image size larger than your file size, go back to your original digital camera image and edit it for color correction and size it to the desired output. If the original camera image is smaller than you want, you're stuck and can't get a quality print that greatly exceeds your camera's capture capabilities.

Printing from Windows

Follow these steps to print from the native color space in Windows:

1. **Choose File⇨Page Setup.**

   The Page Setup dialog box opens.

2. **Select the orientation of your print.**

   Your choices are either Portrait or Landscape.

Figure 14-5: Click the orientation matching your photo, and then click OK.

3. **Click the Printer button to open a second Page Setup dialog box. From the Name drop-down list, select your printer, as shown in Figure 14-5, and then click OK.**

4. **Click OK again to dismiss the Page Setup dialog box.**

5. **Choose File⇨Print to open the Print dialog box.**

6. **Click the Show More Options check box to display the color management options, as shown in Figure 14-6.**

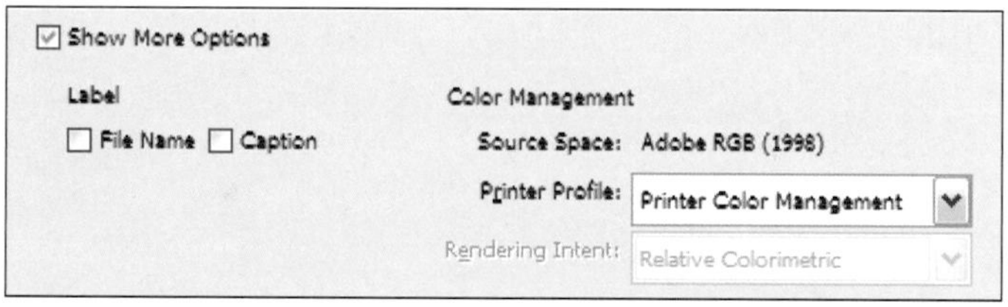

Figure 14-6: Select the Show More Options check box and select Printer Color Management from the Printer Profile drop-down list.

By default, the color management options are hidden.

7. **From the Printer Profile drop-down list, select Printer Color Management.**

   This choice uses your current workspace color and later converts the color from your workspace to the printer output file when you open the printer driver dialog box.

8. **Click Print in the Print dialog box.**

   The file doesn't print yet. Rather, the same second print dialog box that appears in Step 3 opens again.

9. **Verify that your target printer is still selected in the Print dialog box (the second Print dialog box) and click Properties.**

   The printer driver dialog box opens.

   Each printer displays a different dialog box after you click Properties in the second Print dialog box. Figure 14-7 shows you the Epson Stylus Photo R320 Series Properties dialog box. Although many Epson printers use an identical dialog box, you find that some Epson printers, especially the high-end devices, display different dialog boxes. Furthermore, printers from other manufacturers appear with completely different settings in the printer driver dialog box.

10. **Set print attributes.**

    In our Epson example, select Premium Glossy Photo Paper (or another paper from the Type drop-down list that you may be using), and then click the Best Photo radio button, as shown in Figure 14-7.

    Now, it's time to color manage your file. This step is critical in your print production workflow.

11. **Click the Advanced button, and then, in the warning dialog box, simply click Continue.**

    The Advanced Settings dialog box opens, as shown in Figure 14-8.

12. **A few choices need to be made in this dialog box. The most important are**

    • *Select a paper type.* You selected paper already? The second drop-down menu in the Paper & Quality section of the dialog box determines the application of inks. Choose the same paper here as you did in Step 10.

Figure 14-7: Select the paper type from the Type drop-down list and the Best Photo option for printing photos.

Figure 14-8: Click Advanced, and then click Continue to access the advanced settings in the Epson printer driver.

- *Turn color management on.* Because you're letting the print driver determine the color, you need to be certain that the Color Controls radio button is active. This setting tells the print driver to automatically select a printer profile for the paper type you selected.

- *Set the color mode.* Do not use Epson Vivid. This choice produces inferior results on photos. Choose the Epson Standard setting (refer to Figure 14-8).

If you frequently print files using the same settings, you can save your settings by clicking the Save Setting button.

13. **To print the photo, click OK and then OK again in the Print dialog box.**

Your file is sent to your printer. The color is converted automatically from your source workspace of sRGB or Adobe RGB (1998) to the profile the printer driver automatically selects for you.

Printing from the Macintosh

On the Macintosh, the Epson printer driver offers you some different settings, although the process is quite similar. Again, we use the automatic method for color conversion and let the print driver handle the conversion.

Follow these steps to print from the Mac:

1. **Follow Steps 1 through 7 in the preceding section.**

   Make a choice for paper orientation and select Printer Color Management in the Elements Print dialog box (just like Windows users).

2. **After making choices for paper orientation and color profile in the Elements Print dialog box, click Print.**

   A second Print dialog box opens, as shown in Figure 14-9.

3. **From the pop-up menu below Presets, select Print Settings.**

   Choices available to you from the pop-up menu shown in Figure 14-9 are specific to your printer type. If you use a printer other than Epson, and sometimes other than a specific Epson model, your menu choices change.

Figure 14-9: Select Print Settings in the printer driver dialog box.

4. **In the Print Settings dialog box, select the paper type from the Media Type pop-up menu. Click the Advanced radio button and select Best Photo from the pop-up menu (see Figure 14-10).**

   Note that you may have some other options choices for Quality if you're using another Epson printer. If so, choose the best quality from the list you see on the menu.

   Now it's time to select the color management method.

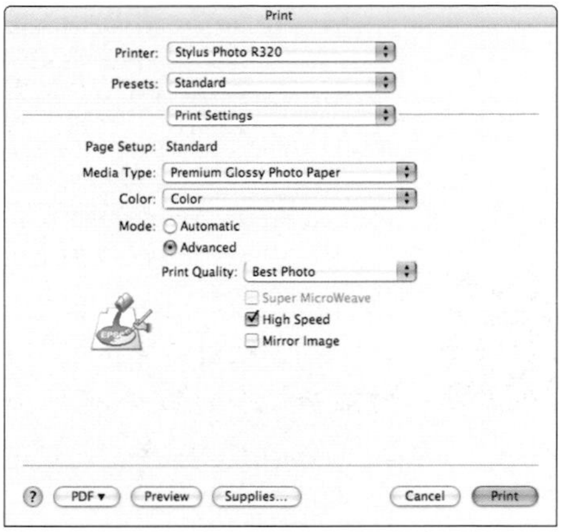

5. **From the pop-up menu where you now see Print Settings, click to open the menu and select Color Management, as shown in Figure 14-11.**

6. **Click Color Controls.**

   Making this choice tells the print driver to manage the color.

7. **Select Epson Standard from the Mode pop-up menu.**

8. **Click Print to print the file.**

   The file is sent to your printer with an automatic color conversion from your workspace color to the printer color profile.

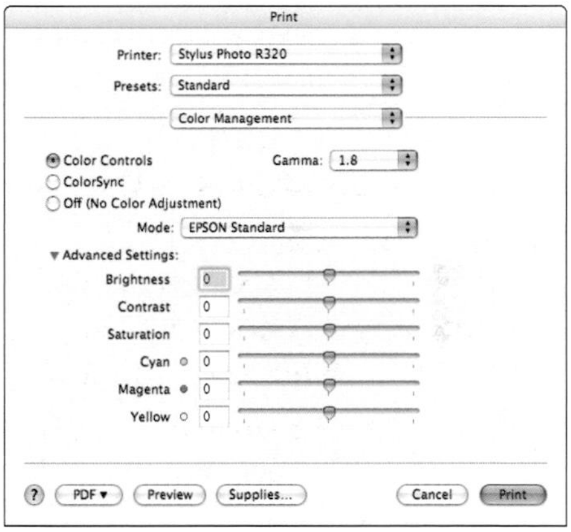

Figure 14-10: Select Media Type and Best Photo in the Print Settings dialog box.

Figure 14-11: Open the Color Management dialog box.

Selecting a printer profile

Another method for managing color when you're printing files is to select a printer profile from the available list of color profiles installed with your printer. Whereas in the earlier section "Automatic profile selection for Epson printers" you used your printer to manage color, this time you let Photoshop Elements manage the color. Again, the Windows options and Macintosh commands vary a little, so we discuss how to print by selecting a profile for each operating system.

Printing using a printer profile in Windows

The steps in this section are the same as the ones described for printing files for automatic profile selection when you're setting up the page and selecting a printer. When you choose File⇨Print, you open the Elements Print dialog box as described in the previous section. Your steps now change when you let Elements handle the color conversion, and you proceed to move through the Print dialog box as follows:

1. **From the Printer Profile drop-down list in the Print dialog box, select the color profile designed for use with the paper you have chosen to print your image.**

   In this example, we use a heavyweight matte paper color profile, as shown in Figure 14-12. (Note that custom color profiles you acquire from a profiling service come with recommended color-rendering intents. For this paper, Relative Colormetric is recommended and is selected on the Rendering Intent drop-down menu, as you see in Figure 14-12.)

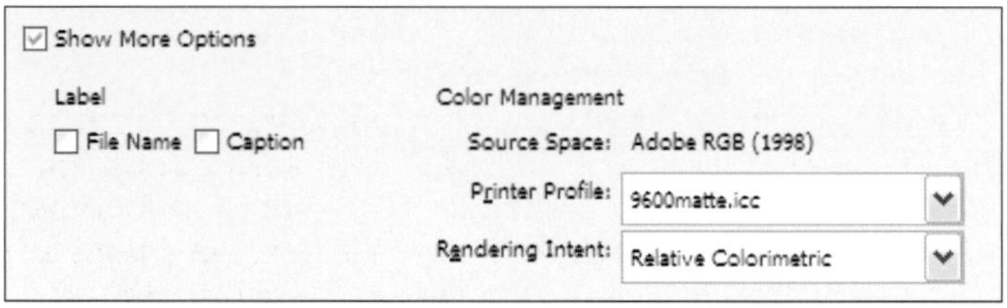

Figure 14-12: Choose a printer profile that matches the paper you use.

2. **Click Print.**

   The second Print dialog box opens.

3. **Click the Properties button.**

   You arrive at the same dialog box shown earlier in this chapter, in Figure 14-7.

4. **Click the Best Photo radio button. From the Type drop-down list, select the recommended paper choice.**

   Custom color profiles are also shipped with guidelines for selecting proper paper.

5. **Click Advanced and click Continue to arrive at the same dialog box shown earlier, in Figure 14-8.**

   The paper choice selection is automatically carried over from the previous Properties dialog box (in Step 2 in the steps in the preceding section). The one different setting you make is in the Color Management section.

6. **Click the ICM (Image Color Management) radio button and click No Color Management, as shown in Figure 14-13.**

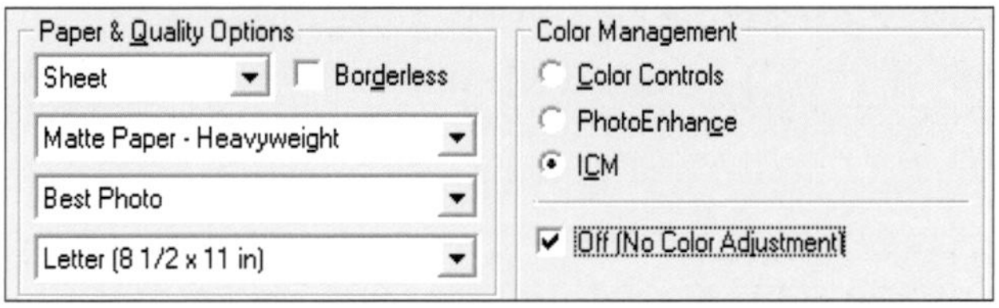

Figure 14-13: Click ICM and click No Color Management.

Because you selected the color profile in Step 1 and you're letting Elements manage the color, be sure that Color Management is turned off. If you don't turn color management off, you end up double profiling your print.

Printing using a printer profile on the Mac

On the Mac, you follow the same steps in Elements to select a printer profile in the Elements Print dialog box. When you select Color Management as we described in Figure 14-11, select the Off (No Color Adjustment) radio button. You make all other settings choices by following the same steps described in the section "Printing from the Macintosh," earlier in this chapter.

Printing with a custom profile

Printing with a custom profile is very simple. Just remember that you must use the profile with exactly the same settings as you used to print the test target when the profile was created. For custom profiles, you always use no color management throughout the output process.

Let us make this concept even clearer. When you generate your test target for the profiling service where you may order a custom profile created for your printer, the service requires that you print the target without color conversions of any kind. The target has to reflect the actual colors generated by your printer from a known sample file with no modifications whatsoever for a known printing condition and media type. The resulting profile tells the color engine exactly how to modify the output data to match the colors as closely as possible to your working space or a different previously embedded color profile.

For all this to work properly, the printer can't be allowed to modify the printing data in any way. All the work has to be done by Photoshop Elements. So, assuming that you have a custom profile ready to use, here's the setup:

1. **Use a profile converter to convert color.**

   In Windows, use a utility like the Dry Creek Photo Profile Converter, and on the Mac use an AppleScript to convert color. (For details, see "Converting color to a printer profile," earlier in this chapter.)

   If you have obtained a custom profile from a media supplier, you must use the specific media and intent settings it recommend for your printer, although all other instructions in this section are the same.

2. **Open the converted file in Elements and choose File⇨Print.**

3. **In the Print dialog box, select Same As Source for your printer profile, as shown in Figure 14-14.**

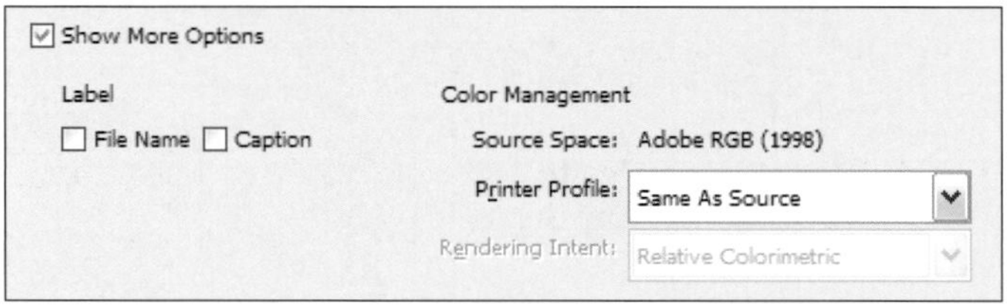

Figure 14-14: Select Same As Source when you print files with converted color.

4. **Turn off color management.**

   Use the same settings for printing when you let Elements determine color. Be certain to turn off color management, the same way we show you in Figure 14-13, in the section "Printing using a printer profile in Windows."

Printing to HP Inkjet Printers

Regardless of the printer you use, the process for printing follows the same logic as we describe for printing to Epson printers. Unfortunately, each manufacturer uses different dialog boxes and different menu command names that can leave you completely confused if you try to apply the steps you use in printing on one printer to a second, different printer.

The three methods for managing color (described in the section "Understanding how Elements uses color profiles," earlier in this chapter) apply to all printers, but the dialog boxes, buttons, and menu choices appear differently.

If you own an HP printer, you probably know where to make your paper selection and your best photo selection. The most obscure setting is likely to be the color management choice. Rather than step through each detailed step for printing to an HP low-end desktop printer, take a look in the following section at how to manage color.

Printing to HP printers in Windows

As with all printers, you have three choices for managing color with an HP printer:

- ✔ **Let your printer determine color.** Follow these general steps:

  1. **Choose File⇨Print to open the Print dialog box.**

  2. **Click the Show More Options check box to display color management options (refer to Figure 14-6).**

  3. **From the Printer Profile drop-down menu, select Printer Color Management and then click Print.**

     A second Print dialog box opens.

  4. **Click Properties to open the printer driver dialog box.**

  5. **On the Advanced tab, click Graphic and click Image Color Management. From the ICM Method drop-down menu, select ICM Handled by Printer, as shown in Figure 14-15.**

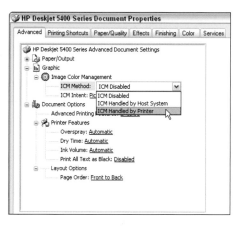

Figure 14-15: Click the Advanced tab and select ICM Handled by Printer.

- ✔ **Let Elements determine color.** Follow the preceding steps, but this time select a color profile in the Print dialog box (refer to Step 3) and select ICM Disabled on the Advanced tab (refer to Step 5).

- ✔ **Print a file with converted color.** Follow the preceding steps, but select Same As Source in the Print dialog box (refer to Step 3) and select ICM Disabled on the Advanced tab (refer to Step 5).

Printing to HP printers on the Macintosh

If there's a way to manage color by using one of the HP Deskjet 5400 series of printers, we haven't found it. HP and Windows go together like bread and butter, but HP printers and Macintosh computers leave a lot to be desired. Among the problems with using an HP printer on the Macintosh is the inability to turn off color management. Therefore, the only surefire method of printing to an HP printer on the Mac is to let the printer manage the color. Don't attempt to use a specific color profile, and don't try to convert color before printing.

Follow these steps to print to an HP printer on the Mac:

1. **Follow Steps 1 through 3 in the preceding section ("Printing to HP printers in Windows").**

2. **Select Print Settings.**

3. **In the HP printer driver dialog box, shown in Figure 14-16, select the Paper Type/Quality from the pop-up menu below Presets, and then choose your paper type.**

   Be aware that you'll want to use just HP papers and make a selection for the HP paper type you use, as shown in Figure 14-16.

Because the HP printer driver determines the options in the Mac OS Print dialog box, you don't have an option for Color Management, like you do when you're using a printer like an Epson. When you use the HP printer driver, no color management options appear on the pop-up menu in the Print dialog box, as shown in Figure 14-16.

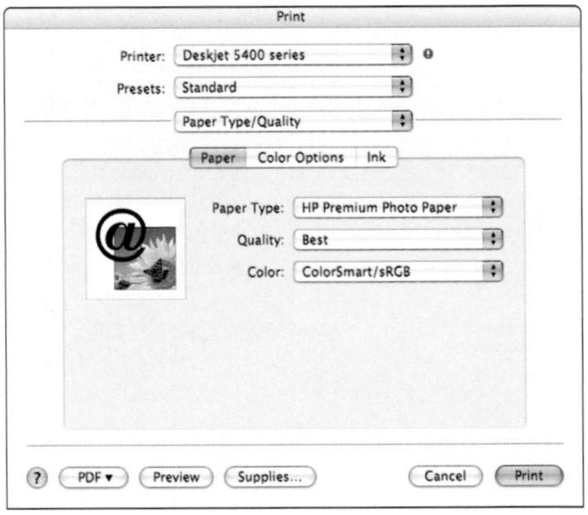

Figure 14-16: Select an HP paper in the Paper Type/Quality dialog box.

Printing to Canon Printers

As with Epson and HP printers (described earlier in the chapter), you follow the same logic and choose to either enable or disable color management when printing to Canon printers. With Canon color printers, the area in the printer driver dialog box is even more hidden than you find in Epson and HP desktop printers.

Printing to Canon printers in Windows

When printing to Canon printers in Windows, you control color management as follows:

✓ **Let your printer determine color.** Follow these steps:

1. **Choose File⇨Print to open the Print dialog box.**

2. **Click the Show More Options check box to display color management options (refer to Figure 14-6).**

3. **From the Printer Profile drop-down menu, select Printer Color Management and then click Print.**

   A second Print dialog box opens.

4. **Click Properties to open the printer driver dialog box.**

5. **On the Main tab, click Manual in the Color/Intensity area, as shown in Figure 14-17.**

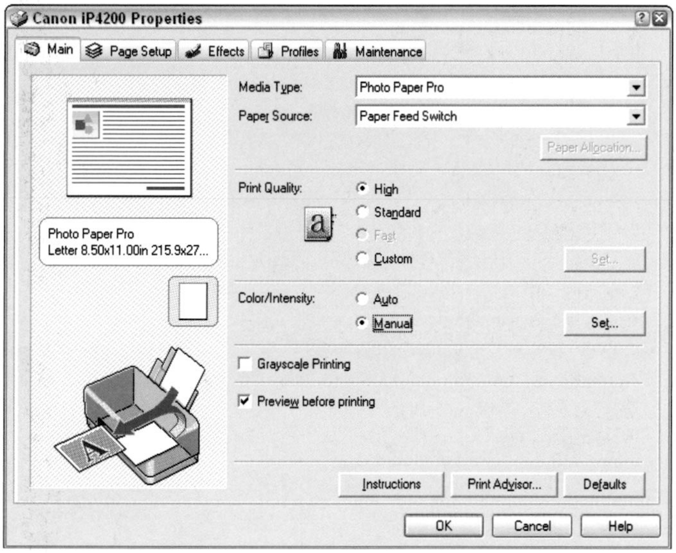

Figure 14-17: Click the Manual radio button for Color/Intensity.

6. **Click the Set button to open the Manual Color Adjustment dialog box.**

7. **Select the Enable ICM (Windows Color Management) check box, shown in Figure 14-18.**

✓ **To let Elements determine color:** Follow the preceding set of steps and deselect the Enable ICM (Windows Color Management) check box in Step 7.

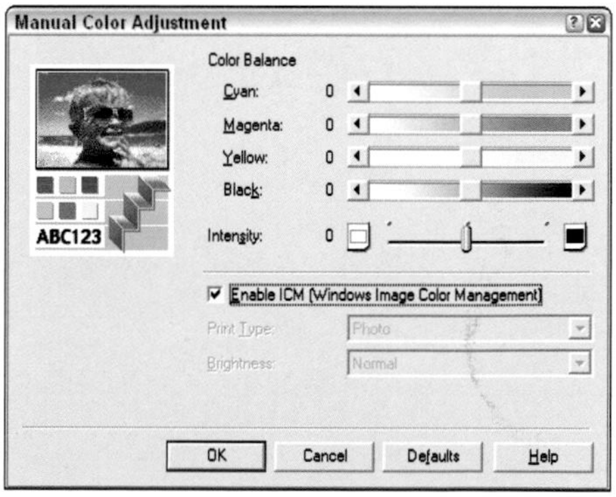

Figure 14-18: Check the Enable ICM (Windows Image Color Management) check box.

✒ **To print a file with converted color:** Select Same As Source in the Print dialog box in Step 3, and deselect ICM (Windows Color Management) in Step 7.

Printing to Canon printers on the Mac

You make the same choices on the Mac as you do in Windows for how you want to manage color on a Canon printer. If you let the printer manage the color, you make a paper choice in the Quality & Media section of the Print dialog box, shown in Figure 14-19. This dialog box appears after you click Print in Elements and after you select Quality & Media from the pop-up menu, below the Presets menu.

From the pop-up menu below the Presets menu, select Color Options. You select BJ Standard when you're letting Elements determine color and select None when you select a printer profile in the Elements Print dialog box; or, select Same As Source when you're printing a file with converted color. The options are shown in Figure 14-20.

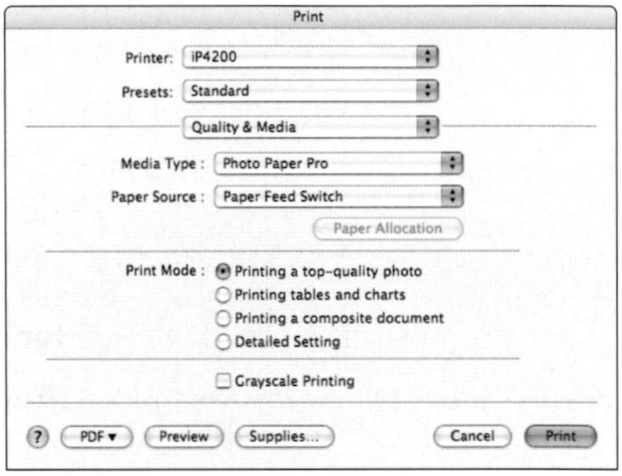

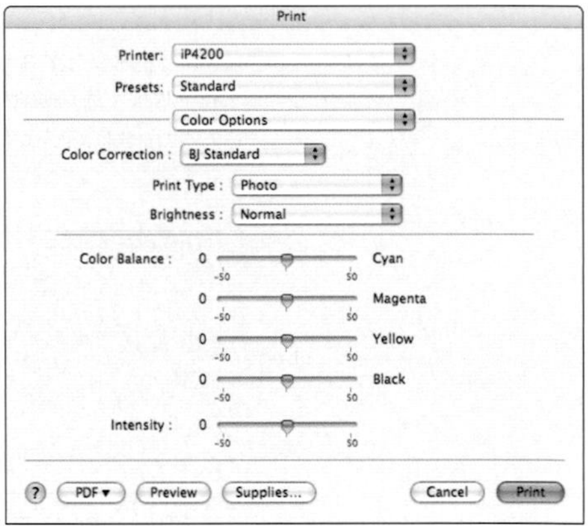

Figure 14-19: Make a paper choice in the Quality & Media dialog box.

Figure 14-20: Select BJ Standard for printing when you want Elements to determine color, or turn off color management by selecting None.

Submitting Files to Service Centers

On provider Web sites, you can usually find guidelines for acceptable file formats and the recommended resolutions and dimensions of your images. If you don't see these guidelines on Web sites, be sure to call and inquire about which file attributes are acceptable.

As a general rule, here are some things you should consider when you're submitting files if guidelines aren't provided:

✔ **Color workspace:** Always ask providers what workspace it prefers to use to convert color. Online services generally recommend that you use sRGB as your color workspace.

✔ **Resolution:** For photo printing machines, be certain to submit files at 300 ppi (pixels per inch). See Chapter 3 for more information on image resolution.

✔ **Dimensions:** As a general rule, size images to the print size. For example, if you want 4-x-6-inch prints, be certain that your images are sized to 4 x 6 inches at 300 ppi.

✔ **File format:** Some centers may take only JPEG images. If TIFF isn't acceptable, open the converted images you saved from the Dry Creek ICC Profile Converter (in Windows):

1. **Open the TIFF file or files in Photoshop Elements and choose File⇨Save As.**

2. **Be certain that the ICC Profile check box is selected in the Save Options in the Save/Save As dialog box. Select JPEG for the format and click Save.**

   Notice that the profile used with the Dry Creek ICC Profile Converter is listed as the ICC Profile. In Figure 14-21, you can see a profile embedded for a Costco print center. (See the section "Converting color to a printer profile," earlier in this chapter, for more on the Dry Creek Converter.)

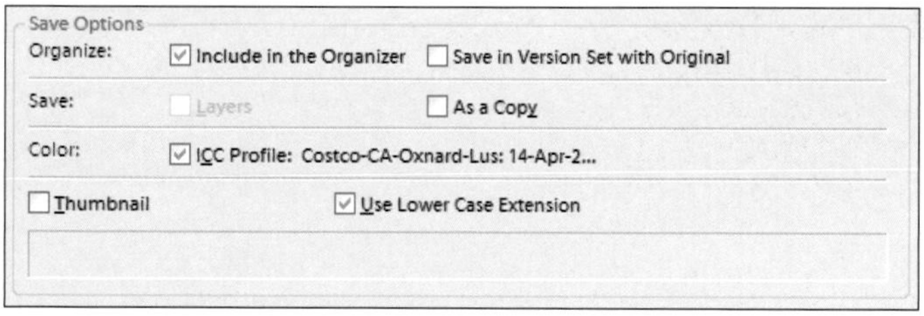

Figure 14-21: You can change file formats from TIFF to JPEG and preserve embedded profiles when you're saving from Elements.

If you're a Mac user, you can convert color by using a JPEG format, and you don't need to be concerned with saving files in a different format in Elements.

✔ **Media storage:** If you walk into a FedEx Kinko's store and go to the self-serve photo-printing machines, you don't see support for any external USB hard drives or removable USB drives. All the print centers support a wide range of media cards used by digital cameras. Be certain to use your memory cards and not USB devices when placing orders. If you use Compact Flash II, memory sticks, or other media sources used by digital cameras, copy your files to these sources when you place orders as a walk-in customer.

Vendors that host Web sites with downloadable profiles and order information are likely to accept file uploads online. This capability saves you the time spent fighting crowds when you're placing orders. In some cases, you can have service centers mail your images back to you so that you don't need to wait when you're picking up orders, either. This online ordering stuff is another matter that we talk about in the next section, however.

Using Online Printing Services

Photoshop Elements supports the Adobe Photoshop Services program, which is a joint effort between Adobe Systems and Kodak EasyShare (formerly Ofoto), a division of Kodak. The Services program offers online ordering of prints and sharing of photos and projects, and it has a huge array of different print products for consumers and professionals.

As of this writing, you get ten free prints, so it's worth taking a little time to check out the service — especially if you want to order prints and have them mailed directly to your home or office. No lines, no hassles, no fighting high-rising gasoline costs — this service offers great prints and an abundance of convenience.

To use the service, follow these steps:

1. **Select files in the Organizer much like you would select files for printing.**

2. **In either editing mode or the Organizer, choose File⇨Order Prints.**

   The Kodak EasyShare Wizard opens, as shown in Figure 14-22. The first screen shown in the wizard is a form for you to create an account.

   If you try to place an order from your office where the IT department prevents you from connecting to some external sources, you may need to have your firewall settings adjusted. Talk to someone in your IT department to help you make a connection.

3. **If you haven't set up an account already, fill in the information and step through the wizard by clicking the Next button on each page. If you have set up an account, supply your logon information.**

   The selected files in the Organizer are automatically loaded in Step 1 of the wizard order page.

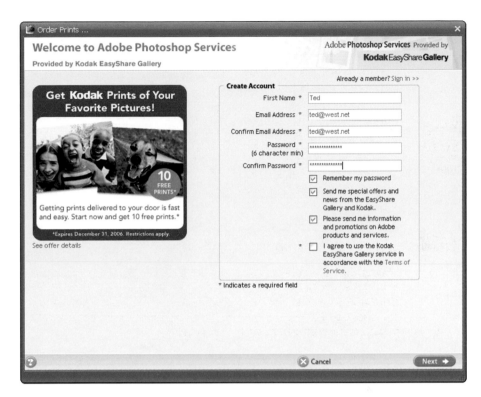

Figure 14-22: Choose File⇨Order Prints and the Kodak EasyShare Wizard opens.

4. **You can modify your order by deleting files from the order and specifying different print sizes and quantities.**

   One nice feature in the service is the option for sending duplicate prints to another party. You can keep an address book on the provider's Web site and specify whom you want to receive an order. This feature is helpful if you're away spending your children's inheritance on a Caribbean cruise and want to send all your kids photos of the great time you're having. Just pop open your laptop on the pool deck, load the digital camera images, and connect via a wireless connection. Before you return to Buffalo in midwinter with a suntan, your kids will frown as they fan through the prints they received a week earlier.

5. **Continue stepping through the wizard to upload your files and confirm your order. Click the Finish button on the last pane and your order is complete.**

Exploring Other Print Options

Photoshop Elements provides you with other options for printing things like video images and contact sheets, adding borders and trim lines, and inverting images for heat transfers like the ones you may use for iron-on T-shirt designs. You find these options in the Print dialog box. Most of these print options are intuitive and easy to use. Just poke around, experiment, and have fun. When it comes time to print, just follow the recommendations we offer here for getting your color right.

Showing It On-Screen

E lements is a great packaging tool that you can use to deploy your photos and creations for screen viewing. And that's not just your computer monitor. You can edit photos or assemble creations that are exported for Web viewing, too, and you can even prepare files to show on your television.

In Chapter 3, you find out about resolutions and color modes. The output requirements for printing files, which we cover in Chapter 14, are much different from what you use for images output for screen viewing.

In this chapter, we cover the options for Web and screen viewing that get you started with basics, including saving images for the Web (or for screen viewing), setting up a slideshow, and burning your images on CDs or DVDs.

Getting Familiar with the Elements Sharing and Printing Options

Before we delve into telling you how to make creations for screen viewing, you should be familiar with your available options for not only screen images, but also sharing and printing. When you open the Organizer and look at the Shortcuts bar, you see three icons. For lack of a better term to globally describe these options, we refer to them as *packaging* your files.

In Figure 15-1, you can see the menu options for the respective items:

- **Printing:** The first menu offers you options for ordering online prints.

- **Sharing:** The second menu provides a number of different sharing options, such as e-mail, e-mail to a mobile phone, Adobe Photoshop online services, and other types of services.

- **Making photo creations:** The third menu (Create) contains commands for a variety of different printing options locally on your desktop printer, options for creating screen presentations, and a few services you can order online.

Figure 15-1: Three menus provide a number of different sharing and printing options.

In Chapter 14, we talk about ordering online prints using commands on the first drop-down menu and sharing options on the second drop-down menu. In this chapter and later in Chapter 16, we cover various commands on the Create drop-down menu.

Creating a Slide Show

This *Million Dollar Baby* is no *Mystic River* — it's simply *Absolute Power!* Well, maybe you won't travel the same path from Rowdy Yates to multiple Academy Award–winning director and filmmaker Clint Eastwood, but even Mr. Eastwood might be impressed with the options for moviemaking with the Photoshop

Elements slide show creations. When he's not rolling out his Panaflex camera, he may just want to take photos of the grandkids and do the directing and producing as well as the editing right in Photoshop Elements.

For the rest of us, we can be our own Clint Eastwood wannabes by using the powerful features of the Photoshop Elements Slide Show Editor to create PDF slide shows and movie files. It's so easy that Elements promises you won't be *Unforgiven.*

Creating a project

You create a project file in the Slide Show Editor and can then export it for a number of different uses. In this section, you find out how to create and save your project. In the next section, you dive into exporting.

Here's how to create a slide show project that you can edit and export later:

1. **Open the Organizer and select the pictures you want to use in your slide show.**

2. **Click the Create button on the Shortcuts bar and choose Slide Show from the drop-down menu.**

   The Slide Show Preferences dialog box opens. Just about everything in the dialog box can be adjusted in the Slide Show Editor, so don't worry about making choices here. If you want to keep the Slide Show Preferences dialog box from reappearing when you make slide creations, deselect the Show This Dialog Each Time a New Slide Show Is Created check box.

3. **Click OK in the Slide Show Preferences dialog box.**

   The Photoshop Elements Slide Show Editor opens, as shown in Figure 15-2.

4. **If your Slide Show Editor doesn't show you a screen similar to the one shown in Figure 15-2, maximize the window by clicking the Maximize button in the upper-right corner of the Editor window.**

   This way, you can see the Storyboard at the bottom of the screen and the Palette Bin on the right side of the editor.

5. **(Optional) Create a Pan and Zoom view.**

   As slides are shown, you can zoom and pan a slide. Click the Enable Pan and Zoom check box and click the Start thumbnail. A rectangle appears in the preview area. Move any one of the four corner handles in or out to resize the rectangle. Moving the cursor inside the rectangle and clicking the mouse button enables you to move the rectangle around the preview.

Figure 15-2: The Elements Slide Show Editor is where you create slideshows.

For the end zoom position, click the End thumbnail and size the rectangle to a zoomed view or a view that you want to stop the zoom. Notice in Figure 15-3 that the End thumbnail is selected and the rectangle is sized down to the zoom area on a portion of the photo.

6. (Optional) Add a graphic.

A library of graphics appears in the Extras pane in the Palette Bin. Drag a graphic to a slide. If you want a blank slide to appear first and then add text and graphics to the blank slide, click Add Blank Slide on the Shortcuts bar at the top of the editor.

7. (Optional) Add text.

Figure 15-3: Open the Slide Show Editor and choose your options for a slide show.

Click the Text tool in the Extras pane in the Palette Bin and drag a text style to the blank slide or the opening slide in the slide show. After you drag text to a slide, the Properties pane opens in the Palette Bin. The text you drag to the slide is placeholder text. To edit the text, click Edit Text in the Properties pane. You can also select a font, a font point size, a color for the text, text alignment, and a font style. After setting the type attributes, click inside the text and move it to the position you want.

8. (Optional) Set transitions.

The icons between the slides in the Storyboard (at the bottom of the Slide Show Editor) indicate a default transition applied to the slide show. You can change transition effects for each slide independently or to all the slides in the show. Click the right-pointing arrow on the right side of a transition icon to open a pop-up menu containing a number of different transitions. If you want to apply the same transition to all slides, choose Apply to All from the menu commands.

9. (Optional) Add audio and media.

You can add audio to the slide show by choosing Add Media⇨Audio from Organizer (or from Folder). Select an audio file and click OK.

You can also add movie files to your slide show. A movie file can be added on top of a slide or on a new slide. When the slide show is played, the video file plays. Choose Add Media⇨Photos and Videos from Organizer (or from Folder).

This same set of commands can also be used to add more pictures to the slide show.

10. **(Optional) Record your own sounds.**

   If you want to add narration, click the Narration tool in the Palette Bin, and the Extras pane changes to provide you with tools to record a sound or import a sound file. Note that this option requires you to have a microphone properly configured on your computer.

11. **(Optional) Fit slides to the audio.**

   If you have 3 minutes of audio and the slide duration is 2 minutes 30 seconds, you can, with a single mouse click, fit the slide duration uniformly to fit the 3-minute audio time. Just click the Fit Slides to Audio tool below the preview image.

   If you want to manually adjust time for slide durations, click the down arrow on the time readout below the slide thumbnails in the Storyboard.

12. **Click Save Project on the Shortcuts bar and then, in the dialog box that opens, type a name and click Save.**

   Your project is added to the Organizer and is available for further editing later. Or, you can open the project to save in a number of different output formats, as we explain in the next section.

13. **Preview the slide show.**

   Before exporting the slide show, you can see a preview by clicking the buttons directly below the image preview area. If you want a full-screen preview, click the Preview button on the Shortcuts bar and click the Play button.

Exporting to slides and video

After creating a project, you have a number of different output options. You can write a project to disc for archival purposes and include slide shows on a VideoCD (videodisc) or DVD. You can e-mail a slide show to another user, share a project online, write a project compatible for display on a TV, or save to either a PDF slide show or Windows movie file.

To write a PDF slide show or a movie file, follow these steps:

1. **In the Organizer window, double-click the project thumbnail.**

   The project opens in the Adobe Photoshop Elements Slide Show Editor.

2. **Click the Output tool on the Shortcuts bar.**

   The Output Your Slide Show Wizard opens, as shown in Figure 15-4.

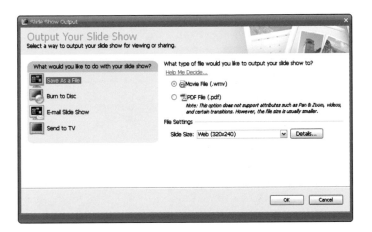

Figure 15-4: Select Output in the Photoshop Elements Slide Show Editor, and the Slide Show Output Wizard opens.

3. **Select the type of file you want to export to.**

   Select Movie File (.wmv) to export a Windows media video file. Your exported video can be viewed in Elements or in the Windows Media Player. You can import the video in all programs that support .wmv files.

   Select PDF File (.pdf) if you want to create a PDF slide show. If you create a PDF slide show, some of the animation features, such as zooming slides and transition effects, aren't shown in the resultant PDF document.

4. **In the dialog box that opens, which prompts you to add your output file to the Organizer, click Yes.**

   You can now easily view the file by double-clicking it in the Organizer window.

Opening multipage PDF files in Elements

If you create a slide show and export the slide show to a PDF document, you can open individual PDF pages in Elements. Elements can open any PDF document created from any PDF producer. Here's how:

1. **In the Organizer, select a file to open and click the Standard Edit option on the Shortcuts bar.**

   Be sure to select the file and click Standard Edit. Don't double-click the file in the Organizer; that action opens the file in Adobe Reader.

When the file is opened in Standard Edit mode, the Import PDF dialog box opens, as shown in Figure 15-5.

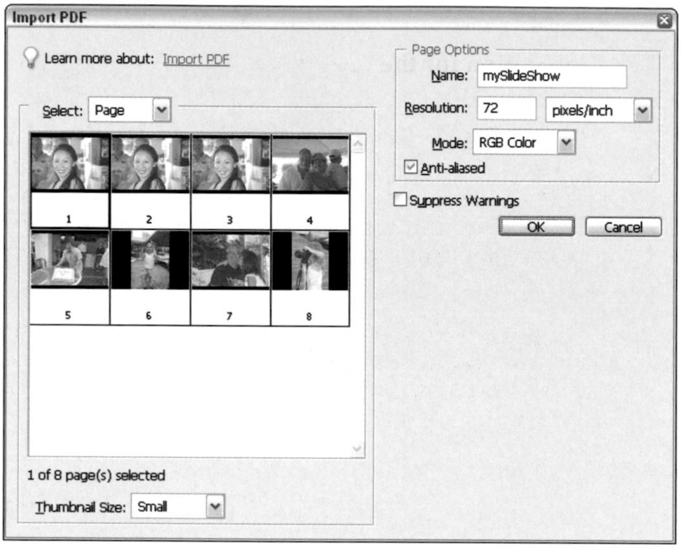

Figure 15-5: Select a PDF file to open in Elements and the Import PDF dialog box opens.

2. **In the dialog box, you can select one or more pages and specify the resolution and color mode.**

   If you want to select several pages in a noncontiguous order press Ctrl and click the pages you want to open.

3. **Click OK to open the PDF pages in individual Image windows.**

Writing Creations to CDs and DVDs

You can output creations, such as slide shows and images you optimize for TV, to a CD or DVD by using the Slide Show Output Wizard. If you have a movie but don't have a DVD burner, most DVD players sold today enable you to view videodiscs written to CDs. The CDs just don't hold as much content as DVD do.

To write to a CD or DVD, follow these steps:

1. **Open a project in the Slide Show Output Wizard by choosing File⊅Open Creation in the Organizer window.**

2. **Click Output in the Slide Show Editor.**

3. **Click Burn to Disc in the Slide Show Output Wizard.**

4. **Select an option for the type of output you want to use — VCD or DVD (see Figure 15-6).**

   - *To create a CD:* Select VCD (Lower Quality; Works on TV or Computer). When you select this option, your project is converted to a movie file (.wmv in Windows) or QuickTime movie file (Mac) during the write process. If you want more files added to the CD, select the Include Additional Slide Shows I've Made on This Disc check box.

   - *To burn a DVD:* Check the option DVD (Higher Quality; Works on TV or Computer) in the Slide Show Output window. Using this option requires you to have Adobe Premiere Elements installed on your computer (Windows).

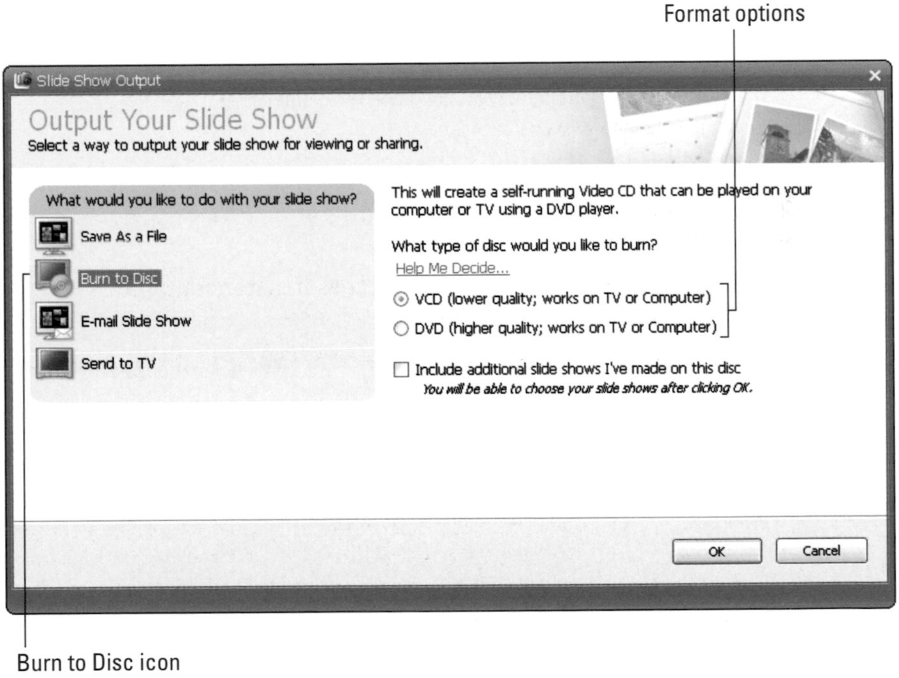

Format options

Burn to Disc icon

Figure 15-6: Type a name and select the format to export in the Slide Show Output Wizard.

5. **Click OK.**

   The Burn dialog box opens, as shown in Figure 15-7.

6. **Click the video format (either NTSC or PAL) and click OK.**

   The status bar shows the writing progress.

After the CD or DVD finishes writing, pop open your CD/DVD drive and remove the disc. Place the disc in your DVD player and press Play. The movie automatically starts playing, like any commercial videodisc.

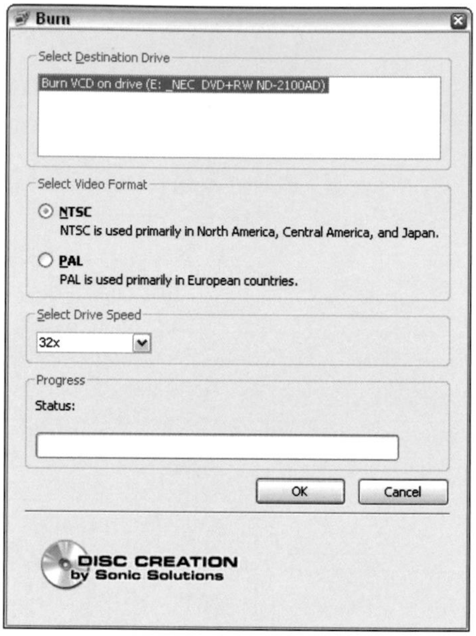

Creating a Flash Gallery

Another option for screen-viewing your photos is to display them on the Web. With Photoshop Elements, you don't need to know a hoot about Web page design and HTML coding. Elements creates all you need to upload attractive collections to your personal Web site. This is all accomplished by using the Flash Gallery menu command, which you select from the Create drop-down menu.

Figure 15-7: Click Burn to Disc in the Slide Show Output Wizard to open the Burn dialog box.

To see how easy it is to create a Web page showing off your photos, follow these steps:

1. **Open the Organizer and select the photos you want to display on your Web site.**

2. **Click Create on the Shortcuts bar and choose Flash Gallery from the menu options.**

   The Flash Gallery Wizard opens.

   When you open the Wizard window, you see a scrollable list of the photos you selected in the Organizer window.

3. **Click a template in the Choose a Template section of the Flash Gallery Wizard and click a style to select it.**

   You can scroll horizontally for templates and styles. Just click the thumbnails you want to use, as shown in Figure 15-8.

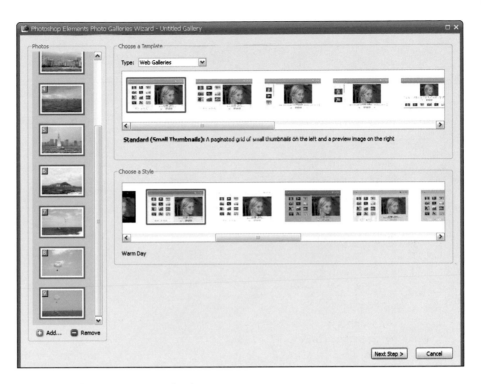

Figure 15-8: Click a template and style.

4. **Click the Next Step button.**

   You arrive at the second pane in the Flash Gallery Wizard.

5. **Set the attributes for the Flash Gallery.**

   You can add titles, choose slide durations, pick transition effects, set background colors, and preview your creation. Play around with the options in the Wizard window and add the effects you want for your Flash presentation.

6. **Click the Browse button and locate a folder where you want to save your files. Type a name for your creation in the Save Gallery As text box, as shown in Figure 15-9.**

7. **Click Share to save the creation.**

   Elements automatically creates an HTML file and copies your pictures as JPEGs to a separate folder. In addition, a number of subfolders with different assets are created. You don't have to worry about the files Elements creates for you because they're all neatly tucked in a folder according to the name you identify in the Flash Gallery Wizard window. Just remember the location and folder name you provide for your creation.

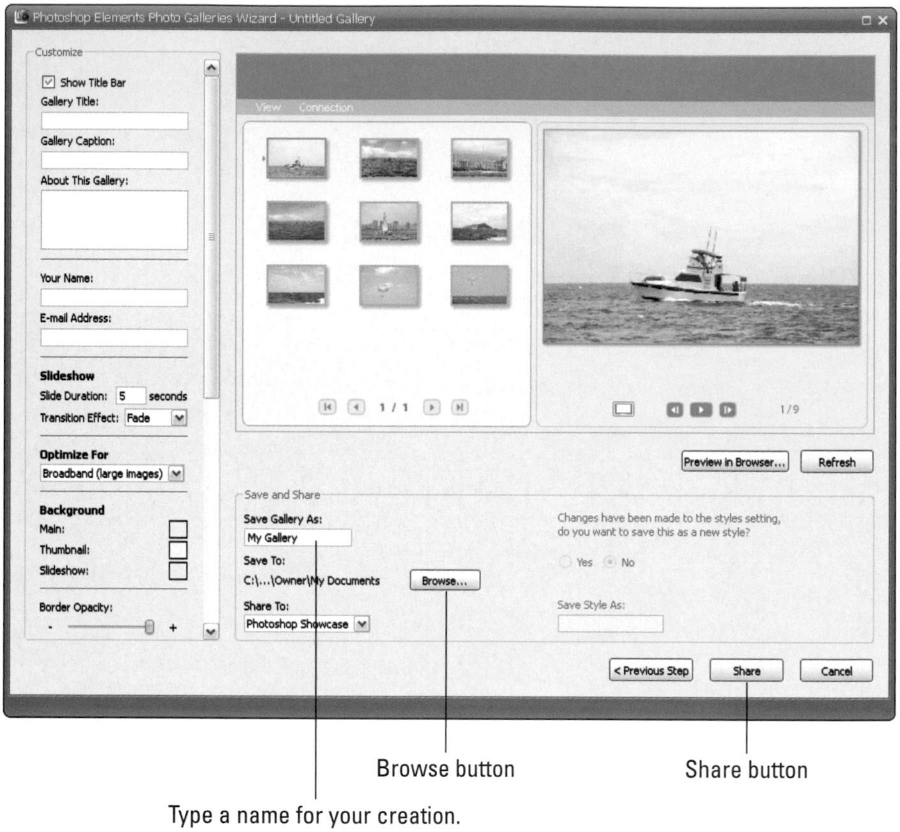

Browse button

Share button

Type a name for your creation.

Figure 15-9: Click Browse to identify a folder, type a name for the creation, and click Share.

8. **Preview your Flash Gallery.**

Open your Web browser and choose File⇨Open. Locate the `index.html` file inside the folder that Elements created for your presentation. Click the thumbnail images in the Browser window, and the corresponding larger image should open in the larger browser window, as shown in Figure 15-10.

To upload your creation to your personal Web site, use an FTP program to upload files. Be certain to upload the entire folder that Elements created for you. Inside this folder is the `index.html` file Elements created. You can add links from other Web pages to this file and host a series of different creations, all made visible with different Web links.

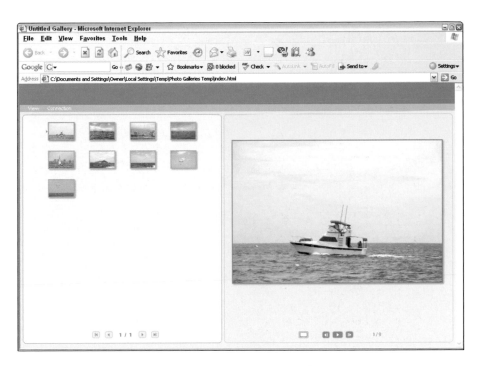

Figure 15-10: Preview your creation in a Web browser.

Flip 'Em Over with Flipbooks

Photoshop Elements 5 offers you a new creation feature that helps you create flipbooks. If you want to create a quick little video that shows off your photos by flashing stills on your screen or your TV set, you can quickly create a flipbook. Here's how you do it:

1. **Open the Organizer and select the files you want to use.**

   Note that you must select at least two files in order to create the flipbook.

2. **Click Create on the Shortcuts bar and choose Video Flipbook.**

   The Photoshop Elements Video Flipbook opens, as shown in Figure 15-11.

3. **Set the playback speed by typing a value in the Speed text box or moving the slider to the desired speed.**

Figure 15-11: The Photoshop Elements Video Flipbook dialog box permits you to select a speed and movie file size.

Note that flipping through photos looks best at low speeds, such as 1 or 2 frames per second (fps). Also, you can select the size for your video file from options on the Movie File Size drop-down menu.

4. Click Output.

The Save Video Flipbook dialog box opens,

5. Type a filename and click Save.

Your file is written as a .wmv (Windows) file. You can use Microsoft Movie Maker (Windows) to write the file to a CD or DVD.

Making Creations and Sharing

*A*dobe Photoshop Elements offers you a number of creations that can be shared on-screen or in print. From the Create drop-down menu on the Shortcuts bar, you have a number of menu choices for making creations.

In Chapter 15, we look at creating files for screen and Web viewing. In this chapter, we talk about creations designed for print and sharing. It's all here in Elements, but shhhhh. Don't tell the Photoshop people because Photoshop doesn't have all these wonderful creation features.

Aloha!
Wish you were here

Getting a Grip on Assembling Creations

In Chapter 15, we talk about slide shows, videodiscs, and Flash Galleries. These creations offer different output options, such as e-mailing, burning files to disc, and creating HTML documents — as well as printing and PDF creation.

The remaining creations you work with by using options you choose from the Create drop-down menu, including Photo Book Pages, Photo Layouts, Album Pages, Photo Calendars, and Photo Stamps. All these creations are designed for output to your printer or for sending off files to an online printing service.

At the top of the Create drop-down menu, seven different commands are listed, ranging from Photo Book Pages to CD/DVD Label. All these creations use a very similar wizard to prepare your files and, ultimately, make the creation. Choosing any one of the first seven menu commands opens a wizard like the one shown in Figure 16-1 when you click Photo Book Pages.

The items you choose in the wizard when you're making creations for print include

🖛 **Select a Size:** From the drop-down list, you can select the sizes supported by the creation type. In some cases, only one size is available.

🖛 **Select a Layout:** Choose a template you want to use from the thumbnails in the scrollable window.

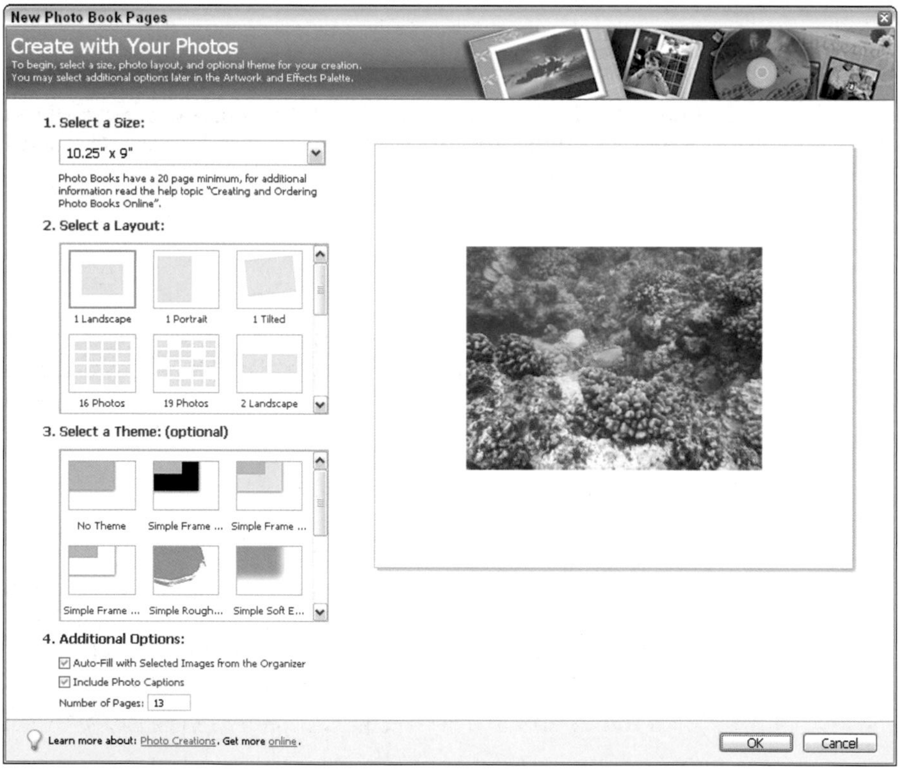

Figure 16-1: A similar wizard window appears for the first seven creation options.

⨽ **Select a Theme:** Also from thumbnails in a scrollable window, you can add borders and drop shadows by clicking a theme thumbnail.

⨽ **Auto-fill with Selected Images from the Organizer:** Select this check box if you select photos in the Organizer and want to include the selected photos in your creation.

⨽ **Include Photo Captions:** Select the check box if you want the photo captions to appear on each page under their respective photos.

⨽ **Number of Pages:** Elements automatically creates the number of pages to accommodate the number of photos you selected in the Organizer. If you reduce the number, Elements creates additional files to accommodate all selected photos.

After assembling your creation, click the OK button. Elements then adds the selected photos to the layout and theme you specified in the wizard. Be patient and wait for Elements to complete the task.

After a creation has been made, the document appears like any other image you open in Elements. You can crop, modify images, print, and more. Using an Elements file, you choose File⇨Save to open the Save As dialog box. Type a name and click Save.

Creating the Family Photo Album

Elements provides some fancy ways to create pages for a photo album. Album pages support all output formats except sharing services. Elements offers options for printing pages that look just like pages in a fancy photo album that you may purchase at your local drugstore.

Follow these steps to create Album Pages:

1. **Select files in the Organizer and click Create.**

   The procedure for all creations is the same. You first select files in the Organizer (or an editing mode) and then click the Create button on the Shortcuts bar. If you forget files that you want to add to a creation, the creation wizards provide options for adding photos.

2. **From the Create drop-down menu, select Photo Book Pages.**

   The New Photo Book Pages Wizard opens.

3. **Select a size, layout, and theme.**

The only size available for Photo Book Pages is 10.25 x 9 inches, which appears as the default page size.

Click a layout from the Select a Layout scrollable window.

Click a theme from the Select a Theme scrollable window. (Note that this choice is optional. If no theme is selected, photos appear without a border or shadow.)

4. **Click Auto-Fill with Selected Images from the Organizer.**

   Selecting this option automatically loads the images you selected in the Organizer window.

5. **(Optional) Click Include Photo Captions.**

   This step is optional if you want photo captions to appear below your images.

6. **Click OK.**

   Wait a few minutes while Elements lays out the page or pages.

7. **(Optional) You can resize and rotate images if you want to modify the design. When you finish sizing and rotating, click the check mark shown in Figure 16-2.**

   Just click an image and drag any one of the handles out or in to size up or down the photo on the page. To rotate an image, grab the lower-center handle on the circle and drag it to change rotation.

8. **As with any other Elements file, choose File⇨Save to save the creation.**

Figure 16-2: Click the check mark icon when you're finished sizing, rotating, or moving a photo.

Greetings!

You can create greeting cards with the New Greeting Card Wizard. As with your options for photo albums, you select a template and a theme.

Here's how to create your own, personal greeting cards:

1. **Open the Organizer and select a photo.**

2. **Choose Create⇨Greeting Card.**

   The New Greeting Card Wizard opens.

3. **Select a greeting card size.**

   From the Select a Size drop-down list, choose either 4 x 6 or 5 x 7 for the card size.

4. **Select a layout and a theme by clicking the thumbnails in the scrollable windows. Then click OK.**

5. **Click the Text tool on the Tools palette and add some text, as shown in Figure 16-3.**

   For more on adding text to photos in Elements, see Chapter 13.

6. **Save the file.**

Figure 16-3: Add some text to your greeting card by clicking the Type tool and clicking the photo.

Calendars

Create your own, personal calendar in Photoshop Elements, and you won't buy any more calendars as each new year rolls around. This tool is helpful for creating calendars for the kids — using pictures of their soccer team, the group at the boys and girls clubs, the 4-H club, that great vacation you took with the family last year — or even for satisfying your own ego by passing out your creations at the office. The calendar options have many uses, limited only by your imagination.

Creating calendars in Elements 5 is handled through the Adobe Photoshop Services, provided by Kodak EasyShare. You assemble your photos and create your layout by using the EasyShare services, and then order the calendar from the service.

Here's how you go about using the EasyShare services for creating calendars:

1. **Select 13 images in the Organizer and choose Create⇨Photo Calendar.**

   The Kodak EasyShare Order Calendar wizard opens.

2. **Log on to Kodak EasyShare.**

   If you don't have an account, you need to create one. Fill in the identifying information and click Next. If you already have an account with Kodak EasyShare, click Sign In and type your logon name and password.

   Your selected photos are uploaded to the Kodak EasyShare Web site after you log in. Your default Web browser is launched, and it opens the Kodak EasyShare Web page, where calendar services are offered.

3. **Follow the instructions on the Kodak EasyShare Web site for placing your order.**

   Kodak provides you with a number of different options for the calendar layout and design. You can additionally choose from a number of attributes, such as month and year to start your calendar and fonts and binding choices. All these options are available in an intuitive format on the Web site.

4. **After making your design decisions, click Buy Prints to place your order.**

   You fill out an online form where you supply your shipping address and mailing information. When you confirm the order, your pictures are printed on a professional-looking calendar and mailed to you.

Creating Personal Postage Stamps

Another new creation feature in Elements 5 is the option to create your own, personal postage stamps. Yes, they're real stamps that you can use for mailing though the post office.

Here's the simple, easy way to use Elements to place an order for your very own personal postage stamps:

1. **Select an image in the Organizer.**

   Your file needs to be less than 5MB. (See Chapter 3 for more on resizing images.)

2. **Click Create on the Shortcuts bar and choose PhotoStamps from the menu.**

   The PhotoStamps dialog box opens.

3. **Click the Upload My Photos button in the dialog box (see Figure 16-4).**

   Your photo is uploaded to the PhotoStamps.com Web site.

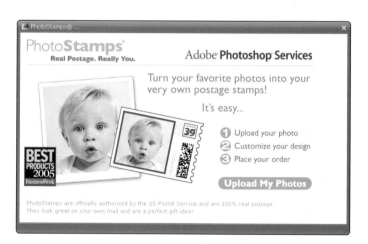

Figure 16-4: Choose Postage Stamps from the Create drop-down menu to open this dialog box.

4. **Place your order.**

   The PhotoStamps.com Web site provides an easy-to-use interface for ordering stamps. After you fill out the order and billing information, your stamps are mailed to you.

Creating CD and DVD Labels

 Another new feature added to the creation options in Elements 5 is the simple, easy way to create CD and DVD labels. From the Create menu, you choose a menu item and choose CD/DVD Label. From templates provided in a wizard, Elements offers you an easy method for printing your own, personal labels for CDs and DVDs.

Spreading the Love Through Sharing

Two methods of sharing your creations are available in Elements. You can place orders with online services, from a variety of online service providers, or you can e-mail your creations to others.

Ordering prints online

Right from within your Photoshop Elements workspace, you can place orders for prints, photo books, and greeting cards and then have your creations mailed to you and any number of friends and colleagues.

You have, under the Sharing button on the Shortcuts bar, three menu options for online orders and sharing:

- **Order Prints:** Click this option to upload photos for which you want photo prints mailed back to you and others. You use the Kodak EasyShare Service to log on and place your orders.

- **Order Kodak Photo Book:** Choose this menu command when you want your pictures displayed in a professional-looking photo book. You can place an order for yourself and have duplicate photo books mailed to other recipients.

- **Order Photo Greeting Card:** You create greeting cards, as we explain earlier in this chapter, and upload your design to the Kodak EasyShare Service for ordering sets of cards.

All these online services work similarly to each other. You select photos in the Organizer and then open the Sharing button on the Shortcuts bar and choose the menu option you want from the commands listed for online creations and sharing.

The Kodak EasyShare Wizard opens, where you add the order information and logon information and then submit your order. The steps are straight-forward and intuitive.

E-mailing creations

After you put together a creation with the Creation Wizard, you can e-mail the creation to your friends, family, or whoever you like by choosing a simple menu command. (We introduce this method and other ways to share creations in the section "Getting a Grip on Assembling Creations," earlier in this chapter.) Additionally, you can e-mail photos to mobile phones. The options are all located under the Sharing button on the Shortcuts bar.

Rather than save your file from Elements and then open your e-mail client and select the photo to attach to an e-mail message, Elements makes the sharing of photos via e-mail as easy as a one-click step.

When you want to e-mail a creation, follow these steps:

1. **In the Organizer, select the photos you want to e-mail to a friend.**

2. **Click the Sharing button on the Shortcuts bar and select E-Mail.**

    The Attach to E-Mail dialog box opens, as shown in Figure 16-5.

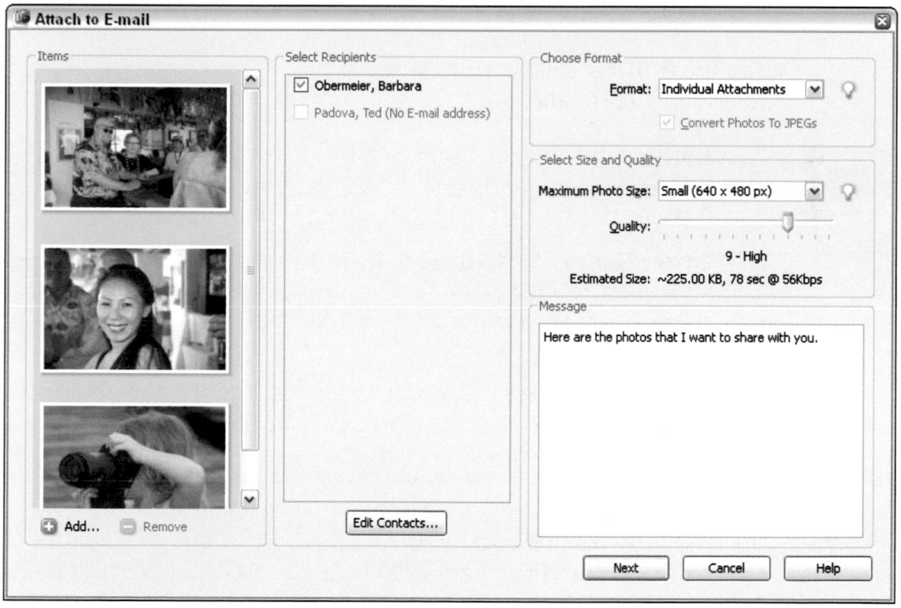

Figure 16-5: Open the Sharing button on the Shortcuts bar and select E-Mail to open the Attach to E-Mail dialog box.

3. **Select recipients and file attributes:**

- **Select Recipients:** You can add recipients by clicking the Edit Contacts button and add names and e-mail addresses. Select the check box adjacent to the name of each recipient with whom you want to share your photos.

- **Choose Format:** From the Format drop-down menu, you can choose to send individual files or other creations you have stored in the Organizer workspace.

- **Select Size and Quality:** For auto-sizing your photos, you can make adjustments from the Maximum Photo Size drop-down menu and select the compression amount for JPEG images.

- **Message:** In an optional item, you can type the text that you want to appear in your e-mail message by adding text to the Message window.

4. **Click Next.**

   Your images are prepared according to the attributes specified in the Attach to E-Mail dialog box. The files you selected are attached to a new e-mail message.

5. **Click the Send button in your e-mail client.**

   The photos are e-mailed to the recipients you identified.

By default, Elements uses your primary e-mail client application, which may or may not be the e-mail program you use. You can change the default e-mail client by pressing Ctrl/⌘+K to open the Preferences dialog box when you're in the Organizer and then clicking Sharing in the left pane. From a drop-down list in the Sharing preferences, select the e-mail client application that you want Elements to use.

Part VI
The Part of Tens

The 5th Wave   By Rich Tennant

"Why don't you try blurring the brimstone and then putting a nice glow effect around the hellfire."

In this part . . .

The Part of Tens offers a couple of fun chapters to help you take your photography and Elements skills a little further. In Chapter 17, you find our top ten tips for composing better photos. Find out about the rule of thirds, framing, and other simple tricks that will make your photos look better than ever. Also, in Part V, we introduce the creations that Elements helps you make, but why stop there? Chapter 18 offers even more ideas for projects you can create for your home or work, such as flyers, portfolios, CD and DVD covers, and more.

Ten Tips for Composing Better Photos

A few things have to come together to make a great photograph. One is being in the right place at the right time. Another is the ability to tell a story. Yet another is excellent composition. Unfortunately, we can't help with your schedule or story-telling, but we can give you several easy tips on how to take photographs that are interesting and well-composed. Some of these tips overlap and contain common concepts. But they're all free; they don't require any extra money or equipment. All they take are an open mind and an eye that's willing to be trained over time.

Find a Focal Point

One of the most important tools for properly composing a photo is establishing a *focal point* — a main point of interest. If too many elements are competing for attention, a photo probably doesn't have a clearly defined focal point. Your eye, therefore, doesn't know where to look. Too many images without a focal point cause the viewer to tire quickly or lose interest. The eye wants to be drawn to a subject.

Excessive background elements, like furniture, walls, tables, fences, build-ings, and even random bystanders, don't add much to the compositional or emotional value of your shot. What you really want to capture are the smiles and expressions of your family and friends.

Keep these tips in mind to help find your focal point:

- ✔ Pick your subject and then get close to it.

- ✔ Include a point of interest in scenic shots. Sunrises and sunsets are pretty, but after you've seen a few, you've seen them all. Try to capture an early morning fisherman casting his line off the pier or a child check-ing out a rogue hermit crab at dusk. That once-ho-hum scenic shot now has some visual punch.

- ✔ When it's appropriate, try to include an element in the foreground, middle ground, or background to add depth and a sense of scale, as shown in Figure 17-1. Just make sure that it's a meaningful element and not random clutter.

Brand X Pictures

Figure 17-1: Including elements in the foreground adds depth to a photo.

Use the Rule of Thirds

After you find a focal point for your shot, the next step is to try to put that focal point, or subject, in a prime location within your viewfinder or LCD display. Those prime locations are based on the photographic principle the *rule of thirds*. If you divide an image into a grid of nine equal segments, as shown in Figure 17-2, the elements most appealing to the eye and most likely to be noticed first are those that fall close to one of the four intersections of the dividing lines.

Corbis Digital Stock

Figure 17-2: Position your subject at one of the intersecting points on the rule-of-thirds grid.

When you're composing your shot, try to mentally divide your frame into vertical and horizontal thirds and position your most important visual element at any intersecting point. When you're shooting landscapes, remember that a low horizon creates a dreamy and spacious feeling and that a high horizon gives an earthy and intimate feeling. For close-up portraits, try putting the face or eyes of a person at one of those points.

If the rule of thirds is too hard for you to remember or employ, when you look through the viewfinder, just repeat the mantra "Move from center." We all have a natural tendency to want to center everything. Get it nice and orderly. But centered subjects are often static and boring. Asymmetry often gives you more dynamic and interesting images.

If you have an autofocus camera, you need to lock the focus when you're moving from center because the autofocus sensor locks on to whatever is in the center of the viewfinder — not on your point of interest. Autofocus can also be problematic when you're trying to do something as simple as photographing two people (in this case, you may want the two people in the center) and your camera keeps focusing on the space in the distance between them. Center your subject in the viewfinder and apply slight pressure to your shutter release button to lock the focus. Then, reposition your subject at an intersecting point on the rule-of-thirds grid and press down all the way to snap the photo.

Cut the Clutter

Contrary to what you see on supermarket tabloid covers, those telephone poles, branches, car antennas, and other everyday objects don't naturally grow out of people's heads. Although these *mergers,* as photographers call them, are good for a laugh, they're not good enough to make it into picture frames and scrapbooks.

Here are some ways you can cut the clutter from your background:

- ✔ **Get up close and personal.** Most people worry about getting their heads cut off when they get their photos taken. But more often than not, people tend to capture too much boring or distracting background. Fill your viewfinder frame with your subject. Although you can always crop your image later, you should try to get your subject to fill the frame when you take the photo.

- ✔ **Shoot at a different angle.** Yes, you can turn your camera! Most photos are horizontal merely because it's easier to hold the camera that way. That's fine for a lot of shots (such as the requisite group photo and some landscape shots), but other subjects (buildings, trees, waterfalls, mountain peaks, giraffes, Shaquille O'Neal) lend themselves to a vertical format.

- ✔ **Move around your subject.** Moving around may help eliminate unwanted clutter. Shoot from below or above your subject if necessary.

- ✔ **Move your subject, if possible, to get the optimum background.** Although there are exceptions, an ideal background is usually free from distracting elements like tree branches, poles, wires, chain-link fences, signs, bright lights, lots of loud colors, busy wallpaper, and so on. Include only what complements your subject.

- ✔ **Use background elements to enhance, not distract.** On the other hand, if your background is interesting and can make your photo stronger, include it. You can use famous landmarks, props, and even decorations in the background to give context to images, as shown in Figure 17-3.

Figure 17-3: Use background elements, like decorations, to help define an event and add ambience to the subject.

- ✔ **Use space around a subject to evoke a certain mood.** A lot of space around a person can give a sense of loneliness, just as a closely cropped portrait can create a feeling of intimacy. Just make sure that the space is intentionally used in the shot.

- ✔ **If you're stuck with a distracting background, you can try blurring it by using a wider aperture (like f/4 rather than f/11 or f/16) on your camera.** This makes the *depth of field* (areas of sharpness in relation to your focal point) shallower so that your subject is in focus but the background isn't.

Because consumer digital cameras use image sensors that are typically one-third the size of a 35mm frame, the lens is very close to the sensor, which really increases the depth of field. This can make it hard to blur the background. Not a problem — you can also blur the background by making a selection and using the Blur filter in Elements. See Chapters 7 and 10 for more on selections and the Blur filter, respectively.

Frame Your Shot

When it's appropriate, use foreground elements to frame your subject. Frames lead you into a photograph. You can use elements like tree branches, windows, archways, and doorways to frame a wide or long shot, add a feeling of depth, and create a point of reference, as shown in Figure 17-4. You don't have to reserve the use of framing for wide and long shots, however. Close-ups can also be framed. Your framing elements don't always have to be sharply focused. Sometimes, if they're too sharp, they distract from the focal point. And, remember to avoid mergers!

ImageState

Figure 17-4: Use elements that frame your subject.

Employ Contrast

Just remember "Light on dark, dark on light." A light subject has more impact and emphasis if it's shot against a dark background, and vice versa, as shown in Figure 17-5. When people view an image, their eyes go first to the area of the most contrast. Obviously, finding contrast in the environment is sometimes beyond your control. But when you're setting up a shot, you can certainly try to incorporate this technique. Keep in mind, however, that contrast needs to be used carefully. Sometimes it can be distracting, especially if the high-contrast elements aren't your main point of interest.

PhotoDisc, Inc./Getty Images

Figure 17-5: High-contrast shots demand attention.

Using Leading Lines

Leading lines are lines that, by either the actual elements in the image or the composition of those elements, lead the eye into the picture and, hopefully, to a point of interest. These lines add dimension, depth, and perspective by carrying the eye through the photo:

- ✔ Diagonal lines are dynamic and evoke movement.

- ✔ Curves are graceful and harmonious.

- ✔ Horizontal lines are peaceful and give a feeling of balance.

- ✔ Vertical lines are direct and active.

The best leading lines are those that enter the image from the lower-left corner. Many elements provide natural leading lines, especially in scenic or landscape photos, such as roads, walls, fences, rivers, shadows, skyscrapers, and bridges. The photo shown in Figure 17-6 of the Great Wall of China is an example of curved leading lines.

Flat Earth

Figure 17-6: You don't have to trek to China to find leading lines, although you may not find a longer unbroken curve than the Great Wall.

Experiment with Viewpoints

Not much in the world looks fascinating photographed from a height of 5 to 6 feet off the ground. Unfortunately, this is the viewpoint of "Snapshotville." Try to break out of this mode by taking photos from another vantage point. Experiment with taking a photo from above the subject (bird's-eye view) or below it (worm's-eye view). A different angle may provide a more interesting image:

✔ **Unexpected angles can exaggerate the size of the subject.** The subject may appear either larger or smaller than normal, as shown in Figure 17-7. Try extreme angles with scenic shots, which otherwise can tend to be rather static or boring.

✔ **Changing your viewpoint can change the mood of the image.** If the photo in Figure 17-7 had been taken from a front angle, it would have been pretty dull. Taken from below, looking up, exaggerates the height and makes for a stronger and more exciting composition, making the cactus seem like nature's skyscraper.

✔ **Use direct eye contact when you're photographing people.** It provides a sense of realism and makes the image more intimate and warm, pulling you into the photo. But remember that children are not at the same eye level as adults. We often shoot down at them, making them appear smaller than they really are. Try kneeling or sitting on the floor and getting down to their level. You will also find that you get a less distracting background in the frame, and the lighting from your flash more evenly covers the face. Do the same for pets and other short-stature subjects, such as flowers.

Corbis Digital Stock

Figure 17-7: Shooting subjects from extreme angles can exaggerate size, resulting in a more interesting shot.

Use Light

When we think of light in regard to photography, the first thing that comes to mind are all those photos we took in the past that are either overexposed (too light) or underexposed (too dark). With lighting, you have to consider not only whether you have the right amount of lighting, but also these factors:

✔ The direction of the light

✔ The intensity of the light

- The color of the light
- Natural light (outdoors) or artificial light (indoors)
- Creative use of lighting to lead the eye and create a certain mood

If the light isn't right for your shot, you have quite a few choices: Hurry up and wait, move yourself, move the subject, add more light with a flash, or diffuse light. Of course, which one you choose depends on the circumstances of the shot and what's convenient or most productive. Here are a few tips to remember about light:

- **The best light for photographs is in the early morning and later afternoon.** The light is warmer and softer, and the shadows are longer and less harsh.

- **Avoid taking portraits at midday.** The overhead sun causes ugly shadows and makes people squint. If you must shoot then, use a reflector to block some of the sunlight or fill in the shadow areas. Or, you can use a *scrim* (white translucent fabric stretched across a frame) to diffuse the light.

- **Cloudy or overcast days can be great for photographing, especially portraits.** The light is soft and diffused and flatters the face.

- **Shooting subjects with *backlighting* (where the lighting comes from behind the subject) can produce dramatic results.** Figure 17-8 shows an example. If you want to see the details of the subject, and not just a silhouette, use a fill flash to lighten the shadow areas.

Corbis Digital Stock

Figure 17-8: Backlighting can yield dramatic images.

✔ **Ensure that the brightest light source isn't directed right into the lens.** This causes *lens flare,* those strange light circles that appear in the photo.

✔ **Take into account the color of the light.** The light at noon is white, the light at sunset is orange, and the light at twilight is blue. The color of the light can make an image feel warm or cool.

✔ **Use a flash when necessary.** Use a flash in low-light conditions. If your built-in flash isn't cutting the mustard, you may want to invest in an accessory flash.

✔ **Get creative with light.** Look for those unique compositions created by the interplay between light and shadow areas or how the light illuminates a particular subject. Lighting by itself can make or break a certain mood or emotion. Think of a simple beam of light coming through the roof of an old barn. Even in the lousiest weather, the most beautifully lit images can emerge. When wet objects are lit, they seem to shimmer, as shown in Figure 17-9.

Corbis Digital Stock

Figure 17-9: Lighting can create drama from the simplest objects.

Giving Direction

When you look at magazines that feature the year's best photos, they all appear as instances of pure serendipity. Sometimes that's the case, but more often than not, the photographer arranged the shot or waited for the right light or a special moment.

As a photographer, you also shouldn't be afraid to play photo stylist:

✔ Give directions on where you want people to stand, how to stand, and so on. For example, tell people to touch each other, bring their heads toward each other, or put their arms around each other, as shown in Figure 17-10.

IT Stock Free

Figure 17-10: Provide direction to the people you're photographing while also trying to capture their personalities.

✔ Designate the location.

✔ Use props, such as trees or cars, to arrange people around.

✔ Use a variety of poses. Have some people sit and others stand.

✔ If you're dealing with a large group of people, rambunctious kids, or excited pets, get someone to help direct. Just make sure that the parties being photographed pay attention and look at the camera.

✔ Try to get people to relax. Although spontaneity can yield great images, you can still get good photos from posed subjects if they aren't hating the experience.

Consider Direction of Movement

When the subject is capable of movement, such as a car, person, or animal, make sure that you leave more space in front of the subject than behind it, as shown in Figure 17-11. Otherwise, the viewer may subconsciously experience a feeling of departure or discomfort. You want to try to give the person or object room to move into the frame. Likewise, if a person is looking out onto a vista, make sure that you include that vista so that the person is given a point of view and the scene is given context.

Brand X Pictures

Figure 17-11: Always include room for your subject to move into the frame.

18

Ten More Project Ideas

In This Chapter

▶ Decorating your computer screen

▶ Advertising in flyers and online auctions

▶ Decorating your duds

▶ Going big with posters

▶ Creating a household inventory or project documentation

▶ Sprucing up your homework

So you posted all your holiday and vacation photos in a Web gallery and made enough albums, slide shows, flipbooks, and cards to keep your family and friends content for months to come? Sounds like you may be ready to take a crack at some other projects. In this chapter, you find some ideas on how you can use your inventory of digital images to make your life more productive, more organized, and more fun. Remember that this chapter just scratches the surface. With a little imagination, before you know it, there won't be anything left in your life that doesn't include your photos.

Wallpaper and Screen Savers

If you like an image so much that you want to gaze at it while you're toiling away at your computer, why not use that image for the background of your computer, better known as the *desktop wallpaper?* If you can't choose just one favorite image, you can use several to create a multi-image screen saver.

If you're serious about image editing, you really should have a neutral gray background. But as long as your wallpaper isn't showing while you do your color corrections, feel free to decorate your desktop with your favorite colorful photo. You use just two easy steps to turn a photo into wallpaper:

1. **From the Organizer, select the photo you want to use.**

2. **Choose Edit⇨Set As Desktop Wallpaper.**

That's all there is to it! Your photo has now been transformed into desktop wallpaper.

If you have two or more photos you want to use, you can create a Windows XP screen saver. Follow these steps:

1. **Select the desired photos from the Organizer.**

2. **Choose File⇨Export⇨As New File. In the Export New File dialog box, choose JPEG as the file type.**

3. **Choose JPEG for your file type, select your photo size, and choose a quality setting.**

   We recommend using a size that matches the resolution setting you're using for your monitor. Use a quality setting of 12 for maximum quality.

4. **Click the Browse button.**

5. **Click the Make a New Folder button and save the photos as JPEGs to that folder. Name the folder something appropriate, like** screen saver.

6. **Choose whether to use the original names of your files or a common base name, such as screen 1, screen 2, and so on.**

7. **Click Export. If all goes well, Elements informs you that it has executed the command. Click OK.**

8. **In Windows XP Professional, choose Start⇨Settings⇨Control Panel⇨ Display.**

   Depending on how your computer is set up, you may have to double-click Display to open it.

9. **Click the Screen Saver tab and choose My Pictures Slideshow from the drop-down menu under Screen Saver.**

10. **Click Settings and choose the folder you created in Step 5 that contains your photos. Define the photo, indicate how often you want the photos to change, and specify all your other options.**

11. **Click Preview to see how the image will appear on your monitor.**

    Move your mouse or press a key to end the preview.

12. **Click Apply and then OK to close the Display window.**

Flyers, Ads, and Online Auctions

Everyone knows that a picture is worth a thousand words. Whether you're selling puppies or advertising an open house, adding a photo to an ad or flyer really helps to drive home your message.

Here are the abbreviated steps to quickly create an ad or flyer:

1. **In the Editor, in Standard Edit (Full Edit on the Mac) mode, choose File⇨New⇨Blank File.**

2. **In the New Document dialog box, enter your desired document specifications and then click OK.**

   We recommend entering the final dimensions and resolution for your desired output. If you want to print your ad or flyer on your desktop printer or at a service bureau, a good guideline for resolution is 300 pixels per inch. For more on resolution and sizing images, be sure to check out Chapter 3. Leave the color mode as RGB and the background as White.

   If you want to fill your background with color, as we did in Figure 18-1, choose Edit⇨Fill Layer and choose Color from the Contents pop-up menu. Choose your desired color in the Color Picker and then click OK.

3. **Open your photos and drag and drop them onto your new canvas with the Move tool. Make sure to choose Window⇨Cascade to view all your canvases at the same time.**

   Your image is automatically put on a separate layer. For more on layers, see Chapter 8. If you want to use only a portion of the image, as we did with the puppy in Figure 18-1, use your favorite selection method to pluck out your element. For more on selections, see Chapter 7.

PhotoDisc, Inc./Getty Images

Figure 18-1: Quickly put together ads and flyers.

4. **Select the Type tool, click the canvas, and add your desired type. Position your type with the Move tool.**

5. **When you're done, choose File⇨Save.**

6. **Choose Photoshop (.PSD) from the Format drop-down menu (Format pop-up menu on the Mac), and make sure that the Layers and Color check boxes are selected. In addition, select the Use Lower Case Extension option. Click Save.**

   If you want to take your document to a service bureau or copy shop, like FedEx Kinko's, you should save your document as a Photoshop PDF (.pdf) file. That way, you don't have to worry about compatibility issues or printing snafus.

If you're preparing photos for online auction sites, like eBay or Yahoo! Auctions, be sure and keep your images at a low resolution — 72 ppi, to be exact — and at 100 percent scale. Save the file as a JPEG to ensure that your file stays lean and mean while preserving colors. Be sure to check the image specifications posted on your online auction site.

Clothes, Hats, and More

Many local copy shops, retail stores, and Web sites enable you to add photos to T-shirts, hats, buttons, tote bags, ties, mouse pads, and many other items. If you can produce it, they can put a photo on it. But it's easy, and less expensive, to tackle this project yourself.

Buy plain white T-shirts at your local discount store or plain aprons and tote bags at your craft or fabric store. Then buy special transfer paper at your office supply or computer store. Print your photos on the transfer paper (be sure to flip the images horizontally first) and iron the print onto the fabric, and you've got yourself a personalized gift for very little cash.

What do you get for the person who has everything? How about a blanket of memories? You can transfer photos onto patches of fabric and create unique memory quilts. What grandparent wouldn't love to have a quilt with photos of her children and grandchildren?

Posters

For special events, important announcements, or maybe just your favorite family photos, you can get posters and large-size prints at many copy shops and service bureaus. Call and talk to a knowledgeable rep at your copy shop or service bureau so that you know exactly how to prepare your file. Here are a few questions to ask:

- What file format and resolution should the file be?
- What print sizes do you offer?
- Do you provide mounting and lamination services?

  In addition to printing large prints, many service bureaus mount prints on foam core or the sturdier *gator board.* These service bureaus also can laminate prints to protect them from scratches and UV rays.

Household and Business Inventories

Don't wait for a natural disaster or theft to get you motivated to prepare an inventory of your household or business assets. Take your digital camera and shoot pictures of your items. Add text to describe the items in the caption section of the Organizer. Be sure to include the makes, models, purchase dates, and dollar values of each piece. Then create a single PDF document from those multiple files by creating a slide show or an album, as shown in Figure 18-2. Upload the PDF file to a Web storage site, or burn a CD or DVD and place it off-site in a safety deposit box or other secure location. If the need arises, the PDF can be viewed by your insurance agent using the free Adobe Reader software.

Laptop, ABC Brand, Purchased Aug 2004, SN2359980, $2,200

PhotoSpin

Figure 18-2: Create an inventory of your assets.

Project Documentation

Nothing helps to document a process like images. The spoken word and the written word are great, but showing how something comes together is even more effective. Consider using your photographs to help document your projects from beginning to end. Whether it's a project involving home improvement, furniture building, crafts, or cooking, take photos at each stage to record the project. If you're taking a class or workshop and the instructors don't mind, take your camera to class. Documenting the positions or steps of that new yoga, pottery, or gardening class will help you practice or re-create it on your own later, either for yourself or to teach someone else.

Import the photos into the Organizer and create notes on each step of the project, either on the canvas itself or in the caption area. Output the images to a PDF slide show or a PDF file of album pages, as shown in Figure 18-3.

Step 5

Garnish with bell, ivy, ribbon and fresh flowers.

PhotoDisc, Inc./Getty Images

Figure 18-3: Document your favorite projects for easier re-creation later.

Sharing projects

Not into killing trees? Not to worry. You don't have to print every project you make. Any file you create can be left as a purely digital file and e-mailed to other users. From the Organizer, you can select files that you want to send to recipients and choose File⇨E-mail.

In the Attach to E-mail dialog box, from the Format menu, you have these options for sending your file: Photo Mail (HTML), Simple Slide Show (PDF), and Individual Attachments. The first option saves the file as HTML that may be used for a Web page design. Other options are to send the photo as a PDF file or as a file attachment to an e-mail message. Additionally,

you have options for editing your address book, selecting image quality, and downsampling (PDF or attachments only). You can add a message here, or you can choose to type text in your new e-mail message, as shown in the figure.

If you happen to choose Photo Mail as your format, you have additional layout options to choose, such as frames, borders, background color, and shadows.

Click the Next button, and the file (according to the format you choose) is attached to a new e-mail message in your default e-mail program.

School Reports and Projects

There's nothing like some interesting photos to jazz up the obligatory school report. Doing a botany report? Include some close-ups of a flower with text labels on the parts of the flower. Have to write a paper on the habits of the lemurs of Madagascar? Trek down to your local zoo and have a photo shoot. Create a simple collage of lemurs eating, sleeping, and doing the other things that lemurs do. In fact, buying your children their own inexpensive point-and-shoot cameras may give them a little more enthusiasm for school work.

Wait — There's More

Before you start taking your photos to the next dimension, here are a few extra ideas: Make fun place cards for dinner party guests, create your own business cards if you need only a few, design your own gift wrap and tags, or label storage boxes with photos of their contents. The possibilities are endless.

Index